50 HIKES

IN THE OZARKS

OTHER BOOKS IN THE 50 HIKES SERIES

50 Hikes Around Anchorage

50 Hikes in Washington

50 Hikes in Oregon

50 Hikes in the Sierra Nevada

50 Hikes in Northern New Mexico

50 Hikes in Utah

50 Hikes in Orange County

50 Hikes in Michigan

50 Hikes in Michigan's Upper Peninsula

50 Hikes on Michigan & Wisconsin's North Country Trail

50 Hikes in Ohio

50 Hikes in West Virginia

50 Hikes in the North Georgia Mountains

50 Hikes on Tennessee's Cumberland Plateau

50 Hikes in Northern Virginia

50 Hikes in Eastern Pennsylvania

50 Hikes in New Jersey

50 Hikes in the Lower Hudson Valley

50 Hikes in the Berkshire Hills

50 Hikes in the White Mountains

50 Hikes in Vermont

50 Hikes in Coastal & Inland Maine

50 HIKES
IN THE OZARKS

SECOND EDITION

Johnny Molloy

THE COUNTRYMAN PRESS

A division of W. W. Norton & Company

Independent Publishers Since 1923

For information about permission to reproduce selections from this book,
write to Permissions, The Countryman Press, 500 Fifth Avenue, New York, NY 10110

For information about special discounts for bulk purchases, please contact
W. W. Norton Special Sales at specialsales@wwnorton.com or 800-233-4830

The Countryman Press
www.countrymanpress.com

A division of W. W. Norton & Company, Inc.
500 Fifth Avenue, New York, NY 10110
www.wwnorton.com

978-1-68268-013-1 (pbk.)

10 9 8 7 6 5 4 3 2 1

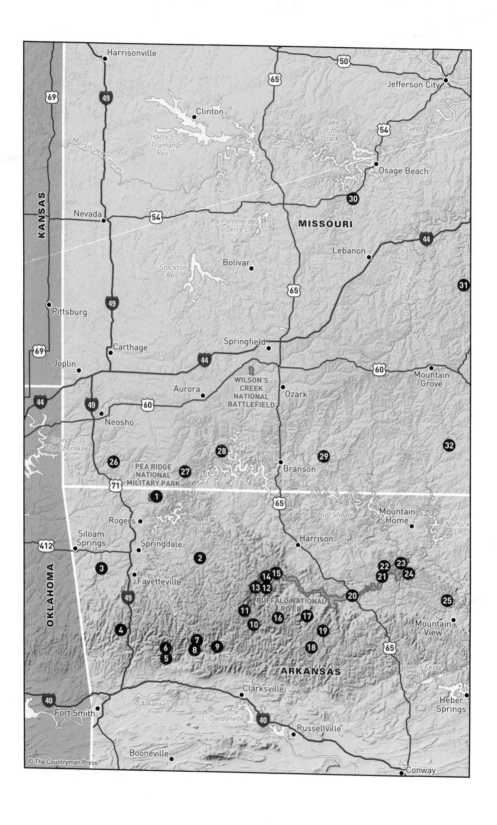

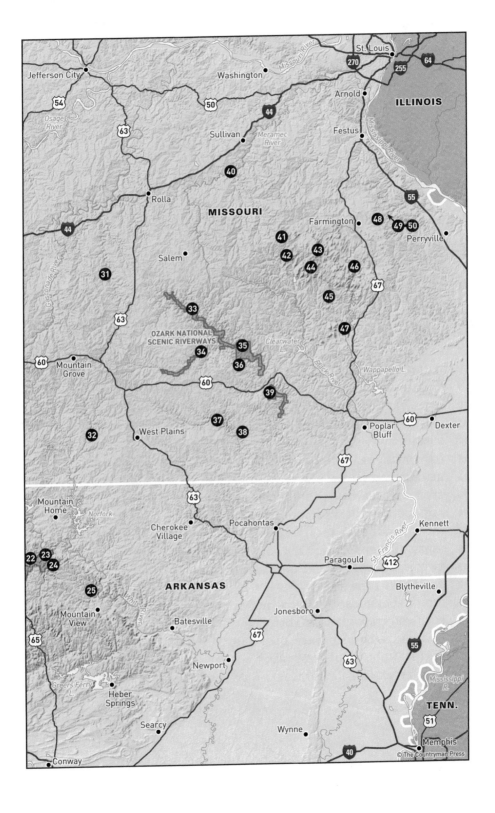

Contents

II. MISSOURI OZARK HIKES | 145

Hikes at a Glance

Hike	City	Distance (miles)	Views
1. Pea Ridge National Military Park Loop	Rogers	3.7	✓
2. Withrow Springs State Park Hike	Fayetteville	2.6	✓
3. Lake Wedington Walk	Fayetteville	4.4	✓
4. Devils Den Geological Walk	Fayetteville	1.3	
5. Shores Lake—White Rock Loop	Mulberry	12.8	✓
6. White Rock Rim Loop	Mulberry	2.2	✓
7. Hare Mountain Vista and Homestead	Ozark	5.2	✓
8. Spy Rock Loop	Ozark	7.8	✓
9. Rattlesnake Rock	Clarksville	6.8	✓
10. The Glory Hole	Fallsville	2.0	
11. Hawksbill Crag Hike	Boxley	2.9	✓
12. Buffalo River Trail End-to-End	Boxley	37.3	✓
13. Lost Valley Trail Hike	Boxley	2.0	
14. Hemmed-in Hollow Loop	Harrison	5.8	✓
15. Cecil Cove Historic Loop Hike	Harrison	7.3	✓
16. Alum Cove Natural Bridge Loop	Jasper	1.2	
17. Sams Throne Loop	Russellville	2.3	✓
18. Pedestal Rocks Scenic Area Double Loop	Russellville	4.0	✓
19. Twin Falls Loop at Richland Creek Wilderness	Russellville	5.4	
20. Tyler Bend Loop	Marshall	4.2	✓
21. Indian Rockhouse Loop with Overlook Addendum	Yellville	4.4	✓
22. Rush Mountain Mine Meander	Yellville	3.6	✓
23. Lower Buffalo Wilderness Loop	Flippin	12.9	✓
24. Leatherwood Wilderness Trek	Mountain View	11.6	✓
25. North Sylamore Wilderness Sampler	Mountain View	4.6	✓
26. Ozark Chinquapin Trail	Pineville	3.1	
27. Roaring River State Park Double Loop	Cassville	5.6	
28. Piney Creek Wilderness Loop	Cassville	6.2	✓
29. Hercules Glades Wilderness Loop	Forsyth	6.6	✓
30. Ha Ha Tonka State Park Loop	Camdenton	3.9	✓
31. Paddy Creek Wilderness Loop	Licking	10.3	✓
32. Devils Backbone Wilderness Loop	West Plains	10.1	✓

Waterfall	Campground	Trail Camp	Kids	Comments
			✓	Preserved Civil War site
	✓		✓	Walk gorge rim above Ozark stream
✓	✓		✓	Recreation area has it all
✓	✓		✓	Trailside cave and rock features galore
✓	✓	✓	✓	One of Arkansas Ozarks' best loops
	✓		✓	Views for miles
		✓	✓	View from high point on Ozark Highlands Trail
✓	✓	✓	✓	This circuit has a little bit of everything
✓		✓		Solitude on Ozark Highlands Trail
✓			✓	Waterfall pours through orifice in rock shelter
		✓	✓	Arkansas Ozark icon
✓	✓	✓		Best long trail segment in Arkansas Ozarks
✓	✓		✓	Geological features aplenty, including cave
✓		✓		Big features, big elevation change
		✓		Old homesites, views
✓			✓	Natural arches
	✓		✓	More views than you can shake a stick at
✓			✓	Unusual rock formations, bluff top views, waterfall
✓	✓	✓		Tough hike along scenic stream to waterfall
	✓		✓	Historic homestead, vistas, good campground
✓	✓		✓	Aboriginal shelter, other trailside highlights
	✓		✓	Historic zinc mining site near Buffalo River
		✓		Wilderness hike to stellar panorama
		✓		Remote area, ford
✓	✓	✓	✓	Part of a larger recreation area
			✓	Solitude at harbor for rare Ozark flora
			✓	Explore fascinating natural areas
		✓		Clear stream leads to lake
		✓		Expansive views, resembles the landscapes of the American West
✓			✓	This hike has it all
	✓	✓		Views and more from big woods
	✓	✓		Solitude-filled classic wilderness hike

Hike	City	Distance	Views
33. Devils Well and Cave Spring Circuit	Eminence	5.4	✓
34. Alley Spring Mill Loop	Eminence	1.9	✓
35. Current River Vista—Blue Spring Double Hike	Eminence	6.0	✓
36. Stegall Mountain Vista via Rocky Falls	Eminence	6.2	✓
37. Boomhole Overlook and Beyond from McCormack Lake	Alton	7.9	✓
38. Irish Wilderness Loop	Alton	18.4	✓
39. Big Spring Loop	Van Buren	7.1	
40. Deer Run Loop at Onondaga Cave State Park	Leasburg	2.6	✓
41. Council Bluff Loop	Potosi	11.7	✓
42. Bell Mountain Wilderness Loop	Potosi	12.2	✓
43. Elephant Rocks State Park Loop	Ironton	1.1	✓
44. Missouri High Point Loop at Taum Sauk Mountain	Ironton	3.0	✓
45. Crane Lake Loop	Ironton	4.8	✓
46. Tiemann Shut-ins via Silver Mines	Fredericktown	5.4	✓
47. Mudlick Mountain Loop at Sam A. Baker State Park	Piedmont	7.4	✓
48. Pickle Springs Natural Area Loop	Farmington	2.0	✓
49. Whispering Pines Loop	Farmington	6.2	✓
50. White Oaks Loop at Hawn State Park	Farmington	4.0	

Water-fall	Camp-ground	Trail Camp	Kids	Comments
✓			✓	Hike combines fascinating geology, views, and an underground lake and cave spring
	✓		✓	Picturesque mill beside spring-fed stream
	✓	✓	✓	Explore wild and scenic Current River plus 310-foot deep spring
✓		✓	✓	Trek superlative portion of Ozark Trail
	✓	✓		Excellent vistas from bluffs above Eleven Point River
		✓		Largest wilderness in Missouri
	✓		✓	Visit truly big Big Spring
	✓		✓	Overlook of Meramec River
	✓	✓	✓	Circle scenic lake, backpacking
		✓		Earn your views on this trek
			✓	Fascinating and colorful granite formations
✓	✓		✓	Hike of superlatives at fine state park
		✓	✓	Shut-ins and more
	✓		✓	Gorge-ous geological and aquatic scenery
	✓	✓		Rugged hike, backpacking
✓			✓	Geological fairyland
✓			✓	Views, shut-ins, backpacking
	✓		✓	Solitude at worth-a-visit state park

LOOKING UPSTREAM FROM VISTA ON TYLER BEND LOOP

Acknowledgments

Thanks to everyone who walked with me on the trails for both the first and second editions of this guide, those who helped back at home, and all the land managers who answered my persistent questions. Thanks to my wife Keri Anne for hiking with me throughout the Ozarks. Thanks to Bryan Delay for backpacking with me on the Buffalo River Trail, and to my brothers for exploring Missouri with me. Thanks to Marie Earwood for hiking with me; Kevin Padgett and Robert L. Cole, too. Thanks to Ryan and Brian at Eleven Point Canoe Rental, and to Jessica Leigh Taylor as well.

BLUFFS RISE FROM SCENIC NORTH SYLAMORE CREEK

Preface

The Ozark Mountains have been a lure for me my entire life. After all, my mother is from Arkansas. When I was a boy we traveled to the Ozarks for getaways. Later I became a full-fledged outdoors enthusiast, eventually turning my passion for the rivers and mountains of our great country into a vocation. In the course of my outdoor evolution I often went to the Ozarks for paddling and hiking trips. On these excursions the great geological beauty of this plateau country revealed itself—the bluffs of the Buffalo River and the grassy glades of Piney Creek Wilderness. Seeing one place did not sate my desire for the Ozarks; rather, it made me want to see more. As a writer, I set my sights for these mountains. I wanted to capture the unique features of the land for others to enjoy.

I pitched the idea for this guidebook, then began systematically exploring the Ozarks for the best hikes. It was a real pleasure (most of the time) to travel these trails, from the bluffs and waterfalls of North Sylamore to the arches of Alum Cove to Missouri's high point on Taum Sauk Mountain to the vistas of Hercules Glades Wilderness. Along the way, too, I found some unexpected hikes that pleasantly surprised this grizzled veteran. I hope the hikes in this guide please you as well.

LOOKING AMID PINES INTO PADDY CREEK WILDERNESS

Introduction

Welcome to the second edition of *50 Hikes in the Ozarks*. The book, which details 50 hikes in the Ozark Mountains of Arkansas and Missouri, has been completely updated and includes several new hikes for readers to explore. In Arkansas the hikes range from Pea Ridge near the Oklahoma state line to the appropriately named town of Mountain View in the east. In Missouri they extend from Big Sugar Creek State Park near Branson to Pickle Creek Natural Area within striking distance of St. Louis—and all the rivers and mountains between. I placed specific emphasis on the most scenic destinations and unique places that make the Ozarks so special—places like White Rock Mountain, with its 360-degree views, and the massive springs along the Eleven Point River.

Many hikes in this book take place on the Ozark Trail and the Ozark Highlands Trail, the two master paths of this rugged land. Others fall within the numerous federally designated wildernesses scattered amid the mountains of Missouri and Arkansas. Treks of varied lengths and difficulties are included. Sometimes you feel like going on a rugged hike; other times an easy stroll will do. Schedule constraints, companions, and time of year are major considerations when choosing a hike. Grandma is not going to feel like fording remote rivers, while a weekend backpack with your old Scout buddy will likely entail challenging terrain.

You'll also find hikes here set within Missouri's Mark Twain National Forest and Arkansas's Ozark National Forest. These federal lands cover over 2.7 million acres and feature not only hiking trails but also campgrounds, waterways to float and fish, special scenic areas, hunting, and more. Some hikes are within boundaries of the Buffalo National River and the Ozark National Scenic Riverways—public lands that grow ever more valuable as the Ozarks become more populated with vacation homes and folks wanting to enjoy the superlative scenery the area offers. Arkansas and Missouri state parks also dot the landscape and are destinations for explorers. No matter what entity manages the land, there is plenty to see—old mines, dramatic falls framed in rich forests, rock outcrops where panoramic views extend forth, and backcountry where bears furtively roam the hollows and smallmouth bass ply the spring-fed streams.

The best way to reach these places is by foot. The rewards increase with every step beneath the stately oaks of the ridgetops or into the deep gorges where waterfalls roar among old-growth trees spared the logger's ax. A respite in the Ozarks will revitalize both mind and spirit. Smelling the autumn leaves on a crisp afternoon, climbing to a lookout, contemplating pioneer lives at an old homesite—these all put our lives into perspective.

That's where this book comes into play. It will help you make every step count, whether you're leading the family on a brief day hike or undertaking a challenging backpack into the reaches. With your precious time, and the knowledge imparted to you in these pages, your outdoor experience will be realized to its fullest.

This book presents 50 hikes from which to choose. Included are some of the classics, such as Devils Den and Elephant Rocks. The majority of the trips described, however, are off the beaten path, offering more solitude on the way to lesser-known yet equally scenic sights like Rattlesnake Rock and Irish Wilderness. This will give you the opportunity to get back to nature on your own terms.

Two types of day hikes are offered: there-and-back and loop hikes. One-way hikes lead to a particular rewarding destination, returning via the same trail. The return trip allows you to see everything from the opposite vantage point. You may notice more minute trail-side features the second go-round, and returning at a different time of day may give the same trail a surprisingly different character.

To some folks, though, returning on the same trail just isn't as enjoyable. There are hikers who simply can't stand the thought of covering the same ground twice, given all the miles of Ozark trails awaiting them. Loop hikes avoid this. Most of these hikes offer solitude to maximize your experience, though by necessity, portions of some traverse potentially popular areas.

Day hiking is the most popular way to explore the Ozarks, but for those with the inclination, this book offers overnight hikes as well. Some of the best locales for overnight stays are detailed for those who want to see the cycle of the mountains turn from day to night and back again. The length of these hikes was chosen primarily for the weekend backpacker. Backpackers should follow park regulations where applicable and practice Leave No Trace wilderness-use etiquette.

The wilderness experience can unleash your mind and body, allowing you to relax and find peace and quiet. It also enables you to grasp beauty and splendor: a wide rock slab with a window to the wooded valley below, a bobcat disappearing into a brushy thicket, a snow-covered clearing marking an old homestead. In these lands you can let your mind roam free to go where it pleases. So get out and enjoy the treasures of the Ozarks.

HOW TO USE THIS GUIDEBOOK

The 50 hikes in this book are divided by state. Each hike is contained in its own chapter and opens with an information box including total distance, hiking time, vertical rise, and maps. Here's a typical hike info box:

SPY ROCK LOOP

TOTAL DISTANCE: 7.8-mile loop

HIKING TIME: 4 hours

VERTICAL RISE: 820 feet

RATING: Moderate to difficult

MAPS: USGS 7.5' Cass, Yale; Ozark National Forest

TRAILHEAD GPS COORDINATES: N35° 40.674', W93° 46.356'

CONTACT INFORMATION: Ozark National Forest, 2591 Hwy 21 North, Clarksville, AR 72830, (479) 754-2864, www.fs.usda.gov/osfnf

This outing, as you can see, is 7.8 miles long. To determine distance I walked (and in many cases rewalked) every hike in this guidebook using a Global Positioning System (GPS). You may notice discrepancies between the distances given in this book and those listed on trailhead signs, in other books, or in trail literature distributed by the governing bodies that administer the trails. Sometimes trail distance is passed down from one government body to the next with no one knowing where it even originally came from. Same goes with trail signs. I have full confidence in the mileages given in this book, since I obtained them myself from my own hiking—field experience, if you will—with GPS in hand. Distances are given from the trailhead to the destination, and not from the parking area.

Our sample hike is a loop: You make a circuit, returning to the trailhead without backtracking. Other hikes could be there-and-back or end-to-end treks. An end-to-end hike requires an auto shuttle between the ends, whereas there-and-back and loop hikes start and end at the same trailhead.

The hiking time—in this case, 4 hours—is based on the actual time you'll likely spend on the trail, with a little leeway built in for orienting and stopping. Hiking times are averages and will of course be different for each hiker and hiking group. Before you take on a particular trip, factor the physical fitness levels of the group, rest times desired, eating and drinking breaks, as well as relaxing and contemplation-of-nature time into your projected hiking schedule.

The Spy Rock Loop features a vertical rise of 820 feet. In this case, it represents the climb from the trailhead to Spy Rock. Vertical rise is calculated as the largest uphill vertical change on a hike; it is not the sum of all climbs during the hike. This rise may come anywhere along the hike, and not necessarily on the first climb from the trailhead. I obtained vertical rise figures from elevation profiles, which I in turn derived from plotting the GPS tracks onto a computer mapping program.

This hike is rated moderate to difficult, based on its elevation change and the fact that this is a well-maintained trail that's mostly easy to follow. Hikes in this book range from easy to moderate to difficult. In rating the difficulty of each trail, I took the following factors into consideration: trail length; overall trail condition, including maintenance and ease of navigation; and elevation changes. Longer, rougher hikes with large elevation changes are rated difficult. In contrast, a short, level, and well-marked nature trail, such as Elephant Rocks, will be rated easy.

Under "Maps," the first items listed are US Geological Survey 7.5' quadrangle maps. These "quad maps," as they are known, cover every parcel of land in this country, divided into highly detailed rectangular maps. Each quad has a name, usually based on a physical feature located within the quad. The Spy Rock Loop traverses two quad maps—Cass and Yale. Quad maps can be obtained online at www.usgs.gov. Other helpful maps are included in this category as well. In this case, the Ozark National Forest map will be helpful. You might also find more detailed maps of wilderness area listed, or state park hiking trail maps. Many governing bodies and organizations also offer online trail maps. If so, those maps will be noted here.

"Trailhead GPS Coordinates" gives you the latitude and longitude of the trailhead location. Therefore, you can simply punch the coordinates into a navigational app on your phone or into a GPS and reach the trailhead. However, readers can easily access all trailheads in this book by using the directions given.

"Contact Information" gives you mail, phone, and Internet resources for learning more about the hike, should your curiosity extend beyond what you find in this book, or you seek information about the destination beyond the scope of hiking.

Following the information box is an overview of the hike: a paragraph or two that gives you an overall feel for what to expect, what you might see, trail conditions, and important information you might need to consider before undertaking the hike, such as permits needed, river fords, or challenging driving conditions. "How to Get There" follows the hike overview and lists detailed directions from a known and identifiable starting point to the trailhead.

"The Hike" is the meat and bones of your trek. A running narrative gives detailed descriptions of the trails used in the hike, including junctions, stream crossings, and interesting human or natural history along the way. This keeps you apprised of your whereabouts as well as making sure you don't miss the best features. With the information included in this guide, you can enjoy an informed, better-executed hike, making the most of your precious time.

In writing this book I had the pleasure of meeting many friendly, helpful people: local residents proud of the unique lands around them, along with state park and national forest employees who endured my endless questions. Even better were my fellow hikers, who were eager to share their knowledge of favorite spots. They already know what beauty lies on the horizon. As the Ozarks become more crowded, these lands become that much more precious. Enjoy them, protect them, and use them wisely.

WHAT IT'S LIKE—HIKING THE OZARKS

It's walking Bell Mountain Wilderness Loop in a thunderstorm;

It's seeing the Glory Hole after a heavy rain;

It's standing under the arch of Alum Cove Natural Bridge;

It's seeing all the homesites in Cecil Cove;

It's entering cool, wet Devils Den Cave on a hot sunny day;

It's pounding your feet on rocky Mudlick Mountain;

It's seeing Alley Spring Mill framed in autumn colors;

It's being eaten up by chiggers while backpacking Irish Wilderness;

It's making ford after ford on Leatherwood Creek;

It's looking down into the Devils Well;

It's being blown away by the concentration of rock formations at Pickle Springs;

It's feeling the raw power of Rocky Falls;

It's wondering how Spy Rock got its name while overlooking an Ozark expanse;

It's wanting to hike the entire Ozark Trail while overlooking the Current River;

It's having the Ozark Chinquapin Trail all to yourself;

It's seeing all the relics left over from the Rush Mountain Mine;

It's watching the fall colors reflect off Crane Lake on a calm evening;

It's being amazed by the continual
views along White Rock Mountain;

It's appreciating all the wildflowers in
Hercules Glades Wilderness;

It's imagining the historic Civil War
battle at Pea Ridge;

It's being disheartened at trash left by
thoughtless hikers;

It's gazing unbelievingly into the depth
and clarity of Blue Spring;

It's passing a hardscrabble Ozark
homestead and wondering what life
was like then;

It's wondering who else sat under the
Indian Rockhouse during a rain;

It's walking along the bluffs of the
Pedestal Rocks on a crystal blue fall
day;

It's looking at Johnson Mountain
rising forth from Council Bluff Lake;

It's seeing the very ruggedness of the
Tiemann Shut-Ins;

It's seeing tree after tree after tree and
appreciating them all;

It's being amazed by the rock walls of
Sams Throne;

It's the sheer numbers of hikers at
Devils Den;

It's the clarity of the Eleven Point River
reflecting the green density of the
forest;

It's watching turkeys scatter on
a wooded hill in Paddy Creek
Wilderness;

It's just being in the Ozarks.

CONTACT INFORMATION

Arkansas

Ozark National Forest
Ozark–St. Francis National Forests
605 West Main Street
Russellville, AR 72801
(479) 964-7200
www.fs.usda.gov/main/osfnf/

Buffalo National River
402 North Walnut Street, Suite 136
Harrison, AR 72601
(870) 439-2502
www.nps.gov/buff

Arkansas State Parks
1 Capitol Mall
Little Rock, AR 72201
(888) 287-2757
www.arkansasstateparks.com

Missouri

Mark Twain National Forest
401 Fairgrounds Road
Rolla, MO 65401
(573) 364-4621
www.fs.usda.gov/mtnf

Ozark Scenic Riverways
404 Watercress Drive
Van Buren, MO 63965
(573) 323-4236
www.nps.gov/ozar

Missouri State Parks
Missouri Department of Natural
Resources
Division of State Parks
P.O. Box 176; 1101 Riverside Drive
Jefferson City, MO 65102-0176
(573) 751-3443
www.mostateparks.com

I.

ARKANSAS
OZARK HIKES

Pea Ridge National Military Park Loop

TOTAL DISTANCE: 3.7-mile loop	
HIKING TIME: 2 hours	
VERTICAL RISE: 300 feet	
RATING: Moderate	
MAPS: USGS 7.5' Pea Ridge; Pea Ridge National Military Park	
TRAILHEAD GPS COORDINATES: N36° 27.295', W94° 1.236'	
CONTACT INFORMATION: Pea Ridge National Military Park, 15930 E Hwy 62, Garfield, AR 72732, (479) 451-8122, www.nps.gov/peri	

This hike takes you through part of a Civil War battlefield. Pea Ridge National Military Park is a preserved parcel of land where the Union and Confederacy fought during March 1862, leaving Missouri in the hands of the North. Today you can explore the area by car and by foot, learning the battle's details. The best time to visit this park is around the time when the battle was fought—March. This particular trek takes you to an overlook offering the grandest view of the park, and then heads for historic Elkhorn Tavern along an escarpment. From the tavern building you will follow old Telegraph Road down past a tanyard and a battlefield hospital locale. You'll walk up a ridgeline to old Huntsville Road, which returns to the tavern—completing your loop. These historic roads are closed to the public and make for good hiking trails.

On your visit make sure to explore the park beyond this track, including a trip into the visitor's center and a tour of the battlefield on the auto road. By the way, bicyclists like to pedal the auto tour road as well, so bring your two-wheeler if you are so inclined.

HOW TO GET THERE

To reach Pea Ridge from Exit 86 off I-540 near Rogers, take US 62 east. After 10 miles, continue forward on US 62; do not turn left on AR 72, which goes to the community of Pea Ridge. Instead continue forward for 2 more miles, for a total of 12 miles, to reach the park on your left. Inside the park, keep left beyond the visitor's center, joining the auto tour road. Travel for 4.9 miles on the auto tour road, and then bear left and drive a short distance to the East Overlook.

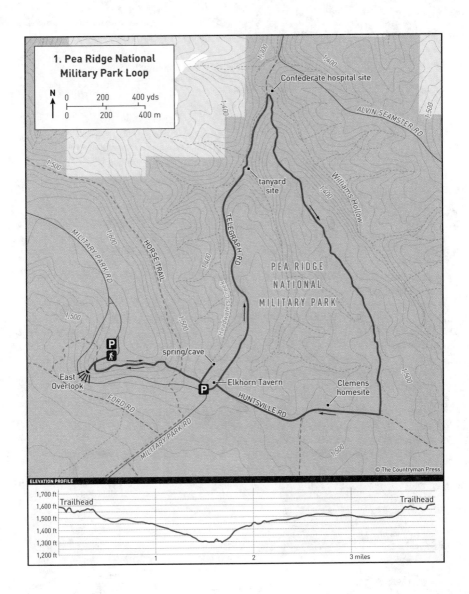

1. Pea Ridge National Military Park Loop

N
0 — 200 — 400 yds
0 — 200 — 400 m

Confederate hospital site

ALVIN SEAMSTER RD

tanyard site

Williams Hollow

PEA RIDGE NATIONAL MILITARY PARK

TELEGRAPH RD

MILITARY PARK RD

HORSE TRAIL

Headwaters Creek

spring/cave

East Overlook

FORD RD

Elkhorn Tavern

HUNTSVILLE RD

Clemens homesite

MILITARY PARK RD

© The Countryman Press

ELEVATION PROFILE

1,700 ft
1,600 ft — Trailhead
1,500 ft
1,400 ft
1,300 ft
1,200 ft

Trailhead

1   2   3 miles

THE HIKE

Leave the parking area and follow the concrete path heading toward the East Overlook. Pass a stone bench on your right, and then reach the overlook. Gaze to the southwest. Many rock outcrops are just below, as are the fields and fences of the battlefield's heart. The visitor center is visible; beyond, the Ozarks stretch as far as the eye can see. Take a minute to absorb this overlook; interpretive information gives you the layout. Backtrack just a short distance and take the trail leading right, walking easterly back toward the parking area along an escarpment covered in cedars and other trees.

Curve below the parking area. The rocks, cedars, oaks, and drop-offs make

LOOKING OVER PEA RIDGE BATTLEFIELD FROM EAST OVERLOOK

for quite a scenic walk here. Finally leave the ridgeline on some steps, cutting through a crack in the cliffs—it's a narrow passage. The single-track path now descends toward Headwaters Creek. Continue forward and reach a wooden fence. Before you head to the Elkhorn Tavern, turn left here and walk down to see the tavern spring and cave. The spur trail to the cave will be on your left, but the park service does not allow exploration—the cave is closed. Just downstream from it lies the spring that once served the Elkhorn Tavern. Backtrack just a bit, and then take the spur trail up to Elkhorn Tavern.

With luck, the Elkhorn will be open for your visit, and you can check it out. The building is open when there are volunteers to man it. When you are done looking around, get oriented. Face the tavern front. The track behind you is Huntsville Road, your return route; the road to your right is Telegraph Road, which is the best way to make the loop. Control of these two roads was key to the 1862 battle. From the tavern, descend Telegraph Road to reach the tanyard at 1.4 miles. Explore around this creekside site. The stone foundation of the tanyard building and also the old well—now partially filled in—are visible. Leave the tanyard clearing and continue downstream, crossing an intermittent streambed. As you cross, look left toward Headwaters Creek and see the walled stones forming an old bridge abutment. Headwaters Creek, the stream you've been following, is now developing some bluffs as it cuts deeper into the hillside. Giant sycamores rise above the other trees of the watercourse. The trail turns acutely right at 1.6 miles. Head just a short distance farther down Telegraph Road to

ELKHORN TAVERN

Withrow Springs State Park Hike

TOTAL DISTANCE: 2.6-mile balloon loop	

HIKING TIME: 1.5 hours

VERTICAL RISE: 200 feet

RATING: Moderate

MAPS: USGS 7.5' Forum; Trails at Withrow Springs State Park

TRAILHEAD GPS COORDINATES: N36° 9.018', W93° 44.413'

CONTACT INFORMATION: Withrow Springs State Park, 33424 Spur 23, Huntsville, AR 72740, (479) 559-2593, www.arkan sasstateparks.com/withrowsprings/

Take an excellent family hike at a fun state park in the Ozarks. Start your walk at War Eagle Creek, walking along rock outcrops and bluffs above the scenic stream. Climb higher, emerging atop a cliff presenting views of winding War Eagle Creek, framed in the hills beyond. Soak in a second view before turning away from the cliffline, heading deeper into Withrow Springs State Park. From there, pick up the Dogwood Trail, looping through hilly woods, briefly emerging alongside AR 23 Spur before completing a loop. Finally, backtrack along the cliff above War Eagle Creek, grabbing encore panoramas on your return to the trailhead.

HOW TO GET THERE

From the intersection of US 412 and AR 23 just north of Huntsville, Arkansas, take AR 23 north for 2.0 miles to cross War Eagle Creek on a road bridge. Immediately turn left here, into a parking area for the War Eagle Trail that also has a launch for canoes and kayaks floating the creek.

THE HIKE

The Ozarks are renowned for their water features—from wild and scenic rivers to bluff-topped turquoise creeks to massive chilly springs. During the nineteenth century, a certain spring that emerged from a base of a bluff then ran into nearby War Eagle Creek attracted a transplanted Tennessean by the name of Richard Withrow. The settler staked out his ground in 1832, and as a result of his efforts to settle the land, the springs now bear his name. Richard Withrow was never exposed to the concept of a state park, so he certainly couldn't imagine such a preserve named after him.

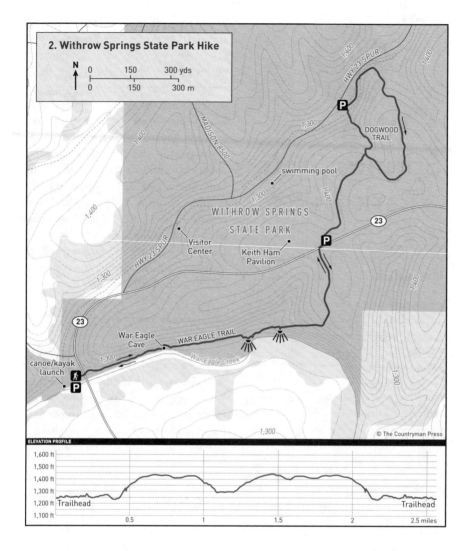

2. Withrow Springs State Park Hike

But that is what happened in 1962, when Arkansas Governor Orval Faubus—who happened to be from the county where Withrow Springs flows—talked his friend and then-landowner Roscoe Hobbs into donating Withrow Springs to the state for a park. The natural features were already there: the springs, the bluffs towering 150 feet over War Eagle Creek, the fish plying its waters, the dense ranks of woods elsewhere. Improvements were made—

picnic areas and campgrounds created, trails laid out, even a swimming pool added. Today, the park is home to a fine campground suitable for tents and RVs. A canoe and kayak launch lies along War Eagle Creek. Picnic shelters hosts families and other groups.

And the trails, though somewhat limited in distance, continue to draw in hikers, walkers, and families. Our hike takes the park's favored trail, the War Eagle Trail, following its singletrack

LOOKING DOWN ON WAR EAGLE CREEK

path under AR 23. Soon, the trail uses rock bluffs as a footbed while heading upstream, looking down on War Eagle Creek. Cedars, walnut and hickory trees partly shade the path, despite the abundance of open rock that makes the trail so alluring.

Below you, War Eagle Creek flows around tan gravel bars and fallen trees. The general paddling season for this stream is March through June, though the waterway can remain floatable through the summer in wetter years. Withrow Springs State Park offers canoe rentals and shuttles while War Eagle Creek is floatable. A trip down this Ozark stream will complement a hike at Withrow Springs State Park.

By 0.2 mile, layered bluffs are a regular part of the trail. Ahead, pass a small cave. There is another, better cave just

ahead—War Eagle Cave. Formerly, visitors could trek almost 200 feet back into its maw, but the cave is now closed in an effort to curb the spread of the bat disease known as white-nose syndrome. Most backcountry caves are shut down these days, though privately operated show caves are still open.

At War Eagle Cave, the trail suddenly climbs, circling atop the opening before continuing along the bluff. Ahead, wire cable aids passage along a particularly narrow stretch of path as it tightropes along a line of rock. At .4 mile, the trail comes to a wider outcrop and you can look over the stream, flowing about 30 feet below.

From here, the trail keeps climbing along the bluff, well above the creek. Reach your first elevated view at 0.5 mile. Below, War Eagle Creek seems smaller, as you stand on a craggy perch of weathered rock. Continuing uptrail, pass a second viewpoint. This one is even higher and allows upstream glimpses around a bend as well as downstream. War Eagle Creek is a tributary of the White River.

The War Eagle Trail climbs up additional craggy slope, then changes character as it turns away from War Eagle Creek. Here, the path enters a grassy, brushy glade, where berries ripen in early summer. Keep going to reach AR 23 and an alternate trailhead, as well as the Keith Ham picnic pavilion at 0.8 mile. Join the Dogwood Trail after the road crossing. True to its name, the path is rich with white blossoms in spring, while the red berries and reddish-maroon leaves provide additional color in fall.

Descend to reach an intersection at 1.0 mile. Head left, beginning the loop portion of the hike. Wind down a narrow vale, crossing a likely dry drainage to reach AR 23 Spur and another parking area at 1.1 miles. Keep right along the road, then pass around a pole gate. Follow the doubletrack, then split right again at a signed turn. Here, the Dogwood Trail climbs through thick woods. Finish the loop part of the hike at 1.6 miles. From here it is a 1-mile backtrack to the trailhead. Enjoy that second round of views from the cliffs above War Eagle Creek.

Lake Wedington Walk

TOTAL DISTANCE: 4.4-mile there-and-back

HIKING TIME: 2 hours

VERTICAL RISE: 110 feet

RATING: Easy

MAPS: USGS 7.5' Wheeler, Rhea; Lake Wedington Recreation Area

TRAILHEAD GPS COORDINATES: N36° 5.804', W94° 22.296'

CONTACT INFORMATION: Ozark National Forest, P.O. Box 76, 1803 North 18th Street, Ozark, AR 72949, (479) 667-2191, www .fs.usda.gov/osfnf

A walk on the Lakeshore Trail is just one component of this multifaceted recreation area west of the college town of Fayetteville, Arkansas. Nonetheless, the walk stands alone as a good one. Start in a cove of Lake Wedington, then saunter along the shoreline, soaking in the Ozark lake scenery. Cross the lake dam, then view a 20-foot waterfall below the lake. Resume the lakeside stroll, then climb to an overlook and historic gazebo, built by the Civilian Conservation Corps. Enjoy more aquatic scenery before backtracking. Include post-hike time to view other historic structures, swim, fish, paddle, picnic, and even camp at this desirable destination.

HOW TO GET THERE

From exit 64 on I-49 in Fayetteville, take AR 16 west for 11.2 miles to the trailhead on your left, 0.6 mile before the Lake Wedington Recreation Area Campground entrance. Coming from Fayetteville, the correct trailhead will be the first thing you reach on Lake Wedington. The main Lake Wedington Recreation Area entrance is 0.2 mile beyond the campground entrance.

THE HIKE

You should enjoy more than just this hike here at such a multifaceted agglomeration of outdoor scenery and activities in the Ozark National Forest. The entire recreation area was developed back in the 1930s by the Civilian Conservation Corps, finished in 1938. The trademark wood and stone structures, now on the National Register of Historic Places, are seen throughout the Lake Wedington area, including the gazebo at the overlook above Lake Wedington; the lodge, where weddings and other gatherings

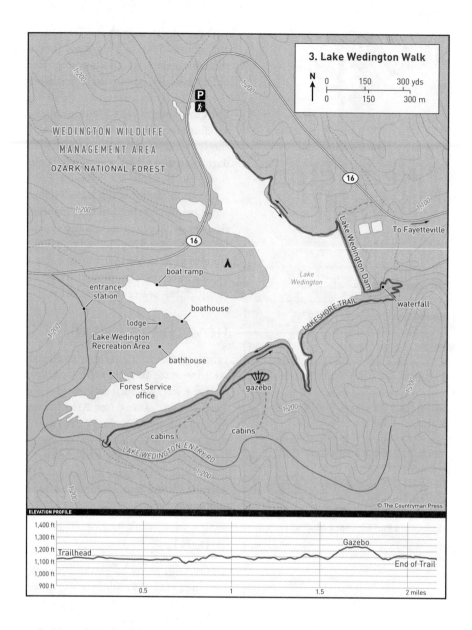

WEDINGTON WILDLIFE
MANAGEMENT AREA
OZARK NATIONAL FOREST

1,200

16

1,100

To Fayetteville

Lake Wedington Dam

Lake
Wedington

LAKESHORE TRAIL

waterfall

boat ramp

entrance
station

boathouse

lodge

Lake Wedington
Recreation Area

bathhouse

Forest Service
office

gazebo

1,200

cabins

cabins

LAKE WEDINGTON ENTRY RD

1,200

1,200

© The Countryman Press

ELEVATION PROFILE

1,400 ft						
1,300 ft					Gazebo	
1,200 ft Trailhead						
1,100 ft						End of Trail
1,000 ft						
900 ft		0.5	1	1.5		2 miles

are held; and the bathhouse, still used by those relaxing on the shoreline on a hot summer afternoon. Rustic cabins from that era dot the rising hills. Still other structures include the boathouse and forest service office.

Lake Wedington spans 102 acres, stretching out in three arms above sloping wooded shoreline. Bass, bream, and crappie are sought-after species. Paddling is very popular here, though no motors higher than 10 horsepower are allowed. Large picnic sites are set in both sun and shade. Overall—if the weather is cooperating—it is hard not to have a good time at Lake Wedington.

And that includes hiking the Lakeshore Trail. The best access is at the

WATERFALL TUMBLES IN STAGES BELOW LAKE WEDINGTON DAM

northernmost arm of the impoundment. Here, the trailhead also serves as a popular bank-fishing area. Pick up the singletrack path, with rising pine and oak woods to your left and open lake to your right. Anglers may be seen plying their trade in small clearings, especially close to the trailhead.

At 0.2 mile, the path curves around a little embayment, fed by a seasonal streamlet. More of the lake opens ahead, with views of the historic CCC buildings across the water. At 0.5 mile, you reach the dam. Here, a spur path leads out to AR 16. The Lakeshore Trail, however, continues southeast, cruising atop the arrow-straight dam. Come to the dam outflow, where the unnamed tributary of the Illinois River continues its journey after filling Lake Wedington. Turn away from the dam, following the stone spillway wall downstream.

Reach a surprising 20-foot waterfall as it careens over a stratified stone wall. In spring this uniform wall of white can be a real gusher. Below the falls, the area can be confusing, since multiple user-created trails make the way unclear. To stay on track, cross the creek below the waterfall, then look for a blazed track that switchbacks uphill, coming near a power line clearing. The Lakeshore Trail then returns you to the shoreline, across from Lake Wedington's 17-site campground, standing proud on a peninsula.

Walk southwesterly, as a hill rises to your left. At 1.1 miles, the path leads you into an intimate embayment, where a narrow valley provides a secluded spot, and cross the streamlet creating the embayment. Avoid a now-closed trail leading up to the gazebo, and turn out to the main lake. A summer Saturday will find swimmers and sunbathers across the water near the bathhouse. At 1.6 miles, come to a trail intersection. Here, make a sharp left on an improved wide gravel path heading up to the historic gazebo.

CCC-BUILT SHELTER ON RIDGE ABOVE LAKE WEDINGTON

Another trail angles up a hillside before turning back toward the stone and wood structure. Tall trees screen the view somewhat, and the vista will be better in winter. A path leads here from the cabins, too. Take a moment to visualize young men constructing the facilities at Lake Wedington during the Great Depression, living on-site, while they erected the iconic stone and wood structures that so many of us associate with parks and recreation areas in the Ozarks and throughout the country. The structures at Lake Wedington underwent restoration in 2016, and hopefully they will persevere for future Ozark hikers and recreationalists to enjoy.

Rejoin the main trail at 1.9 miles. Continue along Lake Wedington, soaking in more waterfront scenery. After leaving the waterfront, the Lakeshore Trail comes to the recreation area road leading to the cabins at 2.2 miles. If you are interested, you can walk around to the main recreation facilities. And if you choose to loop around the lake you will have to walk the roads a bit to make it happen. I recommend backtracking to the trailhead, making a 4.4 mile there-and-back hike exclusively on hiking trails. Then load up your vehicle and enjoy the rest of the fun things to see and do at Lake Wedington Recreation Area.

Devils Den Geological Walk

TOTAL DISTANCE: 1.3-mile loop	

HIKING TIME: 1 hour

VERTICAL RISE: 200 feet

RATING: Easy

MAPS: USGS 7.5' Winslow, Strickler; Devils Den Trails

TRAILHEAD GPS COORDINATES: N35° 46.791', W94° 14.953'

CONTACT INFORMATION: Devils Den State Park, 11333 West Arkansas Highway 74, West Fork, AR 72774, (479) 761-3325, www .arkansasstateparks.com/devilsden/

This hike travels through one of the most geologically interesting areas in the Natural State: the Devils Den, deep in the valley of Lee Creek. Though the trail is only 1.3 miles in length, it packs quite a punch. Furthermore, if you are reluctant to travel here due to the short length of the hike, know that there are over 20 miles of other trails nearby, including the Yellow Rock Loop, which offers a very good vista. Also, this state park has more, including a campground, Lake Devil, mountain biking trails, and cabins. Remember to bring a flashlight with you on this hike so you can go into the Devils Den Cave, if the park has it open.

Be apprised that this is the most popular trek in the entire state park as well as in this book. The trail will be busy on nice weekends. Plan this hike for the early morning or evening if it's a weekend. You will enjoy the water features of this hike more in winter and spring and following heavy rains.

HOW TO GET THERE

From Exit 45 off I-540 near Winslow, take AR 74 west for 7.0 miles to the visitor's center on your left. The Devils Den Trail starts around the right-hand side of the center as you face it. Alternative directions: From Exit 53 off I-540 south of Fayetteville, follow AR 70 west for 17 miles to the state park.

THE HIKE

Before you start your hike, consider going into the visitor's center to purchase some informational pamphlets explaining the geological and human history of the state park. This trail was originally built by the Civilian Conservation Corps (CCC) back in the 1930s. By the way, the visitor's center is just one

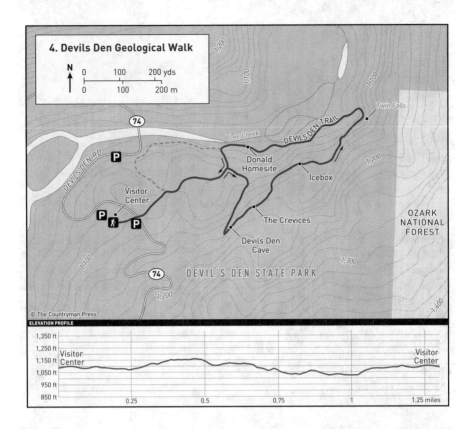

ELEVATION PROFILE

of the many CCC buildings here, said to be collectively the most fully intact of any CCC structures in Arkansas.

As you face the visitor's center, curve around its right-hand side to follow a split-rail fence. Cross AR 74 going down wooden footsteps, which lead to stone stairs down the trail. Cross a streambed, continuing forward to reach the Devils Theater. A spur trail leads left into this walled, roomlike setting. Shortly you'll reach the loop portion of your hike. Stay right here, following the red blazes. The Devils Den Trail travels underneath lush forest as it curves away from Lee Creek and follows a pair of switchbacks to join the ridgeline. The trail then makes a switchback to your left. When it levels off, look for the small hole to your right—the Devils Den Cave. Hopefully you brought a flashlight! Light or no, it's advised that you not enter the cave alone. It may be closed to visitation.

Flashlight in hand, enter the dark passage, a tall and narrow crevice of a cave. The Devils Den area is known for its crevices. It will take a few moments for your eyes to adjust to the darkness and the light from your headlamp or flashlight. In places the passage is so narrow that hikers have to stop in wider spots to allow those exiting the cave to come by. Caves maintain consistent temperatures; this one will feel cool in summer, warm in winter. Continue deeper into the crevice and stop. Listen to the water drip. By this point you will undoubtedly have felt the moisture on the walls of the cave and heard the splattering at your feet. Look around

TRAILSIDE FALLS

with your flashlight. You will see bats here. Five bat species inhabit the park. Your average hiker can head around 200 feet into the cave before having to crawl and get seriously dirty. The entire cave extends back 550 feet before dead-ending, but even the most intrepid hikers get only 330 feet back.

Beyond the Devils Den, back on the outside, reach an overlook to your left.

Then comes a series of features sometimes collectively called the Crevices. On a hot day you can feel cool air blowing from them. I am happy to report that all these features are open for exploration; they aren't fenced and blocked off and such. This means you have to be careful, but it also means you can explore them at will. Look down and see the trails that previous hikers have

HIKERS ENJOY SPRAY BELOW TWIN FALLS

made into the Crevices. You may be tempted to get down and dirty yourself.

Come to the Devils Icebox. This is just one more example of the area's crevices, which geologists believe were formed when the rock fractured and slid, creating the tall and narrow passages 250 to 350 million years ago. Cool air is emitted from this cave, hence the name. Beyond, the trail curves around a crack to your left. Ahead, look at the boulder embedded in the ground, under which lies an opening. This is Bear Cave. Just to the left of this are the Bowls—circular impressions under the overhanging rock shelter. Continue to marvel at the geological features.

Come along a beautiful cliff line that in-season features delicate, spray-filled waterfalls. If you didn't get wet in the Devils Den Cave, here is your second chance. Twin Falls splatters the trailside when flowing heartily. Cross one of the falls on a wooden bridge, and then descend to a second wooden bridge below. Look up for one last view of this aquatic feature, which can run dry in late summer and fall.

Now come alongside of the Lee Creek, heading downstream. Spur trails lead to the water. Pass a spring flowing from under a rock. Look left for a bluff line with elevated catacombs. The trail stays above Lee Creek, which flows in rapids and shoals past gravel bars. You can also look across at the state park campground. Come to the old Donald Homesite, located on a bluff overlooking Lee Creek. Note the stone steps leading down to the water. Shortly beyond the homesite, the trail leads left and away from Lee Creek, returning toward the visitor's center and trailhead. Reach a junction. You were here before. Backtrack to complete your hike.

5

Shores Lake–White Rock Loop

TOTAL DISTANCE: 12.8-mile loop	

HIKING TIME: 7 hours

VERTICAL RISE: 1,000 feet

RATING: Difficult

MAPS: USGS 7.5' Bidville; Shores Lake–White Rock Loop, Ozark National Forest

TRAILHEAD GPS COORDINATES: N35° 38.655', W93° 57.627'

CONTACT INFORMATION: Ozark National Forest, P.O. Box 76, 1803 North 18th Street, Ozark, AR 72949, (479) 667-2191, www.fs.usda.gov/osfnf

This is one of the best loop hikes in the Ozarks. It offers both waterfalls and vistas while traveling through an ultrascenic swath of the Ozark National Forest. You'll start at Shores Lake Recreation Area, which has camping and fishing, and then make your way up the Hurricane Creek Valley, reaching a cascade on White Rock Creek. Beyond this cascade, the trail climbs to the south slope of White Rock Mountain, where views await. Join the Ozark Highlands Trail for a period before dropping into the Salt Fork Valley, which is rampant with rugged beauty. Return to Shores Lake after exploring the Salt Fork.

HOW TO GET THERE

From Exit 24 off I-40, take AR 215 north for 12.7 miles, then veer left onto Forest Road 1505 (FR 1505) and follow it for 1.2 miles, passing Shores Lake Campground on your right. Turn right into the campground, then curve around the camper's loop to reach the trailhead parking area, about three-quarters of the way around and uphill to your right.

THE HIKE

Leave the Shores Lake trailhead, following the blue-blazed trail into oak woods. Prescribed fire has been a tool here, allowing farther-reaching views into the woods, even in summer. You will notice that the forest floor is quite rocky, as is the trailbed. Walk but a few feet, then reach a trail junction: the West Loop and the East Loop. Turn left onto the West Loop. This singletrack path immediately crosses a rocky drainage under oaks with a scattering of pines, aiming for the Hurricane Creek drainage. During warmer seasons, a thick covering of young hickory, oak, maple,

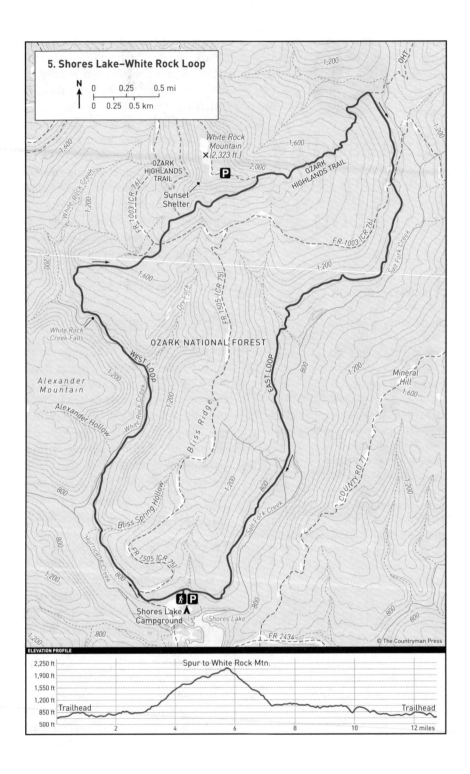

5. Shores Lake–White Rock Loop

N

0   0.25   0.5 mi

0   0.25   0.5 km

White Rock Mountain (2,323 ft.)

OZARK HIGHLANDS TRAIL

Sunset Shelter

White Rock Creek

FR 1003 (CR 76)

OZARK HIGHLANDS TRAIL

FR 1003 (CR 76)

Salt Fork Creek

OHT

White Rock Creek Falls

Dry Fork

FR 1505 (CR 75)

OZARK NATIONAL FOREST

Alexander Mountain

Alexander Hollow

WEST LOOP

White Rock Creek

Bliss Spring Hollow

Bliss Ridge

EAST LOOP

Salt Fork Creek

Mineral Hill

COUNTY RD. 77

Hurricane Creek

FR 1505 (CR 75)

Shores Lake Campground

Shores Lake

FR 2434

© The Countryman Press

ELEVATION PROFILE

Spur to White Rock Mtn.

2,250 ft
1,900 ft
1,550 ft
1,200 ft
850 ft
500 ft

Trailhead

Trailhead

2   4   6   8   10   12 miles

and other trees, along with wildflowers and herbs, carpets the forest floor. At 0.6 mile, cross FR 1505 on a curve. Continue deeper into the Hurricane Creek watershed. The forest floor is exceptionally rocky here. Twist your way among small rocks and boulders, admiring the hard work of the trail builders who cleared the path. Hurricane Creek, off to your left, is within earshot but not eyesight. The trail is curving around the south end of the Bliss Ridge—its slope sharpens.

Ahead, you can see the valleys of Hurricane and White Rock Creeks. Curve away from Hurricane Creek to enter Bliss Spring Hollow. The stream is most often a trickle flowing through a bouldery valley; in times of flood, though, it can blow quite a path through the hollow. Beyond, an impressive cliff line stands tall through the woods to your right. Dead ahead, Alexander Mountain rises forth. The woods perceptibly thicken here while curving into White Rock Creek Valley and Alexander Hollow. A brushy young forest forms a canopy and can be overgrown during summer. Pick up an old roadbed at 1.6 miles.

White Rock Creek comes into sight. Enjoy gazing on that unique sparkling blue-green Ozark water. Just at this point, you'll spot a nice pool that lures swimmers on a hot day. Begin ascending a rocky track with the creek to your left. The stream is also traveling over a rocky bed, in small shoals, riffles, and rapids. The old roadbed you've been following makes a ford, but the hiking trail climbs a slope to avoid it. The steep hillside offers a top-down perspective on White Rock Creek. Dip to meet the old road, then once again leave the creek as the old roadbed makes a ford. Here, the West Loop climbs steeply along the right bank of White Rock Creek. Avoiding the fords is a good thing, since many

hikers tackle this trail in winter and early spring when the water will be up. It comes with a price, however, because the narrow track beats its way up a precipitous rocky slope.

At 2.5 miles, an unmarked and unmaintained spur trail leads left down to the stream and some cascades. Enter a rocky, level bench and continue up the valley, well above White Rock Creek. Look across the creek at Alexander Mountain's bluffs. Return to the streamside flat just before stepping over Dry Fork, a feeder branch. From here, the trail traces the White Rock Creek Valley as it curves to the northwest. The hollow soon tightens to reach a creek crossing just before you reach White Rock Creek Falls at 3.0 miles. Access the falls by heading upstream before the crossing, or make the crossing and head to the falls. They create a 12-foot-high, 25-foot-wide sheet of white that drops into an enticing plunge pool. In the past, there has been a fallen log at this crossing, and there may be one in the future.

Cross over to the left bank and continue upstream. Another view of the waterfall awaits. The pool is more accessible on this side. Cruise past a campsite located just above the falls and continue up the valley to shortly cross back over to the right-hand bank. Climb away from White Rock Creek and curve into a deeply desiccated tributary. Step over a streamlet just above a circular cathedral cascade and clamber above a really steep cascade that is hard to access.

The trail ascends a piney ridgeline, offering a mighty contrast to the moist hollow you've been traveling. The ascent becomes consistent, and White Rock Creek is but a memory as you turn north up the ridge nose before curving east. This moderates the climb under partly canopied woods, opened from the death

WHITE ROCK FALLS

of many oaks due to the red oak borer. This results in a thick summertime understory, leaving the trailside vegetation a hindrance in places.

The path mercifully levels off, crosses a forest spur road, and then passes through a clearing and a large upland flat before reaching gravel FR 1003 at 4.8 miles. The ascent resumes beyond the forest road, joining an old woods track, making the walking easier. A keen eye will spot the shelters atop White Rock Mountain (to hike this mountain, see Hike 6). The loop trail stair-steps its way to meet the Ozark Highlands Trail (OHT) at 5.1 miles. The OHT leaves left for Fort Smith here while this loop continues forward, joining the easterly portion of the OHT, which runs conjunc-

tively with the Shores Lake Loop Trail for the next 0.8 mile. Keep forward on the old roadbed.

Views open to the east, giving you perspective on how much the trail has climbed thus far. At this point the Sunset Shelter on White Rock Mountain is easily visible above. The OHT is actually losing elevation while circling a hollow. Cruise back to the mountain edge with its wonderful views, especially down into the White Rock Creek Valley from which you came. Beyond, the views extend as far as the clarity of the sky allows. Resume the climb, the first since joining the OHT. The mile marker posts on the OHT do not reflect the mileage of this loop. Break the 2,000-foot mark and finally leave the old roadbed, angling left just before intersecting the spur trail leading to the top of White Rock Mountain at 5.9 miles.

Turn right, heading toward Salt Fork Creek, still on the OHT. Snake downward, watching for an old stone fence indicating that this was once farmland, though it's hard to believe now. The path is descending fast, if in fits and starts, and your ears might pop. Cedars become more common along the trailside before you join an old roadbed at 7.1 miles. Keep aiming for the Salt Fork, leaving the roadbed on a singletrack. Just when you think you've missed the turn, reach the East Loop at 7.5 miles. The white-blazed OHT continues to cross the Salt Fork, whereas the East Loop leaves right, heading down the Salt Fork Valley. The OHT dropped over 1,000 feet in that stretch. The blue-blazed East Loop heads southbound on a bench. The prescribed burns in this area have left parts of the woods in scraggly condition as you travel along the bench.

At 8.2 miles, the trail reaches FR 1003. Turn right onto this forest road then leave left, continuing down the Salt Fork Valley. Roller coaster southbound on a narrow track, occasionally dipping into tributaries of the Salt Fork. The Salt Fork Valley lends a real sense of remoteness. You'll be sharing the woods with squirrels, birds, deer, and unseen creatures as well. The trail sidles along the cliff line; you can look below into the depths of the valley. In places, the path will be extremely rocky.

You are walking along the edge of the Bliss Ridge, with Mineral Hill off to your left across the Salt Fork. Drop off an escarpment and reach a major tributary at 10.0 miles. Backpackers, take note of the campsite here. Make a strong climb out of the tributary, eventually regaining the escarpment and joining an old woods track, but watch to your left as the blue blazes angle left off the roadbed you've been following, staying closer to the escarpment edge. Begin working down along a steep slope, finally seeing the Salt Fork below. And what a gorgeous mountain stream it is!

Just when you're close enough for some good views, the trail slices upward between boulders away from the water. The East Loop continues in rolling woods. Pines increase in number. The path continues undulating, often going where you think it won't or shouldn't go. For the hiker, this means unexpected inclines. Since this is the end of the hike and you may be tired, the climbs seem especially unnecessary. Your reward is a trip through a gorgeous boulder field, where naturally placed rocks form a rock garden no man could design. Make a final descent of the mountain slope to cross a small tributary, then complete your loop at 12.8 miles.

White Rock Rim Loop

TOTAL DISTANCE: 2.2-mile loop

HIKING TIME: 1 hour

VERTICAL RISE: 130 feet

RATING: Easy to moderate

MAPS: USGS 7.5' Bidville, Ozark National Forest

TRAILHEAD GPS COORDINATES: N35° 41.370', W93° 57.274'

CONTACT INFORMATION: Ozark National Forest, P.O. Box 76, 1803 North 18th Street, Ozark, AR 72949, (479) 667-2191, www.fs .usda.gov/osfnf

If you're looking for the hike with the most scenery per step taken, the White Rock Rim Loop might be at the top of the list. The entire loop takes place atop White Rock Mountain, a peak with extensive views in all directions from atop sheer vertical bluffs. These bluffs, which circle the mountain, all occur at around the same elevation, so this hike is mostly level. Add in some historic cabins and shelters, and you have one of the Ozarks' most desirable destinations.

The hike leaves the trailhead to shortly join the aforementioned bluff, then begins its journey along the edge of the mountain, first heading north then curving back around to the south end of the crest, where the greatest view occurs from what is known as the Sunset Shelter. Finally, the trail curves back to the trailhead, offering views that extend all the way to the Arkansas River Valley. Bring your camera and try to time your visit with the clear days of spring, fall, or winter to gain maximum appreciation of the extensive vistas. While you're here, you may want to consider renting one of the cabins, a room at the rustic lodge, or a site in the campground. Or at least enjoy the picnic area! For rentals, contact the concessionaire at (479) 369-4128, or on their website, www.whiter-ockmountain.com.

HOW TO GET THERE

From Exit 24 off I-40, take AR 215 north for 12.7 miles, then veer left onto Forest Road 1505 (FR 1505) and follow it for 1.2 miles, passing Shores Lake Campground on your right. Just beyond the campground, the forest road turns to gravel. After 4 more miles FR 1505 veers left. Continue following it for 2.7 miles, then turn right on Bowles Gap Road into

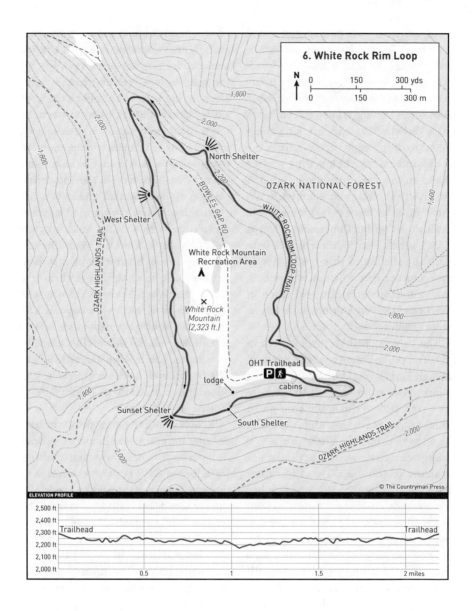

the White Rock Recreation Area. Pass the campground on your right, continue beyond the caretaker's house, and then bear left and reach the Ozark Highlands Trail (OHT) parking area.

THE HIKE

Leave the OHT parking area and take the blue-blazed trail past the final cabin of those grouped here. Descend a lightly forested ridgetop, leveling off just before you join the Rim Trail, which branches out acutely right and forward. Continue just a short distance farther and reach yet another intersection. Here, a blue-blazed spur leads to the Ozark Highlands Trail. Keep forward on the Rim Trail and immediately come upon some major outcrops and views to your right, south.

Enjoy a nice vista point at the end of the rim, then turn back to the west. In many places the trail is open overhead. Pass an old defunct water fountain, the first of many. You may not notice it, however, as the views just keep on coming in every direction. You are cruising along the edge of the drop-off. Look into the cracks and crevices below. Pink azaleas bloom on this rim. Turn away from the rim briefly to circle a streambed. You'll find a circular spring fashioned from rock by the Civilian Conservation Corps (CCC), which also constructed the cabins, the lodge, and this trail. Shortly pass another intermittent streambed. This one drops straight over the cliff line. Look for overhanging bluffs as you curve around the watercourse.

The views continue, primarily easterly. You're looking down the basin of the Salt Fork, which forms Shores Lake before flowing on to meet the Arkansas River. Notice the many spur paths going off the main trail and leading to the edge of drop-offs. There is one you simply can't resist. It's actually not attached to the main rim, but rather divided by a crack of just a few inches that extends downward for many feet. You must bravely step over the crevice. The "cracked rock" leads to your right, and you can look out on the valley mile after mile. Ahead, you'll reach still another vantage from the North Shelter. This is the first of several trailside shelters, also built by the CCC. Notice the handmade stonework and the log roof and benches. Unfortunately, it hasn't been appreciated by everyone, as some feel the need to carve their initials to prove they were here.

The rim of White Rock Mountain narrows. Overhead, the trail is open to the sky, which allows for the development of blueberries aplenty. Reach the recreation area entrance road at 1.1 miles and turn left, briefly going uphill along the road before crossing to the right. Now begin to curve around on the west side of the mountain. Note how brushy the trailside vegetation is, thanks to a fire. Fires are a necessary component of these oak woods. Also notice maple and cherry trees. Briefly join the power line leading to the caretaker's house.

Reach a stellar overlook that offers a 180-degree view of the lands to your west and south. Find the West Shelter, with the Sunset Shelter in the distance. Cruise along the bluff line and shortly reach the West Shelter. Yet another incredible overlook lies just beyond. You can gain a southerly view as far as the sky allows—all the way to the Ouachita Mountains, south of the Arkansas River. The trail travels perilously close to the edge. If you're afraid of heights, don't look down too much!

Reach another outcrop by another defunct fountain. You begin to wonder if the supervisors were just making work for the CCC boys or whether they thought everybody would be especially thirsty along this trail! My bet is on the former. While enjoying views, don't be surprised if you spot a buzzard riding the thermals that rise from the bluff line, especially in the afternoon as the sun warms this wall, creating a thermal chimney.

Curve around to the massive outcrop where the Sunset Shelter stands. This shelter offers a 270-degree panorama of the Ozark countryside, and the most spectacular views among numerous stunners. From here, a trail leads up to the picnic area. Leave the Sunset Shelter and the picnic area, now heading easterly along the south mountain edge. Enjoy more southward views of the greater Arkansas River Valley and the Ouachita Mountains beyond. A sign forbids rappelling. The reason: Numerous people have died here doing it. Reach the South Shelter, then begin passing beneath the cabins. As you pass the first one, look down to your right to glimpse massive boulders that tumbled off the cliff line here. Before you know it, you've completed the loop. Turn left and backtrack to the trailhead.

PEERING OUT FROM ONE OF SEEMINGLY INNUMERABLE TRAILSIDE OUTCROPS

7

Hare Mountain Vista and Homestead

TOTAL DISTANCE: 5.2-mile there-and-back	

TOTAL DISTANCE: 5.2-mile there-and-back

HIKING TIME: 2 hours

VERTICAL RISE: 600 feet

RATING: Moderate

MAPS: USGS 7.5' Cass; Ozark National Forest

TRAILHEAD GPS COORDINATES: N35° 43.563', W93° 45.322'

CONTACT INFORMATION: Ozark National Forest, P.O. Box 76, 1803 North 18th Street, Ozark, AR 72949, (479) 667-2191, www.fs .usda.gov/osfnf

This hike not only offers great views and a trip to an old homestead but also traverses the highest point on the entire Ozark Highlands Trail (OHT). After leaving the Morgan Fields trailhead you'll climb the nose of Morgan Mountain, winding your way north to join Hare Mountain on a well-designed trail. Along the way, the wooded ridge narrows into a rocky razorback, dropping off steeply on both sides, creating great views before you reach the top of Hare Mountain. There, the views really open up. A spur trail leads to a backpacking campsite, near which lies the homesite of an Ozark settler who liked his neighbors lower than him and distant as well. You'll then make a final trek on the OHT, reaching an outcrop that reveals waves of mountains in the distance—an ample reward for your efforts.

You may want to consider bagging two hikes on one weekend. The Spy Rock Loop (see Hike 8) starts near Redding Campground, which you pass en route to this trailhead. Redding Campground has 25 campsites as well as a boat launch for paddling the Mulberry River; it makes an ideal base camp for this hike as well as the Spy Rock Loop. A backcountry campsite located atop Hare Mountain offers yet another camping option.

HOW TO GET THERE

From Exit 35 off I-40, take AR 23 north for 13 miles to reach AR 215. Turn right and follow AR 215 for 3.1 miles to Morgan Mountain Road (FR 1504) just beyond the right turn to Redding Campground. Turn left onto Morgan Mountain Road and follow it for 4.0 miles to the Morgan Fields trailhead, on your right.

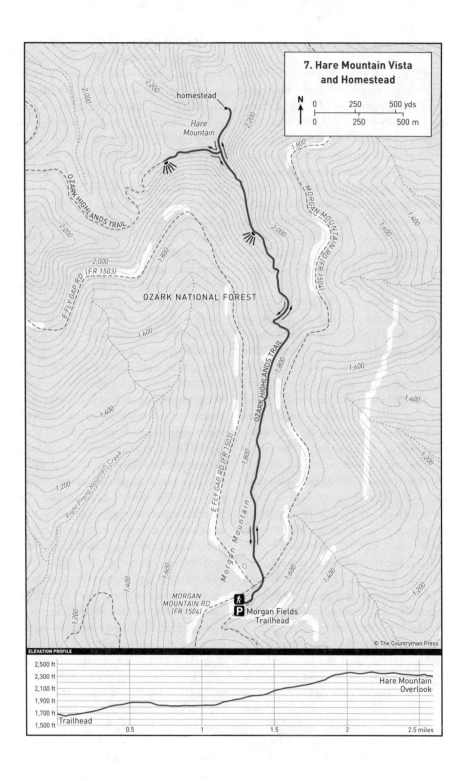

7. **Hare Mountain Vista and Homestead**

N
0   250   500 yds
0   250   500 m

homestead

Hare
Mountain

OZARK HIGHLANDS TRAIL

E FLY GAP RD
[FR 1503]

2,000

MORGAN MOUNTAIN RD [FR 1504]

OZARK NATIONAL FOREST

OZARK HIGHLANDS TRAIL

Right Prong Mountain Creek

E FLY GAP RD [FR 1503]

Morgan Mountain

MORGAN
MOUNTAIN RD
[FR 1504]

P Morgan Fields
Trailhead

© The Countryman Press

ELEVATION PROFILE

2,500 ft
2,300 ft
2,100 ft
1,900 ft
1,700 ft
1,500 ft

Trailhead

0.5   1   1.5   2   2.5 miles

Hare Mountain
Overlook

THE HIKE

Leave the Morgan Fields trailhead, descending on a blue-blazed spur trail connecting you to the OHT. From there, it's 14 miles right to Little Mulberry Creek; this hike, however, takes you left to Hare Mountain. Turn westbound on the OHT. Cruise a rocky slope with scattered picturesque boulders. Immediately pass a little rock overhang with a wet-weather falls. Pass a second stream that's more likely to be flowing—if either of them is—then cross FR 1504. Enter pine woods and bear right, resuming a northbound track.

Take the nose of Morgan Mountain uphill, shortly drifting to the right-hand side of the mountain. Look for an old barbed-wire fence, indicating that this once may have been cattle country, though it's hard to believe given the state of the forest now—oaks stand tall and sturdy. You'll gain obscured views to your east, then shortly regain the crest of the mountain. The valley of Mountain Creek drops off to your left. Looking farther up the watershed, Mountain Creek splits into a Right Prong and Left Prong. A prominent mountain to your left stands between the prongs. The OHT eventually makes it there, but that's beyond the scope of this hike. The OHT slips over to the left side of the ridge, joining an old stone fence. The flat stacked rocks reveal a former Ozark settlement.

Gain the ridgecrest once again. Here, the forest is less thick due to many fallen trees. The trailbed traverses slabs of rock, then scoots over to the right side of the ridge, skirting a clearing to your left. Look for a crumbly stone fence on the right-hand side. Imagine all the work it took moving the stones to add to the fence, day after day, by hand. They didn't

need to join a fitness club back then—life was one continuous fitness test.

Leave the crumbled fence line to begin the climb up Hare Mountain. The OHT switchbacks to the right just before making a break in a cliff line. Once again join the crest of the ridge. The trail designers here did a fine job, taking you by scenic sights yet being practical about the ascent. Keep winding your way up, leaving the ridgecrest again only to rejoin the nose ridge once more—it seems like you're almost at the top. But the OHT keeps climbing. Here, the ridge narrows into a rocky razorback with a few scraggly trees still clinging on. Reach OHT mile marker 43 (as designated from its western terminus near Fort Smith). An outcrop just before you hit mile 43 offers a view into the Mountain Creek watershed and beyond to the Mulberry River Valley. The ascent sharpens. Notice the wind-stunted trees. Clear yet another low bluff line. The Herrods Creek Valley drops steeply off your right. The ridgeline narrows further still, with accompanying shorter and more scraggly trees; shaped by winter winds, these simply cannot grow tall on the razorback. Rock outcrops provide vistas as you reach a trail junction at 1.9 miles.

Head right on the blue-blazed track leading to a campsite, offering a level spot, fire ring, and picnic table. Continue on, passing more campsites beyond, on this nice mountaintop flat. Circle some heavy brush and then reach the stone chimney of a settler who lived up here, atop Hare Mountain. Imagine the solitude. Leave the chimney and backtrack to the OHT, which you rejoin, still heading away from the trailhead. Resume an uphill grade. An old stone fence stands to your right, undoubtedly made by the same person who lived at the homesite. To your left, the ridge of Morgan Moun-

LOOKING OUT ON THE MULBERRY RIVER VALLEY

tain stands in bold relief beyond on either side of Mountain Creek and Herrods Creek. The stone fence goes quite long way, though it has fallen in places and crumbled where trees have toppled onto it.

The OHT becomes squeezed between a bluff line to your left and the stone fence. The path leaves the stone fence area and begins a slight downgrade. Reach an outcrop on your left. This is a good place to enjoy a final vantage and turn around. The views here extend to distant horizons. Mountain Creek forms a huge opening below, allowing you glimpses beyond the Mulberry River Valley into which Mountain Creek flows. This vista, among others, will raise your desire to thru-hike the entire OHT, a 165-mile endeavor.

8

Spy Rock Loop

TOTAL DISTANCE: 7.8-mile loop

HIKING TIME: 4 hours

VERTICAL RISE: 820 feet

RATING: Moderate to difficult

MAPS: USGS 7.5' Cass, Yale; Ozark National Forest

TRAILHEAD GPS COORDINATES: N35° 40.674', W93° 46.356'

CONTACT INFORMATION: Ozark National Forest, P.O. Box 76, 1803 North 18th Street, Ozark, AR 72949, (479) 667-2191, www.fs .usda.gov/osfnf

This circuit offers a good hike through varied woods on a well-marked and -maintained trail that leads to a worthy destination: Spy Rock. The outcrop features superlative vistas, but this trek is as much about the journey as the destination with its everywhere-you-look beauty. Climb away from Redding Campground, a quality camping destination on the banks of the Mulberry River, and curve along the edge of Bowden Hollow before nearing the Ozark Highlands Trail. The track then makes a detour to Spy Rock, offering far-reaching views before resuming its loop back down to the lowlands along the Mulberry River. Redding Campground has 25 campsites and a boat launch for paddling the Mulberry River—an ideal base camp for this trail.

HOW TO GET THERE

From Exit 35 off Interstate 40, take AR 23 north for 13 miles to reach AR 215. Turn right and follow AR 215 for 2.8 miles, passing Redding Campground on your right. You can see the trail heading left into the woods here. However, continue just a short distance more and at 3.1 miles you'll see Huggins Loop Road. Turn right here to reach the official trailhead. If you choose to start the hike at Redding Campground, the trail begins near Campsite 4. Follow the blue blazes. This same parking area also serves the boat launch. The path cuts across the campground between Campsites 20 and 21.

THE HIKE

Leave the trailhead area and immediately descend toward a stream. Cross the streambed and continue in pine woods. Cross an intermittent stream-

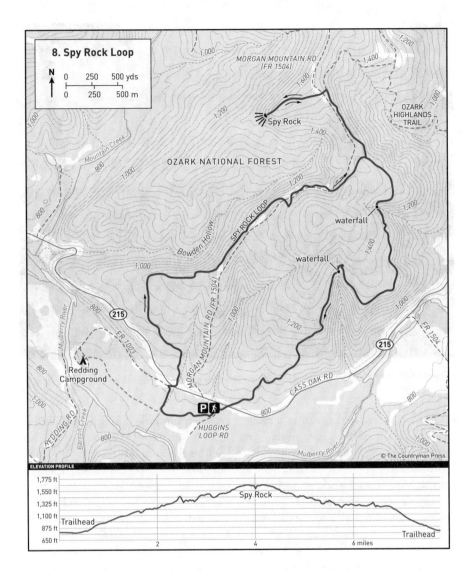

8. Spy Rock Loop

N
0 250 500 yds
0 250 500 m

MORGAN MOUNTAIN RD
(FR 1504)

OZARK
HIGHLANDS
TRAIL

Spy Rock

OZARK NATIONAL FOREST

Mountain Creek

SPY ROCK LOOP

waterfall

Bowden Hollow

waterfall

MORGAN MOUNTAIN RD (FR 1504)

215

FR 1003

Redding
Campground

215

FR 1504

CASS OAK RD

REDDING RD

Barroll Creek

Mulberry River

HUGGINS
LOOP RD

Mulberry River

© The Countryman Press

ELEVATION PROFILE

1,775 ft			
1,550 ft		Spy Rock	
1,325 ft			
1,100 ft			
875 ft	Trailhead		
650 ft			Trailhead
	2	4	6 miles

bed and reach a trail junction. Here, the main path goes left toward Redding Campground, 0.6 mile distant. You turn acutely right, however, continuing the loop. Now cruise up along the intermittent streambed to your right. At 0.5 mile, cross AR 215 and Forest Road 1003, which is the turn into Redding Campground. Begin heading up a small draw on your right amid cedars and pines. The forest floor is covered with needles, lichens, and mosses, as well as small rocks. The singletrack path winds uphill, with the hollow off to your right. Oaks become a more common component of the forest. The blue-blazed trail turns away from the hollow and then turns west to cross a spur of FR 1504. Continue traveling through mostly level woods before curving northeasterly, on the right-hand side of Bowden Hollow; its valley is off to your left.

LOOKING SOUTH FROM SPY ROCK

The Spy Rock Loop resumes a moderate uptick. You have now joined an old woods track, which is bordered by rocks. Skirt the edge of a clearing before turning away from the ridgetop and continuing along the rocky slope of Bowden Hollow. Gain glimpses into the valley as well as the mountains across it. The narrow footbed is sloped in places, making the walking a little more difficult. Still, the slope is what opens these vistas. Blueberry bushes form a thick understory, while pines continue to be the dominant tree cover. You can actually see the ridgeline and the point of Spy Rock across the Bowden Valley. Forest Road 1504 is off to your right. The trail is forced to cross FR 1504 at 2.8 miles; then it continues climbing. Enter a gorgeous wooded flat atop the ridge. The going is easy—you'll enjoy this part of the trek.

Shortly turn away from the flat and cross an unmarked and unmaintained road. Reach a trail junction at 3.2 miles, leaving the loop left toward Spy Rock, northwesterly, soon coming along a mountain drop-off. You can look off to your right in the Herrods Creek Valley. The path quickly resumes an uptick. Make the stony ridgecrest and continue northwesterly to reach another junction at 3.7 miles. From here, it's 0.4 mile right to intersect the Ozark Highlands Trail. To your left is the way to Spy Rock— that's the direction to turn. Immediately cross FR 1504 and make a nearly level cruise through young woods, still following the blue blazes. The ridgeline begins to fall away on both sides. Reach a campsite just before making the final drop to Spy Rock at 4.0 miles.

Spy Rock offers an unbelievably far-reaching view to the south and west. Bowden Hollow lies below; you can see the rock outcrops upon which you hiked earlier. At Spy Rock, pines hang on, as do a few oaks; the open slabs offer the depth and range of Ozark Mountain country, centered on the Mulberry River Valley.

Now backtrack 0.8 mile and return to the loop. Begin circling a little knob to your right while tracing an old roadbed. Dogwoods, maples, oaks, and a lot of Virginia creeper define the woods. The trail makes a moderate descent, curving into a hollow at 5.3 miles. Here, the stream forming the hollow creates a big waterfall over a cliff line. It's difficult to get a really good view of this falls—the trail crosses just above the drop—but they look to be 30 or 40 feet high. A better view opens after you make the stream crossing. Look at how the cathedral into which it falls is covered in greenery.

You've lost the old roadbed beyond the falls. The trail reenters pine-oak woods. Resume a downgrade, curving alongside a drop-off beyond which you can see the Mulberry River and attendant fields growing verdant through the trees. Circle a small clearing at 5.9 miles. After the clearing, the trail comes alongside a lightly wooded bluff with many boulders. Gain obscured views of the valley through the trees to your left as well as the mountains on the far side of the Mulberry.

Trace a rocky, piney slope leading into the head of the hollow. This hollow also features waterfalls, including one directly below the trail crossing, a narrow, thin veil of water dropping 15 or so feet. Another remarkable waterfall lies just down from this one, but is harder to

reach. The falls beneath the trail can be observed from either side of the creek crossing. More craggy bluffs lie just below the trail as you hike on down the Mulberry Valley. Pass another wildlife clearing at 6.7 miles, shortly beyond the last of the falls. These clearings create edges for wildlife and increase food availability for the area's critters. Descend away from the clearing in rocky young woods. Continue angling toward Redding and the Mulberry River, occasionally stepping over shallow, intermittent streambeds. Bisect an old eroded track at 7.4 miles. See how water washing directly down the mountain has worn the old roadbed to its rock face. This is why trails don't go straight up and down mountains.

Enter an interesting point where an intermittent stream flows directly down an open rock slab shaded by cedars. It may run dry in summer. This is yet one more scenic spot on this great loop like. Shortly cross paved AR 215. Enter pine woods, then cross Huggins Loop Road to reach the trailhead, completing your loop.

9

Rattlesnake Rock

TTOTAL DISTANCE: 6.8-mile there-and-back

HIKING TIME: 4 hours

VERTICAL RISE: 900 feet

RATING: Moderate to difficult

MAPS: USGS 7.5' Yale, Oark; Ozark National Forest

TRAILHEAD GPS COORDINATES: N35° 42.061', W93° 38.436'

CONTACT INFORMATION: Ozark National Forest, P.O. Box 76, 1803 North 18th Street, Ozark, AR 72949, (479) 667-2191, www.fs.usda.gov/osfnf

This hike traces a lesser-trod section of the Ozark Highlands Trail (OHT) and is ideal for solitude seekers. It lends a real sense of remoteness, big mountains, and a feeling of being out there. Rattlesnake Rock offers a perfectly framed view of Little Mulberry Creek as it flows toward you, bordered by waves of mountains. Leave Little Mulberry Creek on the OHT after it has just crossed the Little Mulberry Creek on a road bridge. The trail rises, winding its way along the slope of a ridge. It climbs steadily, passing wet-weather drainages and an impressive waterfall (when it's flowing). From here, the trail continues its uptick, traveling beside an old rock fence before reaching Rattlesnake Rock.

HOW TO GET THERE

From Clarksville, take AR 103 north to its junction with AR 215 near Oark. Turn left and follow AR 215 for 4.0 miles, then turn right onto Johnson County 5099 (CR 5099). Cross Little Mulberry Creek on a bridge at 0.9 mile and continue on. At 2.1 miles, stay right as Johnson County 5051 (CR 5051) bears left. Cross the bridge over Little Mulberry Creek at 3.0 miles; you'll see the OHT leading right here. Park just beyond the bridge. Make sure to leave ample room along the road.

THE HIKE

Depart from the bridge, joining the white-blazed OHT as it immediately makes a switchback to the right and curves back downstream along Little Mulberry Creek. The wooded hillside is pocked with large boulders and rocks. At your feet are wildflowers in-season. The trail continues to wind up the mountainside, coursing between boul-

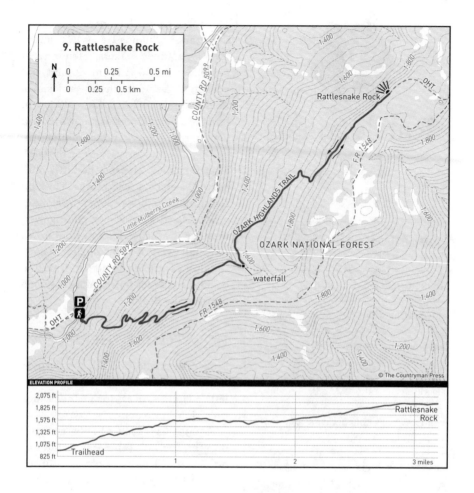

9. Rattlesnake Rock

N

0   0.25   0.5 mi

0   0.25   0.5 km

Rattlesnake Rock

OZARK HIGHLANDS TRAIL

OZARK NATIONAL FOREST

waterfall

© The Countryman Press

ELEVATION PROFILE

2,075 ft
1,825 ft
1,575 ft
1,325 ft
1,075 ft
825 ft

Rattlesnake Rock

Trailhead

1   2   3 miles

ders. The narrow singletrack weaves into drier woodlands. White oaks are the master tree here. The slope has been gentle thus far, and the OHT is making the most of the terrain. It soon levels on a bench, the first of many along which it travels, with steeper-sloping land both above and below you. Cross an intermittent streambed on the steep rocky slope coursing down from the ridgeline at 0.3 mile. Note the beech trees running up and down the hollow. Also look for sugar maple. You can distinguish this tree's leaves because the curves between their lobes

are U-shaped; on the red maple these lobes are right-angled.

The OHT levels off briefly just beyond this beech-filled hollow and resumes switchbacking. Now that you've gained altitude, views of the Little Mulberry Valley open up through the trees to your left. You will see mile markers for the OHT posted on carsonite posts. Ferns and underbrush carpet the forest floor during the warmer times. Continue stair-stepping up the mountainside. The turns become less frequent as you ascend generally northeast. Numerous switchbacks and good

VIEW FROM RATTLESNAKE ROCK

trail routing ease your climb. The trail is furling in and out of small hollows with intermittent streambeds. At 1.4 miles, cross the faint depression of an old roadbed—maybe a wagon track or a very old logging road. Trees are growing up in the middle of it now. Another roadbed leaves shortly thereafter left and downhill. This flat may have been a homesite a long time ago.

The OHT curves right along a cliff line into the most desiccated stream branch yet. It's clearly bigger than the others and has waterfalls and cascades when the water is flowing. You can see a waterfall dropping over a bluff upon entering the watershed. A series of cascades flows upstream of the big drop. In late summer and early autumn this stream may run dry. Cross the stream on a ledge just above a 2- to 3-foot drop. Beyond the crossing, you'll gain a better look at the cascades and pools of this stream. A barely discernible path leads down to a break in the cliff line where hikers have investigated the biggest falls.

The OHT soon leaves the branch and enters flatwoods. Join another rocky cliff line. Pass a campsite on your left in a flat, and then enter a bouldery section of trail. Cedars have joined the forest mix up here. The path is over 1,600 feet in elevation, yet the crest of the mountain

LOOKING INTO THE LITTLE MULBERRY VALLEY AND BEYOND

still eludes. A look across the Little Mulberry Creek Valley reveals mountains higher than where the trail runs.

The walking is easy now, though, and the trail makes a switchback to the right, aiming for the crest; it then crosses FR 1548 at 2.6 miles. Continue ascending, passing OHT mile marker 61 a little way beyond the forest road. You are well above this road, which rises to meet the OHT. The OHT is traveling this path because of a swath of private land just to your right, on top of the mountain. Rejoin, then cross the forest road a final time, watching for an old rock fence on your right just after. This area may have been a homesite as well.

Saddle alongside the fence line, continuing northeasterly at the edge of the escarpment, sensing the serious drop-off to your left. Grassy glades and pines become part of the mix here. The level trail follows a cliff line and a rock outcrop to your left. This is Rattlesnake Rock. Little Mulberry Creek flows to the southwest below you, perfectly framed by the stunted trees growing on either side of Rattlesnake Rock. Beyond, mountains rise on the far side of the valley. The wooded expanse of the Ozark National Forest dominates the setting, a natural view. Beyond here, the OHT continues northeast. This is your turnaround point; retrace your steps to the trailhead.

The Glory Hole

TOTAL DISTANCE: 2.0-mile there-and-back

HIKING TIME: 1 hour

VERTICAL RISE: 380 feet

RATING: Moderate

MAPS: USGS 7.5' Fallsville; Ozark National Forest

TRAILHEAD GPS COORDINATES: N35° 49.695', W93° 23.412'

CONTACT INFORMATION: Ozark National Forest, P.O. Box 427, Hwy 7 North, Jasper, AR 72641, (870) 446-5122, www.fs.usda.gov /osfnf

The Glory Hole is one of the most unusual geological features I have ever seen. And you would never know it's there, judging from this hike's beginning. You start at a modest trailhead and follow an old roadbed before dipping into a valley, where the trail narrows. Reach the upper stretches of Dismal Creek. Upon entering this valley, you'll start to see geological features, beginning with a waterfall and rockhouse. Beyond, the hike continues descending then reaches the upper end of the Glory Hole. Here, the stream you have been following leaves its bed and simply disappears into a circular outlet cut into an overhanging rockhouse. And if you think the top-down view is interesting, the hike leads you around and down to the underside, where you can get the downside-up view of the Glory Hole dropping from its lit tunnel onto the floor of the rockhouse. This whole lower area of Dismal Creek is scenic, with huge boulders pocking the area where several streams converge. If you are lucky enough to catch the Glory Hole following a substantial rain, you will be well rewarded. And when the fall is frozen, the Glory Hole seems surreal.

HOW TO GET THERE

Finding the trailhead may be the hardest part of this hike. It's located on AR 16/21, 2.3 miles from the intersection of AR 16 and AR 21 at Edwards Junction, and will be on your left. If you're coming from Fallsville—the other direction—at the junction of AR 16 and AR 21, the trailhead is 6.1 miles off, on your right. AR 16 and AR 21 run conjunctively at the trailhead. It's unmarked, but there is an abandoned brown house with a metal gate on the far side of the road. Just at the point where the road/trail dumps

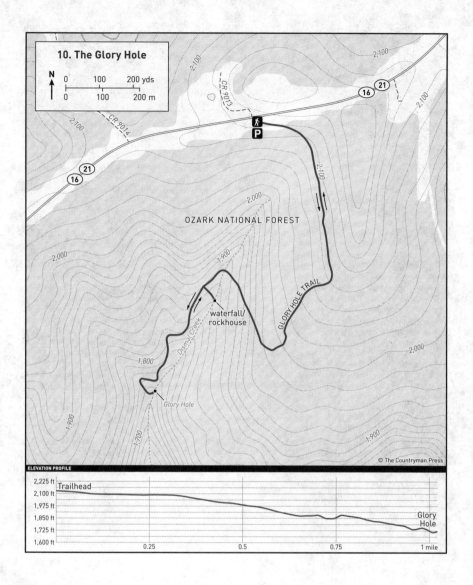

down, you'll see a yellow rectangular road sign indicating an upcoming left turn, if you're coming from Fallsville.

THE HIKE

Follow the old dirt road that leaves paved AR 16/21 and begins to curve away from the pavement. The track is almost level, making for easy walking underneath an oak-dominated forest. When the trail splits, stay right. The trail once served as a boundary for a prescribed burn. In the direction you're heading, the forest to your right wasn't burned; to your left, it was. Begin descending and curving into the upper Dismal Creek watershed, where the Glory Hole awaits.

Reach a stream. If this watercourse is flowing well, your trip to the Glory Hole will be worth it; if not, the thrill will be diminished. Just beyond the

WATER POURS THROUGH THE GLORY HOLE

branch, a spur trail leaves left, where you can observe a waterfall. These falls drop about 15 feet over a ledge into a plunge pool. If the water is flowing, a side branch will tumble over the ledge to your right as you face the falls. About 100 feet below, the same ledge forms an overhanging rockhouse. The rockhouse is very shallow—about 30 feet back and only 2–4 feet from floor to ceiling. Notice how a narrow trail continues down the creek. There are no marked or maintained trails down here; people have just made their own paths. I suggest returning to the main track, to minimize the plethora of user-created trails. Still, I can't blame folks for wanting to walk directly down the creek, as there are beautiful bluffs along it.

The primary trail curves away from the creek in piney woods. Work your way over to the next tributary. At this point the trail is a narrow footpath. You can look down the main stream, which now cascades over rocks. Dismal Creek is quite a scenic view in its own right. Continue down the rocky track and reach the Glory Hole. It's about 5 or 6 feet in diameter; the water plunges directly through it. You can see that before the Glory Hole was formed, the stream just went directly over the ledge of the rockhouse rather than cutting a hole through it. In times of extreme flow it may still go over the ledge, in addition to dropping into the Glory Hole. Contemplate the time that it took to wear down this hole. Maybe it started with just a small crack; maybe it took

a pebble rubbing a hole combined with freezing and thawing and the patience of Mother Nature to create such a thing. And to this moment the water continues plunging through the Glory Hole, creating an ever-larger chasm in the span of geological time in which your life is a mere blink of an eye.

The rock outcrop allows you to look into the Glory Hole. This will spur you on to more views from the downside. Cross a spring seep rife with wildflowers, including shooting stars. Turn around to cross another feeder branch. You're working around a cathedral that has formed at the base of the rockhouse.

Continue down and circle another feeder branch with a waterfall. Descend farther into this amphitheater of beauty, where a sheer bluff stands on the far side of the stream. Reach the base of the rockhouse and head upstream toward the Glory Hole cutting through the rock shelter. If you catch Dismal Creek after rain, with the sun shining through the Glory Hole, your efforts will be rewarded manyfold. Walk underneath the rockhouse to where the Glory Hole plunges through and splatters onto rocks, echoing its incessant obedience to gravity's will. Take some time to absorb the setting. You may want to continue downstream a little way and explore the immense boulder field that stands below the Glory Hole and rockhouse. These gigantic boulders are the final complement to an Arkansas treasure.

When you're ready, retrace your steps to the trailhead.

11

Hawksbill Crag Hike

TOTAL DISTANCE: 2.9-mile there-and-back

HIKING TIME: 2 hours

VERTICAL RISE: 280 feet

RATING: Moderate

MAPS: USGS 7.5' Boxley; Ozark National Forest, Upper Buffalo Wilderness

TRAILHEAD GPS COORDINATES: N35° 53.888', W93° 27.482'

CONTACT INFORMATION: Ozark National Forest, P.O. Box 427, Hwy 7 North, Jasper, AR 72641, (870) 446-5122, www.fs.usda.gov/osfnf

Hawksbill Crag, also known as Whitaker Point, is one of the most photographed vistas in Arkansas, frequently appearing on websites and brochures about the outdoor opportunities in the state. Now you can walk to this destination and see it for yourself. Located in the federally designated Upper Buffalo Wilderness, Hawksbill Crag offers extensive views of Whitaker Creek and the upper Buffalo River drainage. But you will get plenty more views before reaching the actual point—the cliff line beside which you travel will force you to stop to peer out repeatedly. The good news is, these views are easily achieved, as the trail has only a minimal elevation change.

HOW TO GET THERE

From Jasper, just north of the bridge over the Little Buffalo River, take AR 74 west for 14 miles to AR 43. Turn left and follow AR 43 for 4.3 miles to AR 21. Turn left onto AR 21 south; continue for 1.3 miles to the bridge over the Buffalo River. Just before this bridge, turn right onto gravel County Road 5. If you cross the bridge, you just missed the turn. Follow CR 5 uphill sharply, continuing for 5.6 miles, reaching the Cave Mountain Church and cemetery on your right. From the church, continue 0.5 mile farther on CR 5 to the marked trailhead on your right.

THE HIKE

Start the hike, passing an inscribed stone commemorating former Arkansas senator Dale Bumpers for his contributions toward establishing wilderness areas like the Upper Buffalo. Pass a trail register. Descend into woods on a rocky track, shortly crossing a small streambed amid maple-oak-hickory woods with

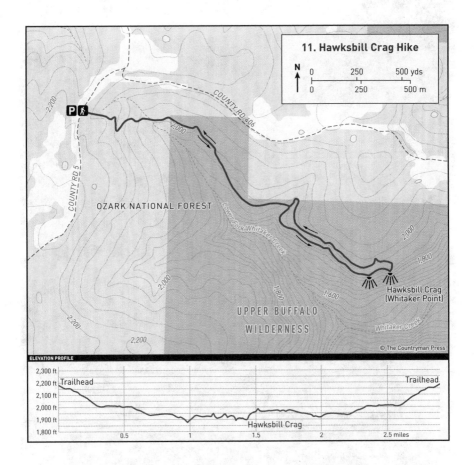

a few scattered beech trees. Step over another streambed on a switchback at 0.3 mile. Continue easterly, crossing more dry drainages flowing from the mountainside to your north.

You can see off to your right through the trees, and it's evident that the land is dropping off sharply. Dip into the largest streambed yet and reach a junction at 0.9 mile. Here in the wooded drainage, one trail leads left, uphill, while another leads right, down the drainage. The uphill route will be your return route; for now, begin heading down the drainage, which becomes increasingly rocky as you near a bluff line. Shortly reach a second, more obscure junction. This time a path goes right along the

bluff line, but the main track heading to Whitaker Point, aka Hawksbill Crag, leads left along the bluff line. Ahead, the drainage drops off to meet Lower Fork, which flows into Whitaker Creek, which in turn flows into the Buffalo River.

Continue easterly. Boulders and outcrops to your right will lure you to exploration. Multiple paths run in generally the same direction—no marked and maintained trails exist here, so hikers have created social trails that work close to the bluff, farther from the bluff, among vegetation, and around boulders.

If you look down from the stone pillars on which you stand, you can see out to Whitaker Creek and other deep wooded canyons, and beyond to other

HAWKSBILL CRAG JUTS OUT OVER WHITAKER CREEK

outcrops. The Upper Buffalo Wilderness, established in 1975, covers 11,000-plus acres at the head of the Buffalo River and tributaries such as Whitaker Creek. Residents once called the bottoms home, but they'd all moved out by 1948.

The main trail climbs a bit as it works around unscalable boulders. The overlooks become too numerous to mention. They are often cloaked in pines and cedars, which gain purchase on the thin soils of the rock, adding close-up beauty to the extensive views. Look closely also at bluffside rocks and boulders, which feature strange eroded holes and openings.

The canyon deepens below as you trek toward Hawksbill. Continue to explore vista points, looking for the best-of-the-best views. Then Hawksbill

VIEW OF HAWKSBILL CRAG AND BEYOND

Crag comes into view, hanging far over the canyon wall, away from the trees and away from the bluff. Worry not: You will know it when you spy this most photographed rock feature in Arkansas. Just before the first view of Hawksbill, the alternative route, your return route, meets the trail you've been walking. Head out to a rock outcrop bordered in smaller pines—and there it is. Earlier settlers called it Whitaker Point, for Whitaker Creek below. Later the name Hawksbill came into use. It's easy to see how this name came to be, as the rock outcrop resembles the beak of a hawk. Look how far out the solid stone extends over the main bluff line.

Continue a bit farther to another vista point. This was the very spot where the pictures you may have seen on brochures were taken. Reach the crag itself at 1.4 miles. Walk out to the promontory. The valley below opens before you. Whitaker Creek lies down below, and a feeder branch of Whitaker Creek known as Boen Gulf Creek opens to the south. The Buffalo River lies to the east, as does another good outcrop. It will lure you to look at Whitaker Point from there. The woods behind this second point are somewhat level and have been used as a camping and picnicking ground, but in normal conditions you must bring your own water.

On your return trip, you may want to consider taking the route that runs a bit back from the bluff line. It climbs away from where it joined the bluff line trail, then veers left onto an old road. The walking is easier here, as the trail works among some boulders, and offers views of wooded bluffs higher on the mountain above. Rejoin the main trail in the aforementioned wooded drainage. From the drainage, backtrack 0.9 mile to the trailhead.

Buffalo River Trail End-to-End

TOTAL DISTANCE: 37.3-mile end-to-end

HIKING TIME: 18 hours

VERTICAL RISE: 900 feet

RATING: Moderate to difficult

MAPS: USGS 7.5' Boxley, Murray, Ponca, Jasper; National Geographic #232 Buffalo National River West

TRAILHEAD GPS COORDINATES: West Terminus N35° 56.739', W93° 23.915' ; East Terminus N36° 3.666', W93° 8.305'

CONTACT INFORMATION: Buffalo National River, 402 N. Walnut Street, Suite 136, Harrison, AR 72601, (870) 439-2502, www .nps.gov/buff

This is arguably the best long-distance section hike in Arkansas. The Buffalo River Trail (BRT) traverses the upper valley of the protected Buffalo National River, covering 37 miles from Boxley Valley to Pruitt. Start by climbing above Boxley Valley, home of elk, to wind through mountainous terrain before returning to the Buffalo near the Villines Homestead. Grab a superb view from Steel Creek Overlook after entering the Ponca Wilderness, where the BRT makes its biggest ascents and descents, passing more vistas along the way. Keep east in the river corridor, reaching historic Erbie, where open fields become platforms for mountain views and settler history, including the Parker-Hickman Homestead. Beyond Erbie, the trail alternately nears the river and rides bluffs above it before ending at Pruitt. The scenery never fails to please, whether it is rockhouses, cliff lines, gravel bars, or springtime waterfalls. The BRT passes several campgrounds and trail accesses along the way, allowing for hikes of various distances to be made, but the entire trip, from end to end, makes for a grand adventure.

HOW TO GET THERE

To reach the east terminus in Pruitt from the junction of AR 7 and AR 74 near the Little Buffalo River bridge in Jasper, head north on AR 7 for 5.3 miles to the Pruitt Picnic Area on the left side of the road, just before the Buffalo River bridge. To reach the west terminus, backtrack 5.3 miles to Jasper and head west on AR 74, following it for 14 miles to reach AR 43. Turn left and follow AR 43 for 4.3 miles to AR 21. Turn left onto AR 21 south; continue for 2.4 miles to the Boxley trailhead on your right. The BRT

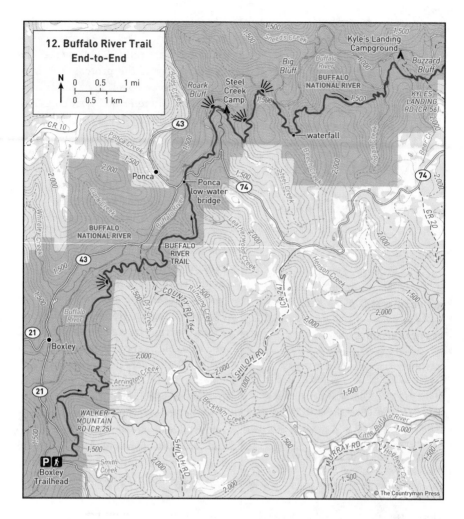

begins on the opposite side of the road from the trailhead.

THE HIKE

The beginning of this hike can be confusing. Cross AR 21, leaving the remnants of a homestead and passing around two gates to cross Smith Creek. Join a singletrack beside a field and stone fence. Turn away from the field along a mountainside, soon ascending this mountainside. Pass a level area for potential late-arrival camping before bisecting a stile-type gate at 0.9 mile.

Level out on a mountainside bench. The trail becomes grassy. You may see elk in the area. Mountains are visible across Boxley Valley. Cross a second fence line, entering an open field. Here, the BRT follows posts, angling downhill and skirting a farm pond before reaching County Road 25 (CR 25), Walker Mountain Road, at 1.9 miles. Turn right on this road and follow it for 0.5 mile, then leave left, descending along a gorge to reach intermittent Arrington Creek at 3.6 miles. Campsites await beneath big beech trees.

Leave the bottom, ascending crum-

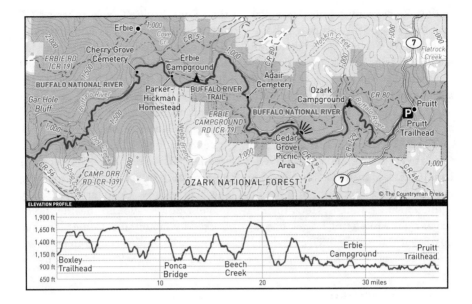

ELEVATION PROFILE

Boxley Trailhead · Ponca Bridge · Beech Creek · Erbie Campground · Pruitt Trailhead

bly cliff lines to level off, joining a northbound old roadbed. Pass a small spring to the right of the trail at 5.1 miles. Look for animal prints around the water. Continue through bouldery woods, leaving the old roadbed, angling left downhill. Cross a drainage to reach an old rock quarry at 6.3 miles. It offers a view into Boxley Valley. The BRT descends to cross a dirt road, then Dry Creek on private land. Ascend to cross CR 164. Here, angle right, uphill, on a roadbed, soon leaving left to cross perennial Running Creek at 7.8 miles. Beyond the creek, the BRT bisects a field and climbs away, circling a steep drainage that offers wet-weather waterfalls. Return to the main Buffalo River Valley, northbound, descending on a thin ridgeline to reach a low-water bridge at Ponca and the spur trail to the Villines Homestead at 11.0 miles.

Pass through bottoms, then ascend a bluff line with views aplenty of the river valley. Slice through a Fatman's Squeeze created by eroding bluffs before dropping to reach Steel Creek Campground

(with restrooms, water, and camping) at 12.8 miles. Circle the greater recreation area, enjoying Roark Bluff before leaving cross Steel Creek, with campsites, at 14.0 miles. Enter the Ponca Wilderness, cutting upward between cliff lines to reach a fantastic overlook at 14.7 miles. Gaze up- and downstream on the Buffalo as it makes a huge bend. Steep bluffs and rounded mountains complement the river. Ahead, you'll reach a point 500 feet above the river before turning south, passing many sinkholes and an overlook of Big Bluff, and then coming across a spur trail leading left down Beech Creek, a perennial stream with campsites, at 17.0 miles.

The BRT crosses Beech Creek above a stair-step, wet-weather waterfall. Cross open rock glades before turning east and making a major climb to a junction at 18.5 miles. The BRT turns left here, on a roadbed, sharing the track with horses to reach an open gap near the old Staley Place at 18.9 miles. The BRT turns right along a level bench in the woods before joining the nose of a ridge dividing the

Buffalo River from Indian Creek. Pass overlooks of both waterways before reaching formerly settled bottomland near Kyles Landing Campground, with water and restrooms. Stay with the BRT signs amid field and forest, coming within 0.1 mile of the campground at 21.4 miles.

The BRT crosses intermittent Bear Creek twice, then climbs to cross Kyles Landing access road at 22.1 miles. Keep east above Buzzard Bluff, dropping to a junction at 23.4 miles. Here, the BRT leaves right, while a trail leads left to Orr Boy Scout Camp. The BRT cuts deeply past fractured rock into Shop Creek, then Rock Bridge Creek, crossing CR 139, and drops to a second Dry Creek. Keep easterly, climbing again, passing wet-weather falls to reach a junction at 25.2 miles. A spur trail leads left to the Old River Trail, a horse path, and riverside gravel bar campsites.

The BRT cuts through another rock squeeze amid rock bluffs and more wet-weather falls to reach the Greater Erbie area at 26.5 miles. Turn left, passing the Cherry Grove Cemetery to abruptly leave right, traveling beside fields backed by mountains. Come along the river; at 27.3 miles a spur trail leads left to head below a rockhouse with the old

ELK GRAZING NEAR BOXLEY VALLEY

VIEW FROM STEEL CREEK OVERLOOK

anchor pins of a swinging bridge still in the stone. A small arch lies just before this split if you look back down the trail where you came. Pass a spur trail leading to Erbie Road, and then at 27.7 miles drift into the Parker-Hickman Homestead, the showcase historic homesite in the Greater Buffalo area. Linger here, enjoying the interpretive information, before leaving the homestead upstream along Webb Branch, which you soon cross on an auto ford. Just beyond, the trail leaves right from the roadbed, and then heads left along a rocky streambed. A spur trail leads to a crumbling wooden outbuilding.

Travel bluffs over to Erbie Campground, with restrooms and water, to cross its access road. You'll reach a spur trail leading left to the campground at

Lost Valley
Trail Hike

TOTAL DISTANCE: 2.0-mile there-and-back	

HIKING TIME: 1 hour

VERTICAL RISE: 360 feet

RATING: Moderate

MAPS: USGS 7.5' Ponca, Osage SW; National Geographic #232 Buffalo National River—West Half

TRAILHEAD GPS COORDINATES: N36° 0.607', W93° 22.485'

CONTACT INFORMATION: Buffalo National River, 402 N. Walnut Street, Suite 136, Harrison, AR 72601, (870) 439-2502, www.nps.gov/buff

This has been consistently rated among the best day hikes in Arkansas. It's located in the Boxley Valley on the upper Buffalo River, within the boundaries of the Buffalo National Scenic River. Lost Valley is a steep and deep canyon full of points of note. Leave the Lost Valley Day Use Area and head up the valley in thick woodland. The valley closes as you pass the Jigsaw Blocks, massive stone blocks that have fallen from the steep rock canyon walls. Next comes the Natural Bridge, where Clark Creek flows through a rock wall.

The canyon tightens upon reaching Cob Cave, a massive rock shelter used for as long as man has been in the Lost Valley. The first of several falls, collectively known as Eden Falls, drops near the cave. Here, a goat trail ascends steeply to reach Eden Falls Cave, an opening from which water pours. Intrepid explorers can continue 200 feet back into the cave to a room where water drops 35 feet; this could be considered the uppermost of the Eden Falls. You will need a flashlight for the cave portion of the hike. A small campground with walk-in tent sites is located at the trailhead. Also, on the way in you will pass through Boxley Valley, a prime elk-viewing area.

HOW TO GET THERE

From the junction of AR 74 and AR 7 in Jasper, take AR 74, located just north of the bridge over the Little Buffalo River, west for 14.0 miles to AR 43 south. Turn left and follow AR 43 for 1.0 mile to the signed right turn to Lost Valley Day Use Area and trailhead. Follow the road for 0.5 mile to dead-end at a parking area. The trail starts at the wooden bridge over Clark Creek at the upper end of the parking area.

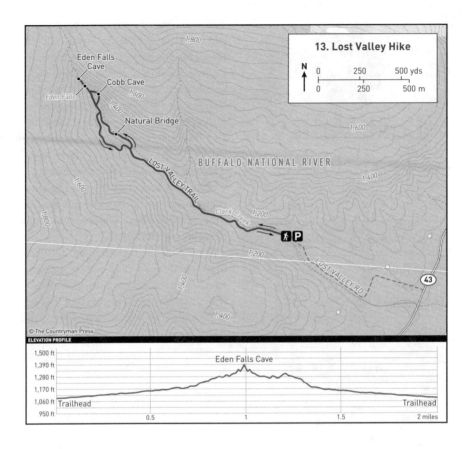

13. Lost Valley Hike

ELEVATION PROFILE

THE HIKE

Immediately trace a wooden bridge over Clark Creek, passing a couple of walk-in tent campsites and the day use area amphitheater. The wide, gravelly track heads up the Clark Creek Valley beneath beech, dogwood, and other vine-draped trees. Clark Creek was named for an early settler of Boxley Valley, Abraham Clark. The streambed is off to your right. Watch for a triple-trunked sycamore tree just to the left of the trail. Cedar, redbud, and cane complement the forest. The smooth-trunked beech trees have been carved on by previous visitors. Ferns grow on the north-facing side of the valley. A spur trail leads right to the creek and a small rockhouse.

The trail splits at 0.7 mile. Keep right, downhill, along Clark Creek. Massive gray and white bluffs rise from the streambed. The Jigsaw Blocks appear to your right. These squared-off stones look as if they could be pieced back together on the bluff from which they fell. The area is quite interesting, as you reach a pool formed by the outflow of Clark Creek through the Natural Bridge. Here, the stream has carved a tunnel though rock, then flows over a rock lip and enters the pool. High bluffs jut forth from the edge. In times of low water, you can walk all the way around the pool. The best view through the Natural Bridge is found to the right of the trail beside the bluff. A small arch is located to the left of the pool as you

LOOKING OUT FROM EDEN FALLS CAVE

face upstream. The trail circles the Natural Bridge with the aid of stone steps. In summer, cool air blows through the Natural Bridge. In my opinion, this feature should be called the natural tunnel.

The valley tightens and becomes more rock than anything else. Look back and you can see through the Natural Bridge from the upstream side. The valley, now a canyon, is extremely scenic here. Rejoin the trail that split left earlier, a detour around the bridge.

Ahead, the trail splits again; keep right, heading toward Eden Falls and Cob Cave. Drop down to a bluff line beside the creek, just across from which stands Cob Cave. This rock shelter is 50 feet high, 150 feet deep, and 250 feet wide. It once housed aboriginal Indians and later white settlers who even held church services here in summer, to take advantage of the cool conditions. Corncob relics from the aboriginal days have been found here—hence the name. Cruise under the enormous overhang. Just ahead is one of the four tiers of Eden Falls, which will dry up in summer and fall. Below this tier, the trail curves left and uphill through a boulder maze via stone steps to rejoin the main footway.

The main trail continues climbing toward Eden Falls Cave. Enjoy more bluff views. The high white bluff, well above you, stands out in bold relief, especially when the sun shines upon it. Climb by switchbacks to reach Eden Falls Cave. Water flows out of the opening to create a cascade of its own. In summer the cave air will seem cool. Conversely, in winter it will feel warm. Even those without a flashlight can enter the cave. But those with a flashlight or headlamp will be rewarded with a trip deep inside the rock maw, where the cave roof lowers before entering a circular room 200 feet back. A waterfall drops 35 feet from the roof of the room to form a small pool before flowing to meet Clark Creek. Be careful—the rocks inside are slick.

Backtrack from the cave, and on your way out you can stay on the upper side of the valley, using the two small loops before making your way back to the trailhead.

Lost Valley has a day use area with picnic tables and restrooms. A ranger station is in the building near the parking area but is usually unoccupied.

Hemmed-In Hollow Loop

TOTAL DISTANCE: 5.8-mile loop

HIKING TIME: 4 hours

VERTICAL RISE: 1,300 feet

RATING: Difficult

MAPS: USGS 7.5' Ponca; National Geographic #232 Buffalo National River— West Half

TRAILHEAD GPS COORDINATES: N36° 4.868', W93° 18.201'

CONTACT INFORMATION: Buffalo National River, 402 N. Walnut Street, Suite 136, Harrison, AR 72601, (870) 439-2502, www .nps.gov/buff

This hike, which takes place in the Ponca Wilderness, is as tough as it is scenic. It starts at over 2,200 feet in elevation, and then descends into the Buffalo River Valley on a steep, rocky track. You'll pass a grand vista into Hemmed-In Hollow and Hemmed-In Falls, your ultimate destination. But looking at and getting to the destination are two different matters, as the trail continues descending to reach the loop portion of the hike. From here, the hike works over rock slabs and broken cliff lines to reach Sneeds Creek and the Buffalo River. Two fords of the Buffalo await. If the water is high, the waterfall will be alluring, but it may make fording the Buffalo too dangerous. If that's the case, skip the loop portion of the hike and head directly to Hemmed-In Hollow and Falls. Pass between bluffs on the Buffalo and across gravel bars before entering the hollow.

This box canyon rises forth and the trail winds its way amid boulders and bluffs, passing small waterfalls before entering the head of the canyon and 240-foot Hemmed-In Falls, which drop over a lip into a colorful overhanging rock amphitheater. This is one of the most scenic spots in the Ozarks, so plan to relax here awhile, simultaneously gathering energy to make the climb out. Emerge from the hollow to complete the loop portion of the hike, finally climbing out of the valley and returning to the trailhead.

HOW TO GET THERE

From Harrison, take AR 43 south of west for 18 miles to Compton and County Road 19 (CR 19), located across from the Compton Post Office (a sign indicates the Compton trailhead). Turn left here and drive for 0.2 mile, then veer right

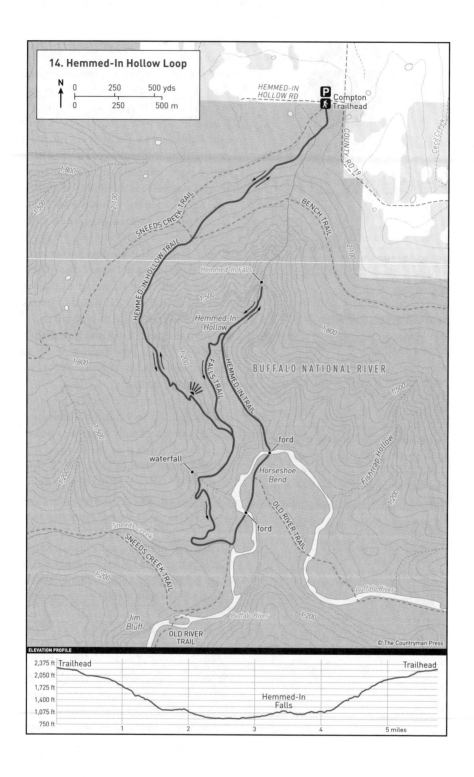

14. Hemmed-In Hollow Loop

N

| 0 | 250 | 500 yds |
| 0 | 250 | 500 m |

HEMMED-IN
HOLLOW RD

P

Compton
Trailhead

COUNTY RD 19

Cecil Creek

1,800

2,100

SNEEDS CREEK TRAIL

BENCH TRAIL

2,100

HEMMED-IN HOLLOW TRAIL

Hemmed-In Falls

1,500

Hemmed-In
Hollow

1,800

1,800

1,200

FALLS TRAIL

HEMMED-IN TRAIL

BUFFALO NATIONAL RIVER

1,500

1,500

1,200

ford

Fishtrap Hollow

waterfall

Horseshoe
Bend

1,200

OLD RIVER TRAIL

ford

Sneeds Creek

SNEEDS CREEK TRAIL

1,200

Buffalo River

1,200

Jim
Bluff

OLD RIVER
TRAIL

Buffalo River

1,200

© The Countryman Press

ELEVATION PROFILE

2,375 ft	Trailhead					Trailhead
2,050 ft						
1,725 ft						
1,400 ft				Hemmed-In		
1,075 ft				Falls		
750 ft						
	1	2	3	4	5 miles	

HEMMED-IN FALLS DROPS 240 FEET BUT CAN BE A TRICKLE IN AUTUMN

at a stone building. Continue on the gravel road for 1.0 mile, heading right at the signed turn for the Compton trailhead. Follow this gravel road just a short distance to the trailhead. Two paths emanate from the parking area. Take the white-blazed foot-only trail, not the yellow-blazed equestrian Sneeds Creek Trail.

THE HIKE

This is one of the best day hikes in the Arkansas Ozarks. Take the white-blazed trail toward the Falls Overlook. No horses are allowed on this trail. Drift downward in pine-oak-cedar woods to cross a wet-weather drainage. Make the slightest of ascents before resuming a downgrade among lichen- and moss-covered boulders scattered in the woods. The going is slow on the rocky track. At 0.6 mile, intersect the Bench Trail, a bridle path. Continue downward southwesterly, passing a dry pond to your right, then join the edge of the wooded escarpment dropping to Hemmed-In Hollow.

Begin working between and over rock outcrops, and between boulders. The trail is very rugged here, but shortly opens onto a campsite at 1.4 miles. A spur trail leads left, sharply downhill, to a fantastic overlook of Hemmed-In Falls and the sheer cliffs that circle Hemmed-In Hollow. Don't be surprised if you can't see or hear the falls, as they will run nearly dry and cannot be detected from this far distance. They are located northeast from the point, above the deepest part of the valley below.

Continue down, opening onto a rock face that offers views down canyon to the southeast, toward the Buffalo River. The trail then reenters woods, grinding through rough country. Reach the loop portion of the hike at 1.7 miles. Here, the Falls Trail leads left toward Hemmed-In Falls and the upper end of the hollow. This is your return route. If the water is roaring, skip the Buffalo River portion of the hike and take the Falls Trail directly for Hemmed-In Hollow.

The main route continues on the edge of the valley. The sound of the moving river becomes audible, and you can glimpse it through the trees. Pass around a wet-weather drainage that forms a waterfall when flowing at 1.9 miles. The falls are hard to see as they drop into a circular rock amphitheater. Stone steps lead you over the lip of a bluff before the trail passes along a lichen-covered rock slab that forms a unique Ozark plant community.

Reach bottomland, saddling alongside clear Sneeds Creek at 2.3 miles. Cross the creek, passing through a campsite to reach the yellow-blazed Old River Trail (ORT), a horse path. The Buffalo River is visible here. Turn left onto the ORT, crossing Sneeds Creek again. Rise forth on a wide track, passing the stone foundation of the old Center Point School. You are heading for Horseshoe Bend, where the river makes a 190-degree curve. The trail leads to a ford, where the water is shallow. Cross the river. Notice the bluffs both up- and downstream. Slice through witch hazel and sycamore on the rocky bottom. Soon reach a junction. Here, the ORT leaves sharply right, while the foot-only white-blazed Hemmed-In Trail continues forward.

Cruise alongside the Buffalo, peering over rocks slabs. Cane grows tall here. Look for a sign leading hikers left toward the second and final river ford. When making this ford, head toward

BLUFFS REFLECT ON BUFFALO RIVER AT HORSESHOE BEND

the noise of the shoals downstream, and cross there. The crossing should be easy in normal summer and fall flows; in spring, when the water is up, it's wiser to avoid this hike. Look for the white blaze on the far side of the river, and enter the rock "gates" on either side of Hemmed-In Hollow. Tall boulders and outcrops rise from the streambed in the tight canyon. Cross over to the left bank at 2.9 miles. The canyon ascent is irregular amid the beech trees, which grow in large numbers here. Step across normally dry tributaries. The main creekbed will have pools year-round.

Reach a trail junction at 3.3 miles. The Falls Trail, your return route, leads acutely left, while the actual trail to the falls continues forward, passing a boulder-laden side creek. Here, two streams converge and—when they're flowing—fall over a lip to create a waterfall. Shortly you'll pass a second waterfall, still rising. Ahead, tan- and charcoal-colored bluffs tower majestically beyond the trees. At 3.5 miles, after walking directly up the streambed, you are there: in the box of a box canyon. Ahead, Hemmed-In Falls drops 240 feet from an overhanging bluff that encircles your viewing point. Rock shelters can be seen above. A pool lies at the base of the falls. This is one of the most beautiful spots in the Ozarks, even if the falls are but a trickle, which is the case more often than not.

Backtrack 0.2 mile, working your way out of Hemmed-In Hollow, now taking the Falls Trail as it crosses a pair of roadbeds fading into the rocky wooded hillside. Climb a bit more to pass a campsite and reach a trail junction at 4.1 miles. From here, backtrack 1.7 miles to the trailhead. This is where you earn your scenery on this hike—climbing over 1,100 feet from this point.

15

Cecil Cove Historic Loop Hike

TOTAL DISTANCE: 7.3-mile loop

HIKING TIME: 4 hours

VERTICAL RISE: 600 feet

RATING: Moderate to difficult

MAPS: USGS 7.5' Ponca, Jasper; National Geographic #232 Buffalo National River—West Half

TRAILHEAD GPS COORDINATES: N36° 5.011', W93° 13.987'

CONTACT INFORMATION: Buffalo National River, 402 N. Walnut Street, Suite 136, Harrison, AR 72601, (870) 439-2502, www.nps.gov/buff

This trek travels through time in the hills and hollows of the Buffalo River, where settlers once lived. Start near Erbie Church along the Buffalo, then head up Cecil Creek. Beyond this beautiful valley, the hike climbs past Jones Cemetery, where former area residents are interred. Cruise along a mountainside with some views before descending to the Farmer Farmstead, where several buildings remain to explore. You'll then ascend bluffs along the Buffalo to enjoy some good overlooks before completing the loop. In addition to the history on the hike, other homesteads and relics are nearby and accessible by car in the Erbie Historic District.

HOW TO GET THERE

From the junction of AR 7 and AR 43 on the south side of Harrison, head south on AR 7 for 8.3 miles to Erbie Road, a right turn just after crossing the bridge over Mill Creek. Turn right onto Erbie Road, County Road 19 (CR 19), staying with it for 7.5 miles as it winds through the mountains. The turns are marked for CR 19. Half a mile before reaching the trailhead, the road makes an auto ford of Cove Creek, which is crossable nearly all the time. You'll then pass Cavers Camp on your left. Keep climbing to reach the trailhead, on your right, near the Erbie Church.

THE HIKE

Leave the trailhead, which has a picnic table and restroom, on the Cecil Creek Trail, traveling a roadbed that was part of the Greater Erbie community. Cedars line the former country lane, open to hikers and equestrians alike. Fields are returning to forest to your right. The descent steepens to reach the bottom-

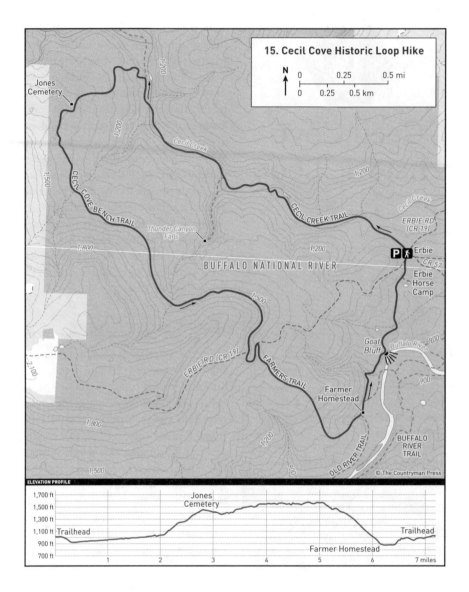

15. Cecil Cove Historic Loop Hike

ELEVATION PROFILE

Jones Cemetery

Trailhead

Farmer Homestead

Trailhead

land of Cecil Creek. Beavers are active in this valley—don't be surprised if you run into a beaver dam here.

The Cecil Creek Trail crosses Cecil Creek into woods of ash, sycamore, and sweetgum. Creekside bluffs are visible. Enter a long field, also transitioning to forest. Sumac, cedar, and hawthorn are doing their best to eliminate the grassland. Cross Cecil Creek at 0.6 mile

before saddling alongside the left side of the widening hollow. Pawpaw thrives in this bottom, where stone piles reveal a farming past. Fertile bottoms such as this were settled early on in the Ozarks.

Cross Cecil Creek. Like most Ozark streams, it runs belowground much of the year. Step over rocky tributaries, shaded by dogwood, maple, sweetgum, and other trees draped in vines. Cross

TRAILSIDE STONE WALL

back over to the left-hand bank at 1.3 miles. Notice the willows and sycamores growing in the middle of the streambed. Continue upstream, passing more bluffs on your right. Ferns, witch hazel, and beard cane spread low to the ground.

Cross to the right bank at 1.8 miles. Reach a prominent and mostly intact stone fence just beyond, then return to the left bank before reaching a trail junction at 2.2 miles. Here, the Cecil Cove Bench Trail leaves uphill and to your left. Another trail leaves right upstream to a campsite beside a large pool and a large, flat homesite with stone fences and stone piles. The flat is where Cecil Creek and a tributary coming out of Bartlett Cove join.

A rough, rocky track of loose stone switchbacks up and away from Cecil Creek, leveling out on a bench dominated by upland hardwoods of hickory and oak. Resume climbing and reach the Jones Cemetery at 2.7 miles. Here, former Confederate soldiers, among others, are interred. More climbing awaits until the trail hits a T-junction. A short path leads right to the old chimney of a hilltop homestead. Note the large oak that once shaded the home. The Cecil Cove Bench Trail leaves left, shortly crossing a perennial stream, and then heads along a long stone fence dilapidated by falling trees. The southeasterly course undulates into and out of drainages flowing off the mountain to your right. Note the massive mossy boulders in the drainage at 3.4 miles. The woods are mixed here, with redbud, ironwood, and other moist species growing in moist soils and oak dominating the drier sites. Pass a second steep, bouldery gorge at 4.3 miles.

From here, the trail climbs, then lev-

VIEW OF MUTTON POINT

els off. Through the trees, views open of the Buffalo River Valley below you and the rampart of Newberry Mountain across Cecil Creek. You'll reach gravel CR 19 and the end of the Cecil Cove Bench Trail at 5.2 miles. The loop turns left, down the gravel road, and follows it for 0.2 mile to reach the signed Farmers Trail, which leaves right, tracing an old pre-park road down a very rocky eroded 600-foot drop nearly to the Buffalo River. Look for small clearings and old wire fences. It's a slow, messy go here, but at least you are rewarded with views of 2,100-foot-high Mutton Point across from you—when you can look up.

At 6.3 miles, the trail reaches bottomland, a junction, and the Farmer Farmstead. The Old River Trail heads both right and left. First, explore the main house and multiple outbuildings of the homestead. To continue your hike, leave left from the junction on the Old River Trail, shortly passing the spring and springhouse that served the Farmer family. Soon you'll leave the Old River Trail and reach another junction. The loop hike leaves left, joining a singletrack foot-only path, cruising along a fence line with a field to your right and a bluff to your left (continue right on the Old River Trail to access the Buffalo River).

Circle a stony streambed, then make your way up a bluff line full of crumbly rocks—their individual layers easily discernible—eroded into stairs seemingly made for hikers. Cedars complement the scenery. Ascend layer by layer to reach a cliff line, Goat Bluff, overlooking the Buffalo Valley. An outcrop extends toward the river to the right of the trail. Mutton Point and the Buffalo Valley are clearly visible. The river itself is below you; the flats of Erbie are to your left.

Soon you'll reach a potentially confusing four-way junction. First, though, enjoy another vista to your right. Junipers, gnarled and draped with old-man's beard, are twisted into interesting shapes along Goat Bluff. Buffalo River country extends below.

Now a major roadlike trail leads left, toward Erbie Horse Camp. Another trail, foot only, continues forward along the bluff line. Still another trail leads left, near a trail sign that points away from the area just before you reach the overlook. This one is a hard-to-find, white-blazed singletrack that cuts through cedars.

The last trail described is the one you want. It heads north toward the Cecil Cove trailhead. This narrow footway travels woods with a field and fence to your right. Step over a rocky drainage, passing a stone fence made from broken slab rock. You are walking over the same flat slabs. Climb a bit, then level off before rejoining CR 19. Follow CR 19 for just a short distance, passing the road leading right to the horse camp, to reach the Erbie trailhead at 7.3 miles.

16

Alum Cove Natural Bridge Loop

TOTAL DISTANCE: 1.2-mile loop

HIKING TIME: 1 hour, 20 minutes

VERTICAL RISE: 250 feet

RATING: Easy

MAPS: USGS 7.5' Deer, Alum Cove Natural Bridge Geological Area; Ozark National Forest

TRAILHEAD GPS COORDINATES: N35° 51.600', W93° 13.971'

CONTACT INFORMATION: Ozark National Forest, 12000 AR27, Hector, AR 72843, (479) 284-3150, www.fs.usda.gov/osfnf

On some hikes you have to go a long way to see a few features. On this hike you go a short way to see many features. The beauty of this trail includes a natural bridge, cave, waterfalls, wildflowers, and more. Begin at a pleasant picnic area with shaded tables, restrooms, and a covered picnic shelter with a grill. From here, the hike dips into Alum Cove with its bridge, a classic arch. Walk atop and underneath it, seeing it from all vantages. During wetter times, you'll see a waterfall here as well, getting an unusual view of this cascade. The hike then dips down to a stream at the base of Alum Cove and climbs to visit more arches and other geological features on the far side of the valley before looping back to the trailhead.

HOW TO GET THERE

From Jasper, take AR 7 south for 15 miles to AR 16 west. Veer right and follow AR 16 west for 1.1 miles to paved Forest Road 1206 (FR 1206). Turn right; continue on FR 1206 for 3.0 miles to reach the right turn into the Alum Cove Picnic Area.

THE HIKE

Leave the parking area, taking stone steps through the picnic area on a gravel path bordered with stone. The track leaves the picnic area to enter upland hardwood forest. Make a big switchback to the left, traveling beneath oaks aplenty, which offer shade for the trail traveler. Beech, dogwood, and red maple complement the oak canopy. Stay with the trail and curve gently down via switchbacks rather than cutting straight down the mountain as others have done before you. This causes erosion on both trail and mountainside, sending soil into

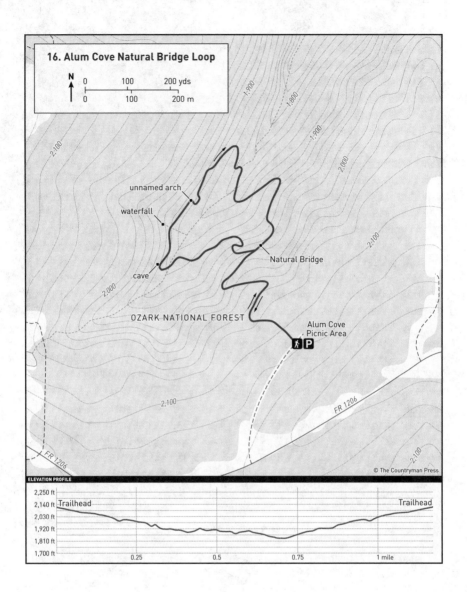

ELEVATION PROFILE

the stream below, which flows into West Fork Shop Creek.

Reach Alum Cove Natural Bridge. The trail continues directly atop the arch. A wet-weather stream drops into this rock span, which may have played a role in undercutting the rock bluff. If the stream is flowing, you can get an unusual vantage point of a waterfall here—from the top looking down, while still facing the falls, rather than the more typical view from the base looking up. And usually, if you're atop the falls, you will be looking outward rather than facing them; here, you get to be at the top and facing the cascade. Explore, but do not cross the bridge—yet. Instead head to your left as you enter, curving back down to the base of Alum Cove Natural Bridge. Notice the steps cut directly into the rock as you descend. Placed stones complement the natural

THE ARCH IS EASILY VISIBLE FROM THIS VANTAGE

rock stairs. Come under the overhang and rockhouse, taking in the immensity of the arch. Arches are truly amazing geological features. Gravity helps keep them together, yet eventually gravity will be their demise, thanks to the incessant downward push. On this arch, some parts of the underside will be dry and others, wet.

Leave the arch area and continue the loop. Descend into the valley below, where a stream flows. Note the abundance of beech trees here, in unusually high concentrations for the Ozarks. You'll undoubtedly notice the carvings in the beech trees, inscribed by previous hikers. Reach the main stream, which at normal flows can be easily crossed. Ascend rock stairs to the bluff line across the stream, where a large cave awaits. At the rear you'll find a very low room and a passage through the cave. The trail turns right here—either cut through the cave or walk around on its outside. Head into the overhang for a moment and let your eyes adjust. Imagine sitting here all day long looking out at snow or rain, as the aboriginal Arkansans undoubtedly did. In wet weather, water will drip into parts of the cave.

Continue along the bluff line, which has dry overhangs. Ahead, a wet-weather waterfall foot plunges 30 feet down a rock face, hits a flat rock slab, then splatters again into a plunge pool. Next you'll reach another rock overhang, this one smaller and bordered by pines. Then comes a small arch, adjacent to an eroded hole. The colors of this bluff line range from orange to gray, brown, and green, depending on the elements, moisture, and exposure. Now reach another large arch. This arch doesn't get much credit, because it's taller than it is wide and has the misfortune of lying so close to Alum Cove Natural Bridge, which is a large, classic arch. This arch is about 30 to 40 feet high and 20 or 30 feet wide, and should get acclaim as well.

Continue on the bluff line, observing more rock features, including still another arch. It's amazing how many arches are found along this one short hike! Leave the bluff line for good, heading back down to the creek in the middle of the valley. Cross the creek on a footbridge, stopping to admire this protected valley—the forest, the stream, the rocks, the moss, the wildflowers . . . all part of the Alum Cove Natural Bridge package.

Begin climbing toward the natural bridge. At this point, just before you reach the bridge, you can go right—under it—or stay left and actually use it as a bridge. When you're ready, backtrack to the picnic area, completing your loop.

Sams Throne Loop

TOTAL DISTANCE: 2.3-mile loop

HIKING TIME: 2 hours

VERTICAL RISE: 400 feet

RATING: Moderate to difficult

MAPS: USGS 7.5' Mount Judea, Lurton; Ozark National Forest

TRAILHEAD GPS COORDINATES: N35° 52.720', W93° 2.678'

CONTACT INFORMATION: Ozark National Forest, 12000 AR-27, Hector, AR 72843, (479) 284-3150, www.fs.usda.gov/osfnf

From where I stand, Sams Throne has the best views in all of Arkansas, and that is saying a lot. A popular destination for rock climbers, the Sams Throne area will not disappoint the most jaded trail trekker. Many of the paths here were built by volunteers who want to see this special swath of the Natural State enjoyed the way it should be while on trails in the best shape possible. The first views come quickly. Cruise along atop a bluff line before cutting to the lower end of the bluff where rock walls, overhangs, and small caves await. Don't be surprised if you pass some climbers doing their thing, especially on weekends. Travel through woods to climb Sams Throne, a rock promontory distended from the main bluff. Here, you can look off in all directions into the Big Creek Valley, the Cave Creek Valley, and the mountains beyond.

HOW TO GET THERE

From Russellville, take AR 7 north 37 miles to Pelsor and Sand Gap. From Pelsor, keep north on AR 7 for 3.6 miles to AR 123 north. Veer right and follow AR 123 north for 10.5 miles. The trailhead is on your left. When entering, stay to your left and reach a parking area. A gravel road at the rear of the parking area may or not be gated. In either instance, go ahead and park before the gate.

THE HIKE

At the far side of the gate and fence, start your hike by following the yellow blazes leaving right. Pass through a little wooded camping area, primarily used by rock climbers. Continue following the yellow blazes here, descending through mostly pine woods. Walk beside a crumbled rock fence—relics of

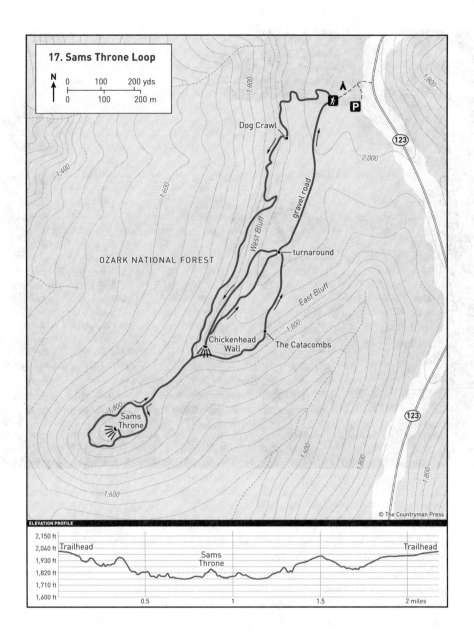

17. Sams Throne Loop

Dog Crawl

West Bluff

gravel road

turnaround

OZARK NATIONAL FOREST

East Bluff

Chickenhead Wall

The Catacombs

Sams Throne

© The Countryman Press

ELEVATION PROFILE

Trailhead

Sams Throne

Trailhead

what was here before the Ozark National Forest came to be. The trail begins curving through the woods and switchbacks downhill to soon reach an overlook at a clifftop. Work south along a bluff line; another vista immediately opens up. The views here are nothing short of spectacular. Continue south along a cliff where other craggy bluffs and overlooks await. Especially scenic are the stunted pines blown by the wind into strange shapes. Below, the fields and houses lie in the Big Creek Valley, with Hudson Mountain rising in the distance. Just beyond this overlook, the trail descends into a break in the rocks known as the

PINES FRAME THE VIEW FROM SAMS THRONE

Dog Crawl. Come alongside the bottom of a bluff line to reach an overhanging rockhouse on the steep bluff. You can go in either direction but continue south, for it leads to Sams Throne.

Watch for a pedestal rock and a Fatman's Squeeze. Most hikers skirt below the squeeze. The trail continues along more gorgeous rocks, huge boulders, and an amazing cliff line. Look below—cabin-sized boulders have broken away from this bluff line, coming to rest. Fewer pines grow here; hardwoods dominate, including moisture-loving species such as tulip trees and red maples, the predominant tree here. The bluffs alter

from gray to iron-colored red to greenish where lichens grow on them. During wetter times, much of the cliff will drip. These cliffs are known to rock climbers as the West Bluffs.

The cliff line ends at a peninsula-like rock extension where fallen boulders form more geological beauty. You have left the rock wall behind and are continuing along the wooded crest of the ridge. When you reach the rock outcrop that is Sams Throne, the trail splits left or right. To your left, look for a big rock crevice and other assorted overhangs. Head left to circle the throne. A sheer wall features a memorial to a climber named Dave Norman. Just beyond, you'll see a rocky track leading up a crack accessing Sams Throne. The last part requires you to travel on all fours.

The views are amazing once you reach the top. Foot trails circle outcrops where you can gain more vantages, especially from a piney point to the south. To the north, you'll see the cliff line under which you walked. Bluffs are everywhere. After circling Sams Throne, once again descend the crack in the rock. Continue circling the lower part of the throne, observing more rock features.

When you're ready, backtrack through the woods and return to the main cliff line, this time heading along the East Bluff. On this side of the wall, azaleas bloom in spring. Completing the loop this way requires a trip through the Catacombs. If you cannot find them or you don't feel comfortable climbing through the rocks, then simply backtrack. The Catacombs is a crack that has fallen rock in it; you must traverse the crack and scramble up a hole in the rocks to emerge onto the main cliff line. A clear trail leads to this feature; if you miss it, the bluffside trails become fainter. Enter a crack and, when your eyes adjust to the semidark, feel for smooth handholds worn from use. As you emerge the sky opens, yet more climbing lies ahead. This is a challenging section, but you're rewarded with unbelievable views at the top. Beyond the Catacombs, follow the yellow-blazed trail to emerge at the turnaround circle of a gravel road. Here is the yellow-blazed Sams Loop Trail, which hikers and climbers use to access the Chickenhead Wall. This trail loops out to the peninsula end and overlooks Sams Throne.

To return, simply follow the gravel road from the turnaround back up to the trailhead, completing your hike.

18

Pedestal Rocks Scenic Area Double Loop

TOTAL DISTANCE: 4.0 miles in two loops

HIKING TIME: 2 hours, 30 minutes

VERTICAL RISE: 300 feet

RATING: Moderate

MAPS: USGS 7.5' Sand Gap; Ozark National Forest, Pedestal Rocks Scenic Area

TRAILHEAD GPS COORDINATES: N35° 43.411', W93° 0.929'

CONTACT INFORMATION: Ozark National Forest, 12000 AR-27, Hector AR 72843, (479) 284-3150, www.fs.usda.gov/osfnf

Pedestal Rocks Scenic Area, part of Ozark National Forest, lives up to is name and then some. This truly scenic area offers far-reaching views, as well as up-close looks at arches, overhangs, rockhouses, waterfalls, and the Pedestal Rocks—tall rock spires capped with level pedestals. Start the first of two loops, taking the Pedestal Rocks Loop past Arch Rock before opening onto a bluff line that offers extensive views and looks down into the fissured rock below. The Pedestal Rocks then appear, just off the bluff you're walking on.

Once you complete the first loop, join the Kings Bluff Loop, with views that go on and on. The trail curves to pass a small waterfall before reaching the actual Kings Bluff, which is an extensive rock slab overlooking a creek below. Another waterfall drops over a rock rim at the far side. Beyond, the trail returns through woods to the trailhead.

HOW TO GET THERE

From I-40 near Russellville, take AR 7 north 37 miles to Pelsor and Sand Gap. From Pelsor, turn right onto AR 16 east and proceed east for 6 miles to the signed right turn to the scenic area. The parking area has picnic tables and a restroom.

THE HIKE

The hike begins by immediately crossing a bridge over a dry wash. Reach a split in the trail, staying left with the Pedestal Rocks Loop. The singletrack path enters classic Ozark hickory-oak woodlands. Stone steps lead down amid maples, oaks, and dogwoods to join an old woods track. Soon you'll reach a second junction, with Pedestal Rocks Loop. Leave left from the old roadbed onto a singletrack, heading toward Arch Rock.

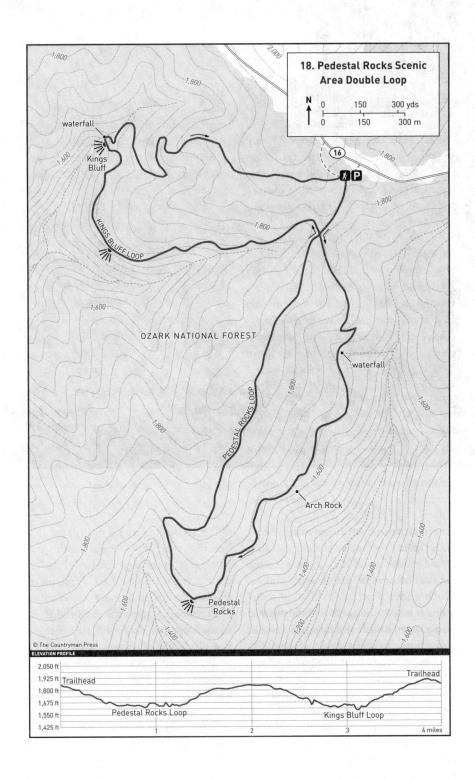

18. Pedestal Rocks Scenic Area Double Loop

N

| 0 | 150 | 300 yds |
| 0 | 150 | 300 m |

waterfall

Kings
Bluff

KINGS BLUFF LOOP

16

P

1.800

1.800

1.800

1.800

2.000

1.600

OZARK NATIONAL FOREST

PEDESTAL ROCKS LOOP

waterfall

1.800

1.600

1.600

Arch Rock

1.600

1.600

1.800

1.400

1.400

1.200

Pedestal
Rocks

1.600

1.400

© The Countryman Press

ELEVATION PROFILE

| 2,050 ft |
| 1,925 ft | Trailhead | Trailhead |
| 1,800 ft |
| 1,675 ft |
| 1,550 ft | Pedestal Rocks Loop | Kings Bluff Loop |
| 1,425 ft | 1 | 2 | 3 | 4 miles |

BLUFF VIEWS APLENTY CAN BE FOUND ON THIS DOUBLE LOOP

The narrow path descends on a slope with the ridgecrest to your right. Join an old roadbed and turn right, continuing the downgrade to cross a streambed, which—if it's flowing—creates a waterfall just below the trail. A rockhouse is also located beside the falls. In summer and fall this may run dry.

Join a wooded bluff line amid cedars, which have joined the woodland fray. The cliff line becomes more sheer as you reach Arch Rock at 0.8 mile. Arch Rock is a distended geological feature to the left of the trail. Water and time have eroded a passage in the large stone setting. If you walk under the rock, you will notice extending downhill the faint bed of a road that once used the arch as a passage through the bluff line. The rock that became the arch eroded away from the main bluff line, then was itself undermined. Cruise along the bluff line away from the direction you came to see other nearby overhangs, an arch, and rockhouses that all beg exploration. This arch is very tall and supports a rock overhang over which the Pedestal Rocks Trail travels.

Backtrack to the main blufftop trail. More pines appear. Vistas begin to open through the trees to the south, where the hills and hollows of the Illinois Bayou

The trail returns to woods. You'll shortly reach a sign indicating that you're halfway along the loop. Pass more outcrops before turning away from the bluffs. Join a woods track and continue gently rising. The hiking is easy, and you reach the junction with the Kings Bluff Loop at 2.3 miles. Turn left here and work your way west through woods. This loop is less traveled than Pedestal Rocks but offers features aplenty, so don't pass it by. Head downhill amid boulders to join a bluff line at 2.6 miles. The piney edge of the rock offers westerly views and down to the hollow to your left. Get ready to stop seemingly every few feet to marvel at the ever-changing vistas. The bluff line becomes wider and more open by 2.8 miles, and has some pedestals of its own.

Watch for the crevices in the wide rock slab upon which you walk. The most open of these crevices are fenced. Look down below for arches and rock formations. The amount of erosion underneath these bluffs is amazing—and shocking. You wonder how these bluffs stay up! Reenter woods, passing a wet-weather drainage that offers a waterfall below the trail, into a dark amphitheater. Open onto the Kings Bluff. This huge, unmistakable rock slab has but a few skimpy pine trees. A rock-and-stone fence borders the sheer cliff. The views aren't as impressive here as before, but the sheer size of the slab will amaze you. Another rainfall-dependent waterfall drops over a lip into a circular rock amphitheater. The Kings Bluff Loop leads away from the center of the bluff, ascending in wide, loping switchbacks between the two streambeds bordering Kings Bluff. Level out and join an old woods road, moderating its curving ways to complete the second loop and arrive at the trailhead at 4.0 miles.

basin extend to the horizon. Soon the first Pedestal Rock appears. Look for a stone column topped by a level rock cap located just off the main bluff line. A view complements the Pedestal Rock. Reach the first of three fenced and developed overlooks in quick succession. More pedestals appear. Look for more arches. The bluff line gets bigger and wider. A geologist would come in handy here. Look for the fenced crevice in the bluff, well back from its edge. Cedars, pines, and lichens cling to life atop this rock slab. Buzzards may be drafting on the thermals rising from the bluff line here. This is a spot to linger . . . .

Twin Falls Loop at Richland Creek Wilderness

TOTAL DISTANCE: 5.4-mile there-and-back

HIKING TIME: 4 hours

VERTICAL RISE: 200 feet

RATING: Difficult

MAPS: USGS 7.5' Moore; Ozark National Forest, Richland Creek Wilderness

TRAILHEAD GPS COORDINATES: N35° 47.914', W92° 55.990'

CONTACT INFORMATION: Ozark National Forest, P. O. Box 76, 1803 North 18th Street, Ozark, AR 72949, (479) 667-2191, www.fs.usda.gov/osfnf

Be prepared for a tough but beautiful excursion. This hike travels through some of the most rugged terrain in this neck of the woods to reach an Ozark icon. Twin Falls, located at the confluence of Big Devils Fork and Long Devils Fork, isn't easy to reach no matter how you get there. This route takes you up one side of Richland Creek and down the other, making a loop of sorts. The trails in this wilderness are not marked or maintained and at times are hardly present. But if you're looking for a challenging track to a rewarding destination, read on.

Before you begin your hike, be apprised that this trail includes some irregular terrain, such as big boulders, steep crumbly slopes, and gravel bars overgrown with brush. It also includes two creek crossings. In times of high water you can go up and back on the same side of Richland Creek, avoiding the crossings.

HOW TO GET THERE

To reach the trailhead near Richland Creek Campground from Russellville, take AR 7 north for 37 miles to Sand Gap and Pelsor. From here, turn right and drive east on AR 16 for 9 miles to Forest Road 1205 (FR 1205)/Pope County Road 68 (CR 68), 1.5 miles beyond Ben Hur. Turn left to follow FR 1205/CR 68 for 9 miles to Richland Creek Campground. Beyond the campground, continue a short distance on FR 1205 to cross Richland Creek on a concrete bridge. From the bridge, continue for 0.4 mile to a parking area on your left, as the rising road curves back to the right. The trail starts at the back of the parking area.

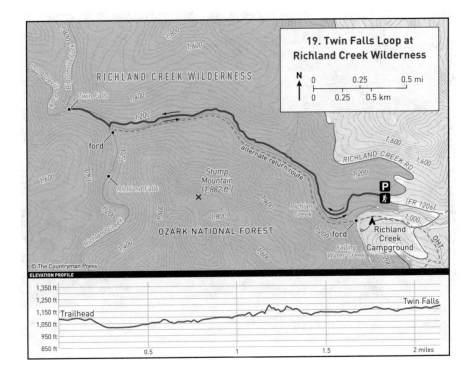

19. Twin Falls Loop at Richland Creek Wilderness

RICHLAND CREEK WILDERNESS

Twin Falls

ford

Stump
Mountain
[1,882 ft.]

Richland Falls

RICHLAND CREEK RD

OZARK NATIONAL FOREST

Richland
Creek

[FR 1206]

ford

Richland
Creek
Campground

Falling
Water Creek

© The Countryman Press

ELEVATION PROFILE

1,350 ft	
1,250 ft	Twin Falls
1,150 ft	Trailhead
1,050 ft	
950 ft	
850 ft	

0.5   1   1.5   2 miles

THE HIKE

Follow the dirt-and-rock path away from the curve of the road, passing a wilderness sign. Richland Creek flows audibly to your left. The trail traces an old settler road through woods punctuated with large boulders. Dogwood, maple, and sweetgum thicken the forest. The trail begins to descend off the hillside back toward Richland Creek in lush bottomland where wildflowers grow rampant in spring. Saddle alongside Richland Creek, cruising up its rich, verdant hollow. At 0.5 mile, the trail enters a full-fledged boulder field, which extends to the stream. Some of these boulders resemble giant children's playing blocks. The graybacks beckon your exploration. Richland Creek does its best to navigate through these massive boulders in cascades, slides, and small falls. Gravel bars form where they

can. The ruggedness of the stream will surprise you.

At times the hike already resembles a boulder scramble. Still, the trailbed is easily discernible here, and as long as you continue up the creek you'll be fine. While you're near the stream, notice the piles of debris left by high water. It's hard to imagine the power and fury of this waterway when such deposition is occurring. Footing is quite rough in places—be prepared for uneven surfaces and boulders and small rocks with very little level terrain. At 0.9 mile, the trail crosses an intermittent branch of Richland Creek, which has its own big boulders. Both the terrain and the river mellow beyond the intermittent streambed, making the walking easier. The bottomland is almost a relief after beating your way through the boulders, though many large boulders lie at the upper end of the flat.

TWIN FALLS

Continue coursing upstream amid these big stones. The trail becomes faint, dispersed, and harder to follow. Waterfall chasers split from one another along the stream, along the slope, and up along a bluff line, making the best route less clear. There is no good way here; each has its own challenges. Pass alongside a steep bluff that drips water and echoes the sounds of Richland Creek. The scenery continues to be outstanding, though you will be kept busy just navigating your way through the rugged terrain.

At 1.7 miles, you'll enter a long flat offering firmer footing. The trail here becomes easier to trace. Finally you'll see the valley began to widen before you; Big Devils Fork comes in on your right. At 2.1 miles, you'll cross this fork. It can usually be done dry-shod. Here, a good path turns right and goes

upstream. Magnificent bluffs rise on the opposite side of Big Devils Fork. Reach Twin Falls at 2.5 miles. This is the point where Big Devils Fork and Long Devils Fork meet, dropping into a singular rock cathedral. The two drops are different. The Long Devils Fork is slender and white, while the Big Devils Fork is a veil of water wider than it is long. Together they form a large plunge pool, with an alluring rock slab that offers both sun and shade for enjoyment of the scene.

Return to Richland Creek. If the water is high and you don't feel like fording, then backtrack the way you came. To make the loop, briefly head upstream on Richland Creek. By the way, if you want to see another waterfall, Richland Falls isn't too far up the creek. Otherwise, go just a short distance until the stream grows smaller with enough rocks to make a safe crossing—but don't count on your

RUGGED RICHLAND CREEK FLOWS BETWEEN BOULDERS

feet staying dry. Once you have crossed, turn downstream and immediately enter a camping area. A relatively good path runs along this bank. The trail is lower to the water, so you'll be doing more clambering over smaller rocks and debris and logs rather than navigating the side of the mountain. In places the path climbs well above the waterway on steep sections. It's definitely more heavily used here; the primary route is much easier to follow—except directly along the river, where flooding tends to wipe it out while depositing limbs and tree fodder. These long, irregular gravel beds—dotted with trees—change with every flood. Enter a large flat at 3.4 miles. Beyond this, leading downstream, a steep bluff pinches the trail down to only a foot or two wide. Reach a very large pool beyond the steep bluff. This quiet pool makes you realize that much of the hike has been along a lively, noisy stream.

The trail rises well above Richland Creek as it makes a big curve. Drop to the confluence of Falling Water Creek and Richland Creek at 4.5 miles. This is the tricky part. I suggest you turn right and head upstream a short way along Falling Water Creek until you find a crossing. It'll be a wet ford. Cross the stream, pass through a rocky overflow area, and then emerge at the lower Richland Creek Campground. Walk through the campground. Leave the campground road and join the forest road upon which you came, reaching the bridge over Richland Creek. This will be your favorite stream crossing of them all. Notice the Ozark Highlands Trail leaving right, just before the bridge. You will actually be on the Ozark Highlands Trail briefly—it uses the very same bridge to cross Richland Creek. Climb the road 0.4 mile farther to complete your loop.

20

Tyler Bend Loop

TOTAL DISTANCE: 4.2-mile loop

HIKING TIME: 2 hours

VERTICAL RISE: 300 feet

RATING: Moderate

MAPS: USGS 7.5' Snowball, Marshall; National Geographic #233 Buffalo National River—East Half, Collier Homestead

TRAILHEAD GPS COORDINATES: N35° 58.541', W92° 45.937'

CONTACT INFORMATION: Buffalo National River, 402 N. Walnut Street, Suite 136, Harrison, AR 72601, (870) 439-2502, www.nps.gov/buff

Tyler Bend is the location of the Buffalo National Scenic River Visitor Center. Here, a series of interconnected trails offer a glimpse into the natural beauty and pioneer past of this Arkansas treasure run by the National Park Service. The loop hike begins at the Collier Homestead parking area. It travels the Buffalo River Trail (BRT) among rich woods and steep hillsides, descending to the Buffalo River Valley. Border a pioneer rock wall in bottomland before bisecting some of the developed facilities of Tyler Bend, including the campground and visitor center. You'll then travel up Collier Bluff, where stellar river and mountain vistas await. Finally, explore the Collier Homestead, where hardy Ozark prepark residents made their lives.

HOW TO GET THERE

From the northern intersection of AR 27 and US 65 in Marshall, take US 65 north for 9.6 miles to the signed left turn into the Tyler Bend Visitor Center. From here, follow the paved road for 1.3 miles to the signed turn into the Collier Homestead trailhead. The hike starts in the back of the gravel loop, near a large white oak.

THE HIKE

Tyler Bend Visitor Center is worth checking out for its interpretive displays detailing the human and natural history of the area. But there's nothing like getting out there and seeing it firsthand. This hike will put your boots on the ground to complement everything you'll learn at the center. It's tempting to leave right from the trailhead toward the Collier Homestead and the Buffalo River Overlooks. But instead, head left, away from the homestead, on the Buffalo

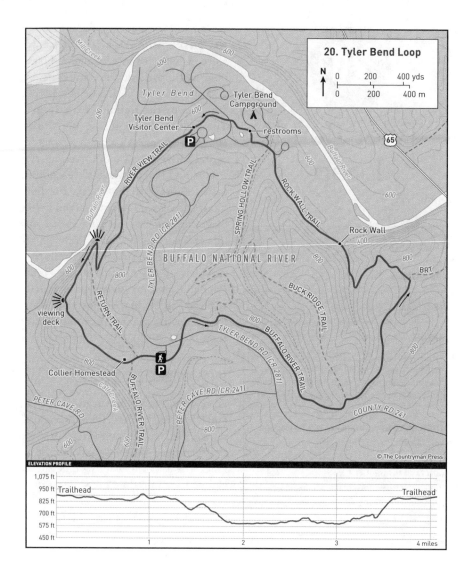

20. Tyler Bend Loop

N

| 0 | 200 | 400 yds |
| 0 | 200 | 400 m |

Tyler Bend

Tyler Bend Campground

Tyler Bend Visitor Center

restrooms

River View Trail

Spring Hollow Trail

Rock Wall Trail

Rock Wall

Buffalo River

65

BRT

viewing deck

Return Trail

Buck Ridge Trail

Collier Homestead

Tyler Bend Rd (CR 281)

Buffalo River Trail

Peter Cave Rd (CR 241)

Buffalo National River

County Rd 241

Peter Cave Rd

Mill Creek

© The Countryman Press

ELEVATION PROFILE

1,075 ft
950 ft — Trailhead
825 ft
700 ft
575 ft
450 ft

Trailhead

1   2   3   4 miles

River Trail. This way, you can get your exercise in before reaching the homestead. Pick up the foot trail as it travels through oak-cedar woods.

Cruise along an oak-dominated slope with a light understory. Look for the blackened trunks at the base of trees here. The National Park Service uses prescribed burns to keep this upland oak-hickory forest in its natural state. Intersect the Spring Hollow Trail at 0.3 mile. It leaves left to reach Tyler Bend

Campground in 0.9 mile, shortcutting this loop. Continue on the BRT, on steep terrain, as the slope drops off sharply down toward Spring Hollow. Begin climbing as the trail curves around the head of a hollow to reach the Buck Ridge Trail at 1.0 mile. This trail leads left to reach the campground after 1.2 miles, also shortcutting the loop.

Stay right on the singletrack BRT, which swings around a hollow. The woods are quite rocky here as your route curves north, then splits through a gap in the ridge. Slip over to the right-hand side of the ridge, now descending, to meet the Rock Wall Trail at 1.5 miles. The BRT keeps forward, but this loop turns left and uphill, toward the campground on the Rock Wall Trail. You are building a little sweat equity for seeing all the features of the last part of the hike. Climb through thin woods before switchbacking downhill, past a grassy glade, into a desiccated hollow. Reach and cross the streambed of the hollow, descending on the left bank amid woods rising in the extremely steep terrain.

The hollow abruptly ends at the bottomland of the Buffalo River at 1.9 miles. The trail turns left and comes alongside its namesake, a settler's moss-covered rock wall. A very large hay field lies between you and the river. A steep wooded hill rises to your left as you travel through rich, viney woods.

Open onto a grassy field on a mown track to reach the Tyler Bend Campground. Ahead, you'll reach the other end of the Spring Hollow Trail. Finding the loop trail in the campground can be confusing. As you reach the road, turn left, uphill along the road, passing the self-pay station. Just beyond, cross the road toward a restroom facility. As you face the facility, walk around the right-hand side of it, finding Campsite 24, a handicapped-accessible site. The trail resumes as a mown path behind this campsite, amid cedars.

Cross the paved picnic road and continue in cedars to soon reach the Tyler Bend Visitor Center, which has water and restrooms in addition to visitor information. To continue the loop,

BUZZARD LAZILY FLAPS ITS WINGS ASTRIDE COLLIER BLUFF

COLLIER HOMESTEAD

walk around to the far side of the visitor center and pick up the River View Trail. Resume woodland walking, crossing a drainage to come alongside a field, walking in woods. A bluff rises to your right. The Buffalo River comes into view before you turn away, circling a tributary. Climb to reach Collier Bluff and a phenomenal view at 3.5 miles. Junipers hang on to the rock promontory. You can look downstream at the bluffs of Tyler Bend, and upstream to where Calf Creek comes in from the left. Fields, mountains, and more of the Buffalo River Valley meld into the distance.

Continue up the impressive Collier Bluff, passing the Return Trail, which leads left 0.4 mile to the parking area and skips the Collier Homestead. The ascent continues, and you'll be tempted to find more vistas before reaching the crest of the bluff and a handicapped-accessible viewing deck at 3.7 miles. Enjoy

vistas upstream along with adjacent bluffs, and fields, and woods, and mountains, and ... you get the picture.

Continue past the observation deck on an easy path, which opens shortly onto the Collier Homestead. Notice the newspaper and magazine paper still stuck on the walls—it was used as insulation. Ol' Sod Collier got this land through the Homestead Act of 1862, moving here from Kentucky in 1928. He and his family were subsistence farmers, living without electricity or indoor plumbing. Later Sod became a fishing guide on the Buffalo. The National Park Service purchased the land in 1978, preserving the structures and grounds of the Collier Homestead. The Buffalo River Trail leaves right at the homestead for Woolum, while you keep forward around the homesite, passing the other end of the Return Trail before completing your loop at 4.2 miles.

21

Indian Rockhouse Loop with Overlook Addendum

TOTAL DISTANCE: 4.4 miles in two loops

HIKING TIME: 2 hours

VERTICAL RISE: 340 feet

RATING: Moderate

MAPS: USGS 7.5' Cozahome; National Geographic #233 Buffalo National River—East Half, Indian Rockhouse

TRAILHEAD GPS COORDINATES: N36° 4.889', W92° 34.139'

CONTACT INFORMATION: Buffalo National River, 402 N. Walnut Street, Suite 136, Harrison, AR 72601, (870) 439-2502, www.nps.gov/buff

This hike is chock-full of features to keep even the most trail-weary walker happy. It's centered at Buffalo Point, originally a state park developed by the Civilian Conservation Corps (CCC) and now part of the Buffalo National River. You'll start out by passing a huge sinkhole, then curve under a waterfall along a tall bluff. Pass an abandoned mine, then cruise a scenic stream, visiting a small cave. From here, head to the Indian Rockhouse, a long-used shelter of large proportions that includes its own skylight. Return via Pebble Springs. Stop at the Natural Bathtub, then visit an old rock quarry used by the CCC boys, who developed the facilities at Buffalo Point. Thus ends the Indian Rockhouse Loop.

If that isn't enough for you, you can add an extra loop hike leading from the same trailhead to an overlook of the Buffalo River, and then traverse extensive cedar rock glades before returning to the trailhead a second time. Informative displays are situated along the Indian Rockhouse Loop. On-site facilities, including cabins, campground, picnic area, river access, and ranger station, make the Buffalo Point area more than just a hiking destination. However, it can be very crowded here in summer.

HOW TO GET THERE

From the intersection of US 62 and AR 14 in Yellville, take AR 14 south for 14.1 miles to AR 268 and the signed left turn to Buffalo Point. Turn left here and follow paved AR 268 for a total of 2.5 miles, passing the ranger station on your right to reach a trailhead parking area on your right. This area also has picnic tables.

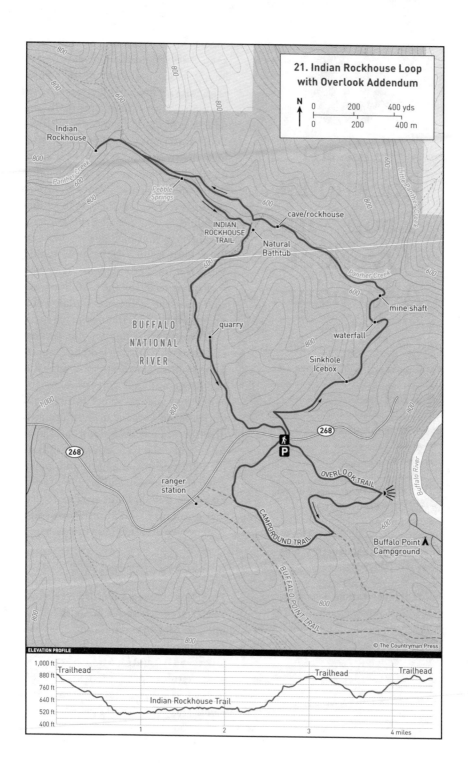

21. Indian Rockhouse Loop with Overlook Addendum

N

| 0 | 200 | 400 yds |
| 0 | 200 | 400 m |

Indian Rockhouse

Panther Creek

Pebble Springs

cave/rockhouse

INDIAN ROCKHOUSE TRAIL

Natural Bathtub

Panther Creek

mine shaft

BUFFALO NATIONAL RIVER

quarry

waterfall

Sinkhole Icebox

268

268

Buffalo River

ranger station

OVERLOOK TRAIL

CAMPGROUND TRAIL

Buffalo Point Campground

BUFFALO POINT TRAIL

© The Countryman Press

ELEVATION PROFILE

1,000 ft
880 ft   Trailhead   Trailhead   Trailhead
760 ft
640 ft   Indian Rockhouse Trail
520 ft
400 ft
                   1   2   3   4 miles

THE HIKE

The Indian Rockhouse Trail starts across the road from the parking area. Begin descending on an old roadbed into pine-oak forest. Curve right into a wooded hollow. Shortly pass the rock face of a sinkhole on your right. A streambed to the right of the trail flows into here. Just ahead you'll reach a bigger sinkhole, known as Sinkhole Icebox for its proclivity to emit cool 56-degree air, which sometimes creates fog in summer. Water flows into here, too. You can see a roadbed to your left that the trail roughly parallels. Meanwhile, the path briefly levels as it crosses a cedar rock glade before descending a rock slab, passing a circular sinkhole on trail left. By now, a waterfall is audible as you curve into a drainage. A spring flows over the lip of a cliff line, dropping 30 feet to a small pool. Usually the water simply disappears underground beyond the pool. The spring appears above the bluff line because it can't flow through it, as it does through gravelly rock of the streambed below.

The trail now travels along an overhanging bluff before resuming a downgrade. Reach a mineshaft on your left. This was an experimental shaft cut during a zinc boom that swept across the Arkansas Ozarks in the 1880s. A successful community and mine came on the scene just miles away at Rush (see Hike 22).

When you reach Panther Creek, turn left upstream. This creek, like many Ozark streams, flows only seasonally. However, notice the ironwood and other trees beside Panther Creek that lean downstream, from the push of torrents that occasionally crash through this lush hollow. Gray boulders contrast with the white and tan rocks in the creek. Keep along Panther Creek, ascending to reach a cave/rockhouse to the left of the trail at 1.1 miles. This cave has a skylight, created when part of its roof collapsed; the collapsed stratum lies directly below the skylight. Technically, this created an arch as well. Climb away from the cave to reach the crumbling asphalt of an old roadbed coming from uphill.

Here, the trail turns right, downhill, and crosses Panther Creek. A short path leads left, connecting to the Return Trail, but save that for later. Continue on the now gravel trailbed farther up Panther Creek, which has cut a mini gorge. Cross Panther Creek to reach the other end of the Return Trail. Keep heading upstream to step over Panther Creek yet again. Through the trees at 1.7 miles stands the maw of the Indian Rockhouse. This is a big rock shelter, and has been in use for 10,000 years. It has dry places, a skylight, and even running water near the back of the cavern! Listen to the water flow. Look at the rock formations in the back of the shelter. Imagine all the nights spent by man over ten millennia. This is truly a special spot in the Ozarks.

From the Indian Rockhouse, backtrack to the Return Trail and cross Panther Creek. Water flow has cut the bedrock, an open slab forming a crevice flow that drops to a pool. You are now on the right-hand bank of the creek, heading downstream to shortly reach Pebble Springs. This is strictly a winter and spring feature. When the water is flowing, it forms a deep pool at the spring mouth; otherwise, it looks like a sinkhole. The pebbles are inside the hole of the springs.

Circle the top of the springs, look-

LOOKING OUT FROM THE MAW OF THE INDIAN ROCKHOUSE

ing into Panther Creek at more carved streamside bedrock. Pass the Connector Trail and reach the Natural Bathtub. Here, on a feeder branch of Panther Creek, water has carved a circular pool that really does resemble a bathtub. It's likely to have water, too, as this tributary of Panther Creek flows more often. Turn up the tributary, bisecting open cedar glades and walking on bedrock. Step over the tributary just above a small waterfall. Leave the creek for steeper terrain, ascending a crumbly bluff line on stone steps.

Reach a roadbed and a split in the trail at 2.7 miles. Head left to see where the CCC boys cut into this bluff for stone to build the structures you see at Buffalo Point. Leave the quarry and follow the roadbed used to access the quarry. Reach a gate to your left. AR 268 is ahead. A foot trail cuts left between

both roadbeds, but as long as you go left, all will lead you shortly to the trailhead, completing the Indian Rockhouse Loop at 3.2 miles.

If you're still feeling feisty, why not tackle the 1.2-mile loop that heads to an overlook of the Buffalo River? Come on! From the trailhead, facing the picnic tables, take the worn trail leading left, toward Cabins 7 through 12. It descends through pine-oak woods. The hillside drops off to your right and opens to a panoramic view at a rock bluff, with a stone wall to keep the kids safe. The river and its gravel bars lie below you, and you can see part of Buffalo Point Campground. Turn right, away from the overlook, to join extensive rock glades that top a cliff line. The bare rock slab makes for interesting walking. Lichens, small cedars, fall wildflowers, and even cacti cling to the thin soil here; as a

LOOKING OUT ON THE GRAVEL BARS ALONG THE BUFFALO

benefit, you can look out below. Cross a wet-weather drainage, leaving the glade behind. Ascend to reach the Campground Trail. Turn right here, still heading uphill into pines. Look to the right of the trail for bricks and other artifacts of a forgotten homestead before turning right at a sign indicating the trailhead. Pass behind some cabins on the hill to your left to emerge at the trailhead, completing your bonus loop for a total hike of 4.4 miles.

22

Rush Mountain Mine Meander

TOTAL DISTANCE: 3.6-mile loop	
HIKING TIME: 2 hours	
VERTICAL RISE: 450 feet	
RATING: Moderate	
MAPS: USGS 7.5' Rea Valley; NPS Rush Historic District handout; National Geographic #233 Buffalo National River— East Half, Rush Historic District	
TRAILHEAD GPS COORDINATES: N36° 7.896', W92° 34.076'	
CONTACT INFORMATION: Buffalo National River, 402 N. Walnut Street, Suite 136, Harrison, AR 72601, (870) 439-2502, www.nps.gov/buff	

In the 1880s, a mining boom swept over the Ozarks, eventually making its way to the hollow of Rush Creek and adjacent Rush Mountain. Zinc was the target mineral. By the time World War I erupted, the price of zinc was high and Rush swirled with hundreds of residents. When Rush was incorporated into the Buffalo National Scenic River in 1974, however, it was but a ghost town. Today you can visit the relics of the community and the Morning Star Mine, learning what life was like in an Ozark mining town.

After leaving the Morning Star Area, this loop hike heads toward the Buffalo River along Rush Mountain, where fenced-off mine shafts and tailings offer mute testimony to the area's past. Next, swing out toward the river, gaining a view or two before turning toward Clabber Creek to see more mine ruins. An unmaintained slender foot trail leads over Rush Mountain back to the trailhead. The unmaintained trail is steep but doable. If you feel uncomfortable with the climb over Rush Mountain, simply backtrack to the trailhead. Rush also has a picnic shelter, a small campground with water and restrooms, and a boat launch.

HOW TO GET THERE

From the intersection of AR 14 and US 62 in Yellville, take AR 14 south for 11.5 miles to the signed left turn into Rush, at Marion County Road 6035 (CR 6035). Follow CR 6035 for 4.2 miles to the Morning Star Mine site and trailhead, on your left.

THE HIKE

Leave the parking area and begin the interpretive trail, wandering through

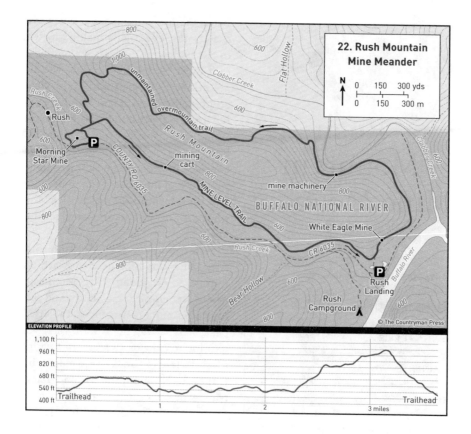

ELEVATION PROFILE

the old Morning Star Mine site. Take the trail heading up along the gravel road, not the one that leads up a step of stairs from the parking area. The old livery barn site is your first stop. Animals were used in all phases of mining. The old smelter is nearby. It was originally built to smelt silver, because the men who discovered the mine thought they had a silver strike on their hands. They were heartsick after the first batch came through and the smelter proved useless. Later they tried to pawn the mine for a can of oysters but were turned down. Ultimately, others saw the potential for zinc and reopened the facility.

Climb a bit more, passing the old blacksmith shop and mine office before turning left and leaving the interpretive trail for the Mine Level Trail. Immedi-

ately begin climbing, passing a sign detailing the trails of Rush. If you look to your left past the sign, you will see a faint trail coming in. This is your return route, if you like following unmaintained trails.

For now, stick with the main trail as it traces an old wagon road used to access the mines; pines and cedars are regrowing atop old mine tailings. This is the first of many mine entrances. All are fenced and gated. Now home to bats, they are closed off to keep fools from entering an old mine on a lark. The trail levels off and begins passing several mines, tailings piles, and trails leading to mines above the level you're walking on. Some of these tailings piles offer views into the Rush Valley below and hills beyond.

OLD MINING CART LIES BY THE TRAIL

The shadeless track continues heading toward the Buffalo River. The mine openings keep on, too. Interestingly, at 0.5 mile, you'll come upon an old cart that was likely used to haul ore from one place to another. The mining was done by hand at first, with picks; as the good ore became harder to reach, more sophisticated machine methods came into use.

The trail drops a bit as a steep ridgeline pinches in the trail. This open area, scattered with unnatural piles of rock, offers more views of the Rush

Valley and Rush Creek below, as well as the access road leading to the Buffalo River. Turn away from the bluff line, dropping sharply into full-blown woods and leaving the primary ore-gathering area. At 1.0 mile, the Mine Level Trail leaves left as the wagon track bears right and downhill. The trail now makes an irregular climb near some tailings and up a gladey bluff that's quite steep. You may hear Rush Creek flowing from this perch—the closer you are to the Buffalo River, the more likely Rush Creek is to be flowing. Winter views of the Buffalo can be had at this point.

The trail passes over a land bridge between a sinkhole to your left and the bluff to your right before reaching a trail junction at 1.5 miles. A short path leads down to Rush Landing, a paddler access and picnic area. This is also the site of the White Eagle Mine, and gravelly tailings lie beneath scattered pines, cedars, and cacti. Pilings also rise forth below the trail of a short-lived 1950s ore-processing mill. Stay left here, leaving the maintained trail, onto a much less used path. Join a broken and erratic cliff line, gaining glimpses of the Buffalo River. You can hear it, too. At 1.7 miles, look for a faint trail leading right, downhill, to an outcrop where you can see the river.

The trail now circles the northeast side of the mountain, entering the Clabber Creek Valley, a clear tributary of the Buffalo, descending to join a roadbed in 2.0 miles. Turn left, keeping Clabber Creek, which is well below, to your right. A sharp bluff line rises just to the left of the trailbed. Come upon some old mining machinery and a fenced mine with a very large opening. This spot also offers good looks into clear Clabber Creek, which flows over wide and smooth rock slabs beside gravel bars. The trail con-

tinues beyond this last mine on a still fainter path.

At 2.3 miles, the old roadbed continues forward, but the overmountain route to the trailhead leads left and uphill as a faint and slender track only a foot wide. Though it isn't maintained by the park service, it's footworn. If you cannot find the path or are uncomfortable with the prospect of following the unmaintained trail over steep terrain, simply backtrack on the Rush Mountain Trail.

The overmountain route leaves the roadbed left, nearly straight up Rush Mountain. Keep an eye on the trailbed and an eye peeled for the blazes on the trees. Occasional limbs and fallen trees obscure the path. Angle uphill, west-northwest, amid boulders in pine-oak woods. Briefly level out before slicing upward through a break in a cliff line at 2.6 miles. The ascent eases up and stays fairly level before reaching a National Park Service boundary marker, a metal stake in the ground, with nearby posted bearing trees.

Keep level a bit more, then ascend to the crest of Rush Mountain at 2.9 miles. Here, veer right and keep atop the mountain, working around occasional blowdowns. The trail apexes on the northwest end of the mountain, then turns left and sharply drops, finding breaks in bluffs to keep downhill. Continue dancing between cliff lines, with views opening across the mountain. Reach and briefly follow an old mining track before turning left off the bed. Wind amid more rocks and cedars to emerge onto the Mine Level Trail at a trail signboard just uphill from the Morning Star Interpretive Trail. Backtrack a short bit, then turn left, exploring more of the interpretive trail and processing mill before descending steps to complete the hike at 3.6 miles.

23

Lower Buffalo Wilderness Loop

TOTAL DISTANCE: 12.9-mile loop	

HIKING TIME: 7 hours

VERTICAL RISE: 680 feet

RATING: Difficult

MAPS: USGS 7.5' Buffalo City; National Geographic #233 Buffalo National River—East Half, Lower Buffalo Wilderness

TRAILHEAD GPS COORDINATES: N36° 9.557', W92° 28.201'

CONTACT INFORMATION: Buffalo National River, 402 N. Walnut Street, Suite 136, Harrison, AR 72601, (870) 439-2502, www.nps.gov/buff

Not only is this wilderness rugged and lesser used, but it's an adventure just finding the trailhead. None of the paths in the wilderness are marked or maintained; if it weren't for some use by backpackers and equestrians, the trail system might disappear altogether. Located near the confluence of the Buffalo and White rivers, this slice of the Buffalo National Scenic River is in the forgotten east end. The loop explores the 22,500-acre federally designated Lower Buffalo Wilderness. It climbs to a gap on Turkey Mountain, then begins a long loop, mostly following old forest roads. First it dips into Cook Hollow, then climbs Granite Mountain. The path heads south and east, eventually dipping into the Cow Creek drainage, passing an old mine site, and approaching the Buffalo River and Elephant Head Rock. From the river, the loop runs north over more old roads and nears the river again at the base of Cook Hollow. A side trip to Stair Bluff offers an arduous climb and superlative views. Return up Cook Hollow, completing the loop.

This route, minus the side trip to Stair Bluff, is also known as the CC-CH Loop, for Cow Creek and Cook Hollow. It touches only the northern part of the wilderness and makes for a good backpacking trek. You could create a longer trek, too, if you're willing to explore beyond the loop. Long pants, a map, and GPS are recommended on this hike.

HOW TO GET THERE

From the intersection of US 62 east and AR 14 in Yellville, take US 62 east for 8.8 miles, passing through Flippin, to meet AR 101 (the mileages to AR 101 may change, as US 62 is being widened

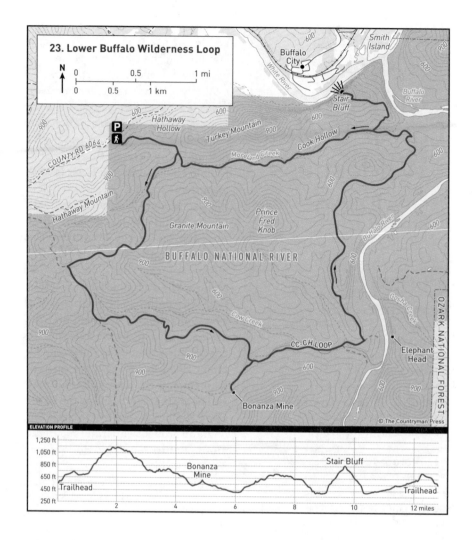

23. Lower Buffalo Wilderness Loop

N

| 0 | 0.5 | | 1 mi |
| 0 | 0.5 | 1 km | |

and rerouted). Take AR 101 toward Rea Valley a total for 11.9 miles to the trailhead, on your left. Specifically, AR 101 ends after 10.9 miles, and the paved road becomes Marion County 6064 (CR 6064). After 11.0 miles, the pavement ends. Pay attention here. Go 0.9 mile beyond the pavement, passing a cabin on your right, and then drive over a normally dry streambed. Watch on your left for two pull-ins to the same grassy area with one large cedar tree standing at the far end—the only tree here.

This is the trailhead. The trail, however, starts in the corner opposite the large cedar, away from the road, and is 0.1 mile beyond the cabin.

THE HIKE

Leave from the parking area southeast on a narrow track, winding uphill southeast through woods. The trail will likely have horse tracks. It parallels a drainage on your left on a rocky and sometimes sandy track along the northeast side of Hathaway Mountain, to reach a gap between Hathaway Mountain and Turkey Mountain at 0.6 mile. The trail becomes wider and stonier. Granite Mountain is visible ahead. About 50 yards below the gap, the trail splits. The trail continuing straight down toward Cook Hollow is your return route. You, however, turn right, southwest, drifting through open cedar glades, aiming for the upper reaches of Cook Hollow, which you cross at 1.0 mile. Ascend through oaks on an extended uptick up the north slope of Granite Mountain on an eroded track, making your way to a gap in the crest at 1.6 miles. Turn right here, heading westerly. Top out on the ridgeline, with thin woods to your right; this was once either pastureland or a homesite, or both. Notice the larger trees mixed in with the younger along this old road.

Drift into a trail junction at 2.3 miles, near oaks with widespread branches. Here, a trail leads right and uphill toward Hathaway Mountain and out to the trailhead access road at a four-way junction. This loop, however, heads left, downhill, to undulate southerly toward the upper reaches of Cow Creek. Trace another old roadbed in pine-oak woods. Many scattered large oaks grow here, amid younger trees. At 2.8 miles, reach a large flat rock to the left of the trail, which has been used as a resting/picnicking spot. An important trail junction lies directly ahead. One trail continues forward on the ridgeline for Dead Horse Gap; this loop, however, veers left and downhill into the greater Cow Creek drainage. If you keep south for Dead Horse Gap, I hope you have a pack on. You could be on the trail for days.

The correct trail joins an old forest road easterly, descending into deeper, thicker woods—well above the creek yet well below the ridge—into the heart of the wilderness. This is good deer country; you may see a whitetail here. At 4.4 miles, the trail begins dropping steeply. Cleveland Knob stands across the Buffalo River. At 4.6 miles, you'll reach a perennial feeder stream of Cow Creek, with camping potential. Just before you cross the creek, a narrow trail leads right, upstream, for 0.3 mile toward the old Bonanza Mine. About halfway there it crosses the creek and opens into a large area of gravelly tailings. This was likely a zinc mine.

Return to the main route, crossing the stream and coming alongside Cow Creek. The trail in this bottom becomes thick and brushy, but keep the faith and keep east to cross Cow Creek at 5.9 miles. Ahead, a side trail leads down to the Buffalo River, while the main trail circles past two rock slab drainages. Begin ascending away from Cow Creek and reach another important trail junction. One trail leads forward, passing an out-of-place old stove before dropping to cane bottoms along the Buffalo; you can fight your way to the river's edge to see the Elephant Head, a rock face in Trimble Bluff across the river. The rock looks more elephantine from the river than from here, however. The correct trail for this loop leaves left and sharply uphill on a gravel track, northbound on an old roadbed. The climb is long and steady on an irregular rocky tread. Small cedars grow in the middle of the old roadbed.

At 7.4 miles, reach a gap east of Prince Fred Knob, where people have camped and rested before. Wind toward the Buffalo River, which has made a big curve at Hudson Bend. Circle behind a knob before making the bottoms again and a junction at 8.7 miles. The trail to your right leads to the river. You stay left, westbound, immediately crossing a small drainage to enter thickly wooded Cook Hollow. Cross Moreland Creek, the stream of Cook Hollow, at 9.0 miles.

Reach another junction. Here, you must go right and take the spur trail to one of the best vistas in the Ozarks at Stair Bluff. Head downstream along the streambed before curving left and uphill on a steep and stony track through partly open forest. A forest fire raged here some time ago, with some big trees surviving. The rest of the forest is growing back. The trail mercifully eases up, moderately climbing through brushy, messy woods. It seems you are almost there . . . but keep climbing. You will see buzzards overhead, but they are not claiming dead hikers and horsemen failing to make the climb, just riding the thermals of the bluff, which you reach at 9.8 miles.

It's worth every step. A cross stands atop the perch. From here, you can look down at Buffalo City, just across the White River. To your left, Turkey Mountain stands out in bold relief, with its own riverside bluffs. The downstream shot of the White River reveals Smith Island, at the confluence of the White and Buffalo Rivers. And for 180 degrees to the north, the views go for as far as the clarity of the sky allows. Obscured vistas to the south show the Lower Buffalo Wilderness and the places you just hiked. You could walk directly here from the trailhead for a there-and-back day hike of 6.2 miles.

Backtrack to Moreland Creek and begin heading upstream. This creek will be flowing in places, offering camping possibilities. Ahead, the stream braids; you cross some of these braids before resuming the right bank against a piney hill. Cross over to the left bank of Moreland Creek on a rock slab at 11.1 miles. Continue up the now tighter hollow to cross one more time just above a small falls at 12.2 miles. After the crossing, take the trail leading straight up

LOOKING OUT ON TURKEY MOUNTAIN AND THE WHITE RIVER FROM STAIR BLUFF

THE CONFLUENCE OF THE WHITE AND BUFFALO RIVERS

the hillside, climbing a stony track to complete the loop portion of the hike. Climb another 50 yards through the gap between Turkey Mountain and Hathaway Mountain, backtracking to reach the trailhead at 12.9 miles.

24

Leatherwood Wilderness Trek

TOTAL DISTANCE: 11.6-mile there-and-back

HIKING TIME: 6 hours, 30 minutes

VERTICAL RISE: 870 feet

RATING: Difficult

MAPS: USGS 7.5′ Norfork SE, Big Flat; Ozark National Forest; National Geographic #233 Buffalo National River—East Half, Leatherwood Wilderness

TRAILHEAD GPS COORDINATES: N36° 4.983′, W92° 22.287′

CONTACT INFORMATION: Ozark National Forest, P.O. Box 1279, 1001 E. Main Street, Mountain View, AR 72560, (870) 269-3228, www.fs.usda.gov/osfnf

This is a tough but rewarding hike for those who want to tackle it. The Leatherwood Wilderness is over 20,000 acres in size, yet doesn't have any developed trails. The trails that do exist are kept open by wilderness users, tracing the old roads of former homesteaders. This particular track starts atop Push Mountain, where a closed fire tower stands. The hike cruises down a rib ridge of Push Mountain and dips into Spencer Hollow, a lush mountain valley. This valley opens to Leatherwood Creek, the wilderness's namesake stream. Upon reaching the creek, continue to enjoy clear waters, bluffs, and raw beauty that make up this wilderness. But you will also be challenged by numerous creek crossings. At times of normal flow most of these can be dry-footed. After the crossings, reach the Buffalo River, where you can see the magnificence of the wild and scenic waterway, especially looking downstream at a 600-foot-high bluff.

Though the trails are not maintained, you needn't worry too much about getting lost while heading down Leatherwood Creek. Once you reach the stream, just stay with it and you'll be fine. The return trip will be a backtrack. I recommend this hike for fall through spring. Be apprised that this wilderness trail will be going around blown-down trees and may become brushy in summer. However, equestrians keep it open. Horse traffic on this trail has its pluses and minuses. The horsemen bring in chainsaws and help keep the trail open, but they also turn some areas into quagmires. Backpackers with time and a GPS could further explore this backcountry.

HOW TO GET THERE

To reach the Push Mountain trailhead at Leatherwood Wilderness from the

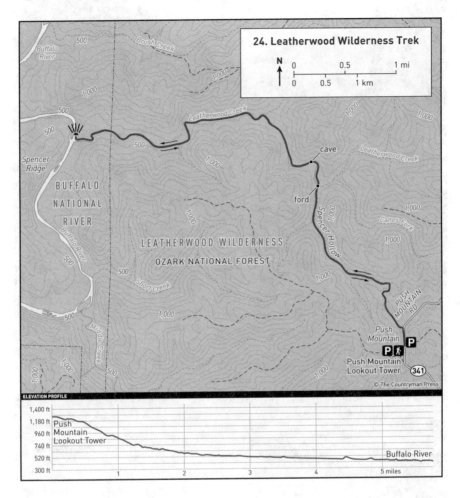

24. Leatherwood Wilderness Trek

N
0   0.5   1 mi
0   0.5   1 km

500
Buffalo River
Brush Creek
1,000
1,000
500
Leatherwood Creek
1,000
1,000
500
500
500
Spencer Ridge
cave
Leatherwood Creek
BUFFALO NATIONAL RIVER
1,000
ford
Spencer Hollow
1,000
Canes Fork
1,000
1,000
LEATHERWOOD WILDERNESS
OZARK NATIONAL FOREST
1,000
Short Creek
500
500
1,000
PUSH MOUNTAIN RD
Push Mountain
1,000
Middle Creek
1,000
1,000
500
1,000
Push Mountain Lookout Tower
341
© The Countryman Press

ELEVATION PROFILE

1,400 ft
1,180 ft   Push
960 ft   Mountain
740 ft   Lookout Tower
520 ft   Buffalo River
300 ft
              1   2   3   4   5 miles

junction of AR 14 and AR 9 in Mountain View, take AR 14 west for 22.4 miles to reach AR 341 north. Turn right and follow AR 341 north for 7 miles to the Push Mountain trailhead. There is trailhead parking on your right as well as below the Push Mountain fire tower.

THE HIKE

Leave the tower parking area and continue down AR 341 north, away from Mountain View. The wilderness information kiosk and horse trailer parking area will be on your right as you walk along the road to pick up a little path that runs parallel to it. Split left onto an old roadbed leading into the woods as AR 341 bears to your right. Pass a tank trap and wilderness sign to begin descending a ridgetop roadbed, working your way into Spencer Hollow under a young hardwood forest—a typical Ozark ridgeline oak-dominated woodland.

Make the bottom of the hollow at 0.8 mile and begin heading westerly, deeper into the watershed. The stream forming Spencer Hollow is likely to be running dry most of the year. As you continue ever deeper into the hollow, you'll begin to notice small bluffs bordering

LEATHERWOOD CREEK FLOWS CLEAR THROUGH REMOTE TERRAIN

the streambeds. At 1.2 miles, a bigger hollow comes in on your left. Note the musclewood and buckeye trees growing in this area. Look for an old roadbed heading up this hollow, which drains Push Mountain.

This hike continues downstream toward Leatherwood Creek. With the addition of another streambed, the creek beside you is now cutting more deeply and exposing more rock. When this stream is flowing, it will be a multitude of small cascades. When it's dry, all you'll see are watery potholes. At 1.9 miles a perennial stream comes in from your left. This stream is born from a ridgetop spring. Keep downstream to reach Leatherwood Creek at 2.3 miles. The forthcoming crossing will likely necessitate taking your shoes off. But it's a spot worthy of

BLUFF RISES TALL BELOW CONFLUENCE OF BUFFALO RIVER AND LEATHERWOOD CREEK

contemplation: The stream you've been following and Leatherwood Creek meet to form a deep, enticing pool. The bottomland here is thicker still, with cedar, sycamore, sweetgum, and dogwood. The sounds of moving water become ever present.

Ford Leatherwood Creek a second time, continuing down the valley where bluffs rise ever higher. Quickly make a third crossing, then come alongside a bluff with a cave at 2.6 miles. Even though the cave isn't deep, it is cooler in summer and warmer in winter than the surrounding air. Make a fourth ford at 3.0 miles. A fifth ford at 3.5 miles takes you to the right-hand bank and a massive flat topped with big pines. However, the trail immediately crosses back over to the left side. You can avoid this fifth and the ensuing sixth ford by continuing on the left bank here. Also on the right-hand side of the stream between the fifth and sixth fords, a spur trail heads up a tributary of Leatherwood Creek and may prove confusing. If in doubt, continue down Leatherwood Creek.

The valley is quite wide and getting wider as you reach the next ford, which crosses a wide, shallow rock slab. You are now continuing downstream on the right bank. Reach ford number eight and the left bank at 3.9 miles. At lower water these can be made dry-shod, except for the very first ford. Here, a tall bluff and accompanying rock glades are visible across the creek. Cedars overhang the rock wall. Another wide rock slab ford is found at 4.6 miles. The trailbed can be alternately sandy or rocky.

The flats are very large, and you can easily see how this was farmland a century ago. More fords continue. Keep downstream along Leatherwood Creek, ignoring any trail junctions. At 5.6 miles the trail dips to cross Leatherwood Creek at an island. Just below the island, the stream makes a very sharp curve to the right and is backed by a big bluff across the water. You are now in bona fide bottomland, with Leatherwood Creek to your left. Close in on the Buffalo River amid sycamore and ash. Cane grows rife in this bottom.

At 5.8 miles, you'll reach the Buffalo River atop of a wooded sandbar. This perch allows for a good view of a downstream bluff on the Buffalo, rising 600 feet above the water. Leatherwood Creek comes in just to your left. Look upstream to gain a wide, sweeping river view, with Spencer Ridge across the water. From the sandbar you can drop 20 or 30 feet to the river's edge. On your way back up, consider what a wild treasure the Leatherwood Wilderness is.

North Sylamore Waterfall Sampler

TOTAL DISTANCE: 4.6-mile there-and-back	
HIKING TIME: 3 hours	
VERTICAL RISE: 160 feet	
RATING: Moderate	
MAPS: USGS 7.5' Fifty Six; Ozark National Forest	
TRAILHEAD GPS COORDINATES: N35° 58.177', W92° 10.318'	
CONTACT INFORMATION: Ozark National Forest, P. O. Box 1279, 1001 E. Main Street, Mountain View, AR 72560, (870) 269-3228, www.fs.usda.gov/osfnf	

Not only is this hike a good destination in and of itself, but it starts at a great place, too—Blanchard Springs Caverns. You can hike and take a cave tour, as well as camp, fish, and swim in-season. This is a popular spot, though; if you're looking for solitude, come on a weekday or during the cooler times of year. The North Sylamore Creek Trail extends for 23 miles one-way. Blanchard Springs Recreation Area is on the lower part of the North Sylamore Creek Trail, and offers quality hikes in both directions.

This hike heads downstream, passing some spectacular bluffs, springs, and tributaries before coming to a waterfall flowing out of Cornfield Hollow. Beyond this waterfall you'll climb to reach an overlook atop a bluff with North Sylamore Creek flowing below, though you'll be seeing a lot of the stream as the trail passes alongside the watercourse flowing clear over gravel beds. Adventurous travelers will continue beyond the overlook at the end of this high to enter Slick Rock Hollow, which has more falling water.

HOW TO GET THERE

To reach the Blanchard Springs Caverns trailhead from the junction of AR 14 and AR 9 in Mountain View, take AR 14 west for 12.3 miles and turn right onto paved Forest Road 1110 (FR 1110). Proceed past the entrance station and continue for 2.5 miles, staying left for the campground. After 0.3 mile, turn left into a parking area signed NORTH SYLAMORE CREEK TRAILHEAD.

THE HIKE

Finding the correct part of the North Sylamore Creek Trail can be confusing.

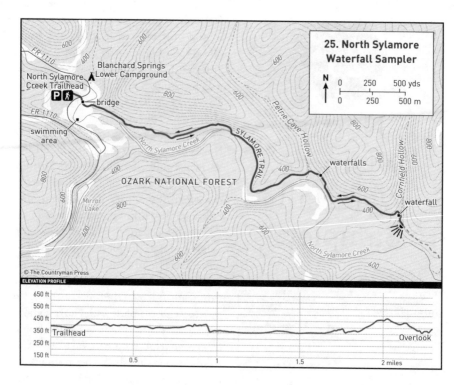

25. North Sylamore Waterfall Sampler

ELEVATION PROFILE

As you face the trailhead picnic shelter, you'll see the North Sylamore Creek Trail going forward. Do not go this way; rather, turn right and follow the blazes through the pine-shaded picnic area. Cross the road leading to the campground, then immediately cross North Sylamore Creek on a road bridge leading to the swim area. Stay left beyond the bridge. Instead of heading for the swim area pavilion, follow the blue-blazed singletrack trail up and away from the parking area to reach gorgeous rock bluffs to your left and North Sylamore Creek to your right. Watch for wildflowers in spring along the bluff here, especially fire pink and pussytoes. Ferns add a green touch to the forest floor.

North Sylamore Creek is flowing clear and alluring below as it winds its way down the valley, bordered by gravel bars. Watch for a little cave in an overhanging bluff to your left. Overhead,

cedar and ever-present oaks canopy the sandy slender track. Soon bluffs began to recede as you continue downstream. A large wooded flat opens below. You may notice old fences. These barbed-wire fences were part of the valley homesteads before national forest acquisition. Intermittent streambeds bisect the trail in places. Pines share space with the cedars. The bluff pinches in at 0.8 mile. Bridge a watercourse flowing off the side of the mountain to your left. This spring once served a small schoolhouse in the vicinity.

Beyond the spring, the path runs very close to North Sylamore Creek. The trail is very sandy here. A gray bluff rises high overhead to your left. When the stream overflows its banks, it will often leave debris atop the path. At lower water you will see an island in midstream piled with logs and other driftwood. The bluff line once again recedes. A wide path

BLUFFS RISE FROM SCENIC NORTH SYLAMORE CREEK

enters the stream. Stay with the blue blazes as other paths spur off. You can also see the last vestiges of fields along the flat. Trees are invading the former farmland. Pale gravel bars shimmer off to your right as the stream noisily follows gravity's orders. Watch for beard cane growing in the moister areas. Occasional glades open in the woods. Pass a steep bluff just before crossing a creek flowing from Petrie Cave Hollow at 1.6 miles. You'll reach the most spectacular bluff of the hike after the creek. This rock wall with a high overhanging shelter features two wet-weather waterfalls dropping into a circular cathedral, then flowing across the trail.

When the bluffs rise, the trail becomes pinched in and thus is forced to the river's edge. Sandbars are usually present across the stream from the bluffs. The trail turns away from North Sylamore Creek as it cuts up a shallow hollow. The sound of rushing water is temporarily lost. Soon enough, the trail climbs to saddle alongside some bluffs, not quite as magnificent as those that are riverside. Make a rib ridge, then begin a downgrade back toward the North Sylamore Creek to reach a feeder branch as it flows clear over slabs of rock. You are now in Cornfield Hollow. This crossing can be made dry footed, save for heavy flows.

Below this, you'll hear a waterfall descending just below the stream crossing. Here it makes a 10-foot drop over a ledge into a catch pool. Interestingly, the stream will often be dry below the waterfall. It seeps back into the streambed, filtering into the honeycombed underground, intermingling with the cave system of the area. Though Blanchard Springs Cave is the most renowned, over 200 caves pock the greater Sylamore area.

The trail continues beyond the falls and reaches another high point. A spur trail leads right to an overlook. If you want to reach the base of the falls, continue beyond the stream crossing for just a short distance—40 or 50 yards— and the bluff line begins to become crumbly. Work your way down to the streambed and walk up to the falls.

Beyond the falls, a spur trail leads right to the creek overlook. If you're close to the edge, remember that you're atop a sheer bluff—be careful! This waterfall and overlook make a good turnaround point. However, the North Sylamore Trail continues beyond the bluff line and crosses a stream flowing from Wolf Pen Hollow, then enters a cedar rock glade en route to Slick Rock Hollow, where more waterfalls await. You can't go wrong on any section of this Ozark treasure.

Consider the other recreational opportunities at Blanchard Springs before coming here. The recreation area has an excellent campground, springs, and good swimming and fishing, in addition to Blanchard Springs Cave, which you can tour. This is but one section of the North Sylamore Trail, which extends 23 miles one-way, passing the most scenic sights along the stream.

BLUFFS RISE FROM SCENIC NORTH SYLAMORE CREEK

II.

MISSOURI OZARK HIKES

26

Ozark Chinquapin Trail

TOTAL DISTANCE: 3.1-mile balloon loop	
HIKING TIME: 1.75 hours	
VERTICAL RISE: 270 feet	
RATING: Easy	
MAPS: USGS 7.5' Jane, McNatt; Big Sugar Creek State Park	
TRAILHEAD GPS COORDINATES: N36° 37.292', W94° 17.647'	
CONTACT INFORMATION: Big Sugar Creek State Park, 7505 Big Sugar Creek Road, Pineville, MO 644856, (417) 847-2539, www.mostateparks.com	

This hike is very long on solitude and natural history. Seldom-visited Big Sugar Creek State Park is the setting for this loop that traverses botanically important hills and hollows on a tributary of Big Sugar Creek. After finding the quiet trailhead, you will head up a rocky hollow, repeatedly crossing a feeder stream that is usually dry and continuing up the hollow as it closes in. You will reach a shortcut path that travels the ridgetops, an area favorable for the Ozark chinquapin tree. Additional important plant and animal life are reasons this stretch of land is designated a Missouri State Natural Area.

HOW TO GET THERE

From exit 5 on I-49 in southwest Missouri, take County Road H east a short distance to US 71 Business. Turn left on US 71 Business to quickly cross the Elk River on a bridge, then turn right onto Jesse James Road. Follow it for 0.3 mile, then turn right on 8th Street in the town of Pineville. Follow 8th Street for 0.3 mile, then curve left onto Big Sugar Creek Road. Stay on Big Sugar Creek Road for 6.3 miles to the signed trailhead on your left.

THE HIKE

Sometimes we don't miss things until they are gone—or don't grow to proportions they once did, as is the case with the Ozark chinquapin tree, a former stalwart of Ozark forests. The range of the Ozark chinquapin extends from Missouri into eastern Oklahoma and northern Arkansas, with a few outliers in Louisiana, Mississippi and Alabama. Ozark chinquapins were once prized for their bountiful nut crops. Animals of all kinds looked forward to the spiny,

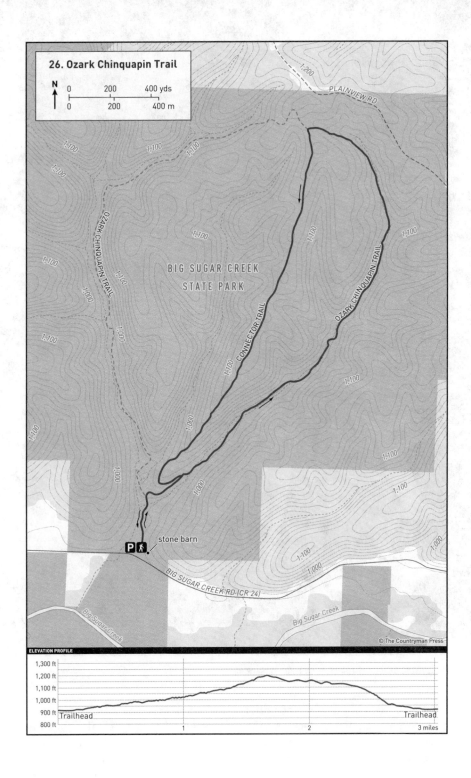

26. Ozark Chinquapin Trail

N
| 0 | 200 | 400 yds |
| 0 | 200 | 400 m |

PLAINVIEW RD

OZARK CHINQUAPIN TRAIL

BIG SUGAR CREEK
STATE PARK

CONNECTOR TRAIL

OZARK CHINQUAPIN TRAIL

1,200
1,100
1,000

stone barn

P

BIG SUGAR CREEK RD (CR 24)

Big Sugar Creek

Big Sugar Creek

© The Countryman Press

ELEVATION PROFILE

1,300 ft
1,200 ft
1,100 ft
1,000 ft
900 ft
800 ft

Trailhead

Trailhead

1   2   3 miles

CONEFLOWERS GRACE THE TRAILSIDE ON A HOT SUMMER DAY

rich nuts of the chinquapin—including bears, turkeys, squirrels, deer, and the two-legged variety as well. Yep, Ozark residents used chinquapin nuts to feed themselves, to sell to others, and to feed their livestock. The rot-resistant wood was valued too, especially for fence posts. However, the chestnut blight reached the Ozarks in the 1950s, decimating the Ozark chinquapin. To this day, shoots rise from stumps in multiple small trunks, but the trees typically live only 4-6 years before getting the blight. Sometimes they produce the nuts before dying, but most of the time they do not. Thus, the Ozark chinquapin is found most often as a shrub. Look for shoots growing from a stump. The leaves are about 5 inches long, serrated, dark green on top, and whitish on their underside.

This hike uses the Ozark Chinquapin Trail, which traverses an important habitat for the Ozark chinquapin. This habitat is the primary reason the 1,600-acre Elk River Breaks Natural Area was established. It encompasses much of the greater Big Sugar Creek State Park. And that is good, because the range of the chinquapin has been greatly reduced. Designated in 2000, the state natural area also harbors the rare and lesser-known Ozark corn salad, a plant typically found on limestone outcrops along streams and in limestone glades.

On this hike, you can watch for the two lesser-seen flora, in the harbor of oaks, pines, and blueberries found here. The Missouri Department of Natural Resources (DNR) is extensively using fire to manage the ridges, as you will see along the way. The hike starts at the grassy trailhead. Look for the old stone structure near the parking area and restrooms. Head north past the trail sign. At 0.1 mile, the Ozark Chinquapin Trail splits; head right. Turn into a hollow that is soon lined with low rock bluffs. It isn't long before you make the first of many crossings of a normally dry creekbed, a tributary of Big Sugar Creek—though parts of the stream may be flowing where water is pushed to the surface.

At 0.2 mile, the Connector Trail enters on your left as a doubletrack path. For now, we stay with the Ozark Chinquapin Trail, crossing the stream and passing through a clearing. The variety of forest and fields adds biodiversity to this already important floral refuge. Small feeder streams enter the main hollow from left and right. Walnut trees, cedars, and hickories rise above the pathway, which rarely strays from the streambed of the main hollow. Wild roses and purple coneflowers, among other colorful plants, brighten the forest.

In places, the streambed itself has been used as a firebreak during managed conflagrations. The creekbed can be rocky to the extreme during some crossings. However, the creek gets smaller and smaller as you continue up the main hollow. At 1.6 miles, leave the hollow and reach a trail intersection. The suggested loop heads left on the Connector Trail. This loop is a little over 0.5 mile shorter than following the whole Ozark Chinquapin Trail, but it also offers a chance for some hilltop hiking, where you can admire the ranks of oaks and other hardwoods—including the Ozark chinquapin—in all their glory.

You are heading south. Winter views open across the hollows that fall away from the unnamed ridge. Sassafras forms a thick understory. The ridgeline descends, then makes a sharp curve to the left, meeting the Ozark Chinquapin Trail at 2.8 miles. From here, it is a 0.3-mile backtrack to the trailhead.

While here, consider combining your hike with a paddle on Big Sugar Creek. An outfitter is located in nearby Pineville. During spring and summer, over 24 miles of the waterway can be floated past tawny gravel bars in the shadow of rising bluffs and tall woods.

Roaring River State Park Double Loop

TOTAL DISTANCE: 1.6-mile loop and 3.8-mile loop

HIKING TIME: 3.75 hours

VERTICAL RISE: 440 feet

RATING: Moderate

MAPS: USGS 7.5' Eagle Rock; Roaring River Trails

TRAILHEAD GPS COORDINATES: N36° 35.302', W93° 50.152'

CONTACT INFORMATION: Roaring River State Park, 12716 Farm Road 2239, Cassville, MO 65625, (417) 847-2539, www.mostateparks.com

This trek is actually two hikes at one state park, accessed from the same trailhead. First you'll take the Devils Kitchen Trail to visit both a cave and a cave spring. Climb over a ridge to reach the Devils Kitchen, a rugged rock formation with a cave spring of its own. This loop includes interpretive stops, which allow for some outdoor education. The second loop travels along the spring-fed Roaring River—with a stop at the interpretive center for more outdoor learning—before entering the Roaring River Hills Wild Area, where you gain a ridgeline and fire tower. From here, head down to the Deer Leap, where views of Roaring River Spring and the adjacent fish hatchery are a final reward on a great second loop. Both trails were constructed by the Civilian Conservation Corps (CCC) in the 1930s.

HOW TO GET THERE

From the intersection of MO 248 and MO 112 in Cassville, take MO 112 south for 7 miles to the state park. Once you're at the bottom of the hill, stay left on Hatchery Road toward the spring, amphitheater, and lodge. Park at the lodge. To access the first loop, Devils Kitchen, walk across the bridge over Roaring River. The Devils Kitchen Trail starts at the kiosk at the edge of the woods.

THE HIKE

This is an interpretive trail, so make sure to stop by the park office to get the interpretive brochure. It will enhance your hike. You can see the trailhead across the Roaring River from the lodge. Once you're on the trail, immediately cross a streambed on a small bridge, then begin slicing up a hollow.

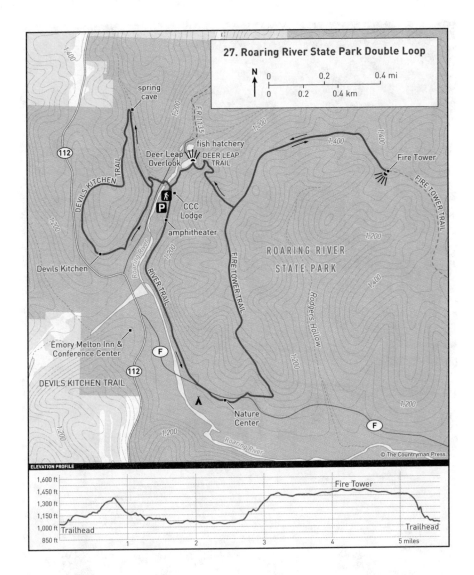

spring
cave

FR 1135

fish hatchery

Deer Leap
Overlook

DEER LEAP
TRAIL

112

DEVILS KITCHEN TRAIL

CCC
Lodge

amphitheater

Fire Tower

FIRE TOWER TRAIL

ROARING RIVER
STATE PARK

Roaring River

RIVER TRAIL

FIRE TOWER TRAIL

Rodgers Hollow

Devils Kitchen

Emory Melton Inn &
Conference Center

112

DEVILS KITCHEN TRAIL

F

F

Nature
Center

Roaring River

© The Countryman Press

ELEVATION PROFILE

	Fire Tower

1,600 ft
1,450 ft
1,300 ft
1,150 ft
1,000 ft Trailhead   Trailhead
850 ft   1   2   3   4   5 miles

Climb well above the stream, then stay right at the trail junction, continuing your ascent; the other route will be your return path. The hillsides here will be covered with wildflowers in spring. Shortly reach interpretive stop 1, where dolomite and limestone meet. A spur trail leads to stop 2, Shelter Cave, a dry overhang used by many a passerby over the ages to stave off precipitation. Drop down to the branch at its confluence with a trib-

utary coming in from your left. Across the creek is a spring cave from which water emerges. The outflow is slowly but surely enlarging the cave's opening.

The trail makes a big curve uphill to the left; pass marker 3 just beyond. The trail curves back into the Roaring River Valley, making a fair climb while you're serenaded by the sounds of the spring run over the rapids. By the way, those sonorant rapids were created by

COLUMBINE GROWS ALONG THE BLUFFS OF THE ROARING RIVER

the Missouri DNR to enhance the put-and-take trout fishing. Often anglers are shoulder-to-shoulder along the stream, casting for trout. Be apprised of the various creel limits and regulations here if you choose to fish. Turn away from the spring run and level out on the ridgeline, passing interpretive stop 5, now atop the Springfield Plateau.

Begin descending a wide track that was once a roadbed, now reverted to trail. Enter a hollow, passing a second trailside spring cave before reaching the Devils Kitchen. The cave spring is part of the beginning of an impressive cliff line.

The Devils Kitchen used to be more of a classic overhang with an entry into the shelter, but some of the boulders at the front fell in 1985, partially closing what was once a hideout for Civil War guerrillas. The big boulders that split off resemble children's play blocks. The trail now begins scurrying along the cliff line back in the Roaring River Valley. Switchback downhill to emerge near a cabin. Turn left here and take the footpath back to the trailhead rather than the road. Watch along this hillside for privet, a planted flowering ground cover common at old homesites, before returning to the trailhead.

To continue your hike—the second loop—cross the Roaring River and return toward the lodge. As you face the lodge, the River Trail leaves to your right, shortly passing the park amphitheater, cruising beside a low bluff. The River Trail then works high on the bluff, directly above anglers fishing on the Roaring River below. Pass a little intermittent waterfall before reaching an overhanging bluff line. Watch for columbine growing along the cliff line in spring. The River Trail ends and you pass a few cabins, then the campground on your right, crossing Highway F. Ahead is the Ozark Chinquapin Nature Center. Stop in the center to enjoy its exhibits.

The Fire Tower Trail starts behind the nature center to its right as you face it. Upon returning to Highway F, turn right, and then cross it left. Reenter woods as the path curves right and begins climbing along the ridgeline, entering the Roaring River Hills Wild Area. Crumbly rocks form your trailbed as you scale the mountainside. Soon you'll turn left near an old building. The climb eases upon leveling out below a cliff line forested with eastern red cedars and hardwoods. Make a break in the cliff line at 2.9 miles (of the total hike). The forest floor has become quite rocky underneath the bed of leaves now. Scattered views open to your left through the trees.

The hike moderates again atop the ridge, where oaks rise majestically and the birds cheer you on while you walk. Intersect the Deer Leap Trail at 3.5 miles. This will be your return route; for now, continue forward on the ridgeline as the Fire Tower Trail curves east to a historic CCC fire tower. The walking is easy and glorious while circling Rodgers Hollow. Reach the tower at 4.2 miles. The trees of the forest have now outgrown the low metal structure; the views aren't what they used to be when the CCC boys built it in the 1930s. Climb it anyway for the added exercise value, gaining a view of the woods from tree level rather than the base of the forest, which hiking trails offer.

Return to the junction with the Deer Leap Trail, immediately nose-diving into the Roaring River Valley. You can see an old eroded path leading left—do not follow this path, which has been permanently closed. The Deer Leap Trail has been rerouted and makes more gentle switchbacks. Stone steps lead down around a bluff line and reach a junction. You can take the trail down to your right to visit the spring and hatchery. The Deer Leap Trail continues forward along the bluff line, where you pass another cave spring. A boardwalk leads around the steepest parts.

You'll reach an interesting overlook of the Roaring River Spring and fish hatchery. This is the Deer Leap. Look for gigantic trout as well as the fish of

VIEW OF ROARING RIVER SPRING AND TROUT HATCHERY FROM THE DEER LEAP

various other trout ponds. The overlook is atop a sheer bluff that makes its way straight down to the spring and provides quite a view. Leave the view, descending via stone steps and passing some cabins on your left. Emerge near the spring. More anglers are vying for the stocked trout put into the Roaring River from the hatchery. Follow the paved path downstream to complete your loop.

28

Piney Creek Wilderness Loop

TOTAL DISTANCE: 6.2-mile loop

HIKING TIME: 4 hours

VERTICAL RISE: 480 feet

RATING: Moderate

MAPS: USGS 7.5' Cape Fair, Piney Creek Wilderness, Ava; Mark Twain National Forest—Cassville and Willow Springs Ranger Districts

TRAILHEAD GPS COORDINATES: N36° 42.185', W93° 36.597'

CONTACT INFORMATION: Mark Twain National Forest, P.O. Box 188, 1103 South Jefferson, Ava, MO 65608, (417) 683-4428, www.fs.usda.gov/mtnf

This hike travels through the Piney Creek Wilderness of the Mark Twain National Forest. It was the first place I ever backpacked in Missouri. I can still remember my delight upon seeing clear and alluring Piney Creek. This loop, different from my original adventure, offers a high-to-low back-to-high hike from the area's crest, the now-closed Pineview Fire Tower. Head down through woods and glades to reach crystalline Piney Creek, which flows east into Table Rock Lake, passing through fields reverting to forest. Several fords are necessary to reach the impoundment, but it makes for a good destination. The return trip ascends a tributary of Piney Creek before making the fire tower. Note: None of the trails here are blazed. The trails are mostly maintained by volunteers and wilderness users.

HOW TO GET THERE

From Cassville, take MO 76 east for 19 miles and turn right onto Lake Road 76-6/Forest Road 2150/Piney Tower Road. Continue for 0.7 mile, turn right onto FR 1139, and follow this forest road for 0.1 mile to the fire tower.

THE HIKE

Leave the parking area and take the trail heading westerly away from the tower, traveling downhill. Begin cruising along a ridgeline that emanates from the tower's high point. Dive deeper into the wilderness on an ever-narrowing ridgeline shaded by pines, oaks, hickories, and cedars. The track is alternately gravel and leaf litter. Valleys drop off on both sides of you.

The descent sharpens and boulders emerge, opening the canopy overhead.

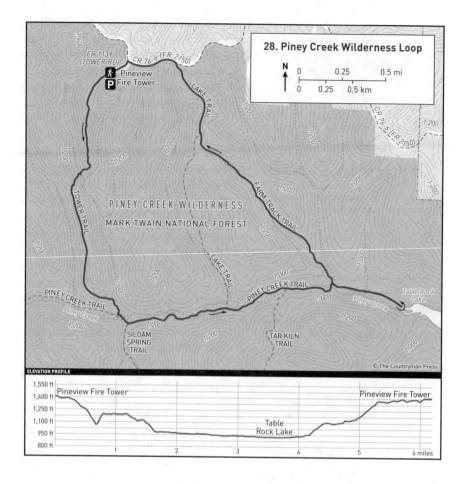

ELEVATION PROFILE

Here you can gain wilderness vistas to the south in an open glade area bordered in cedars. A beautiful rocky glade area continues. Continue descending among open limestone outcrops and grassy glades to reach a clear stream at 0.6 mile. Cross the stream and begin a short but steep climb until you level off in more glades on the far side. Continue south, still paralleling the streambed you just crossed. Ignore a trail leading right, away from the open gravel glade where it levels off. The cedar-lined track is now mostly rock under your feet. In places the limestone is continuous; in others it's more crumbly—dinner-plate-sized rocks. In still others, it's just gravel. The more rock

you see, the higher the likelihood that the forest canopy overhead will be open.

The hiking is easy as the track descends toward Piney Creek near a low limestone bluff. Views open of the upper Piney Creek drainage, to your right. The trail then deteriorates to a rocky, crumbly mess; loose gravel and boulders make the footing challenging. Pass a backcountry campsite on your left just before leveling out in the lower Piney Creek Valley. Moisture-loving trees such as sycamore disclose the valley's lushness. You may get your feet wet crossing Piney Creek in spring and winter. Piney Creek is as clear as a stream can be, flowing over a white bed.

LOOKING INTO PINEY CREEK VALLEY

SHOOTING STARS ADD A DELICATE TOUCH TO THE WILDERNESS SCENERY

At a trail junction turn left and keep downstream—the other path heads up Piney Creek. You can look over the gorgeous creek as it gathers and pools and noisily babbles over rocky riffles. Just ahead, cross the stream emerging from Siloam Spring Hollow, the very spot where I first laid eyes on this lovely locale. Reach another junction. One trail heads up the hollow; you continue downstream as the Piney Creek Valley widens. Cedars and hardwoods grow in scattered pockets alongside clearings. The clearings may become quite brushy later in summer. While traveling downstream, you'll cross occasional overflow channels. The bottom can be lush with wildflowers, including larkspur, in spring. You will also cross gravelly washes from tributary drainages that flow into Piney Creek only during heavy rains. Make the second crossing over to the left bank of Piney Creek. Just below here, you'll see a deep pool luring in swimmers on a hot day.

The third crossing comes in short order. You are now on the right-hand bank, heading downstream. Piney Creek is widening, and the white gravel bars on its edges shine brightly through the woods. Make a trail junction shortly after the third crossing. A trail leads left across the creek, shortcutting this loop. Continue down the valley toward Table Rock Lake. Your fourth crossing comes soon after the trail junction. The valley widens significantly now. Crossing number five leads over to the right-hand bank and a trail junction. The other path leads toward the Siloam Springs trailhead. Continue down in the ever-widening valley. Invasive thorny trees are spreading in the former clearings.

The sixth crossing takes you to the left bank. The path is confusing at first, as you are going upstream along a feeder branch of Piney Creek to reach a trail junction. The trail going up the tributary is your return ticket, but for now, cross the tributary and proceed downstream on Piney Creek. This lowermost section can be muddy following rains. Some of the clearings get quite large down here and are interspersed with more thorny trees. At 3.5 miles, reach the shores of Table Rock Lake. The Piney Creek embayment extends beyond view. This location isn't particularly good for relaxation, as shade is limited. But it does offer a good view and a destination.

Backtrack to the last crossing—not of Piney Creek, but rather of the feeder branch—then turn right, heading north. (The GPS coordinates of this trail junction are N36° 41' 10.07", W93° 35' 11.10".) Join an old woods track heading northwest. Cross a small branch to ascend over a wide tread of crumbly rock. It's hard to imagine taking a wagon over this unbelievably stony bed, much less a car. The track passes by grass and rock glades on its ascent to a small vale. Step over the now tiny streamlet, still in the steep valley. The watercourse may or may not be flowing.

The stream is unlikely to be running when you cross the second, third, and fourth times in rapid succession. The path continues up the shallow valley, making one final jump to the ridgeline. Reach a junction at 5.2 miles and turn right, northbound. Look for the larger old oaks with their widespread arms amid the younger yet taller pines. Emerge onto the pavement of CR 76-6 at 5.6 miles. Turn left here. Walk the pavement, and then turn left onto the forest road—the same road that brought you to the Pineview Fire Tower—to complete your loop.

29

Hercules Glades Wilderness Loop

TOTAL DISTANCE: 6.6-mile loop

HIKING TIME: 4 hours

VERTICAL RISE: 430 feet

RATING: Moderate to difficult

MAPS: USGS 7.5' Hilda, Hercules Glades Wilderness, Ava; Mark Twain National Forest—Cassville and Willow Springs Ranger Districts

TRAILHEAD GPS COORDINATES: N36° 41.099', W92° 57.535'

CONTACT INFORMATION: Mark Twain National Forest, P.O. Box 188, 1103 South Jefferson, Ava, MO 65608, (417) 683-4428, www.fs.usda.gov/mtnf

This is one of the best wilderness hikes in Missouri. Hercules Glades is renowned for its extensive grassy glades, open areas that give the wilderness a western feel. This loop leaves the Coy Bald trailhead and traverses old Cross Timbers Road to reach a nice warm-up vista before curving past an old farm pond, then opening onto a huge grassy glade where the views will exceed even your highest expectations. Beyond, the loop dips to reach Long Creek and a waterfall. Long Creek has widely variable flows, and the falls follow suit. Cross Long Creek and walk through a mix of glades and woods before dropping into the Devils Den, a rocky hollow, crossing Long Creek one last time under high bluffs before climbing back to the trailhead. This 12,315-acre wilderness has over 30 miles of trails and is suitable for backpacking as well as day hiking. Note that you'll be sharing the trail system with equestrians.

HOW TO GET THERE

From Forsyth, take US 160 east for 2.3 miles past the bridge over Beaver Creek (for a total of 7.5 miles) to Cross Timbers Road. Turn left and continue for 1.7 miles, crossing a low-water bridge over Cane Creek; veer right, then left, now following Forest Road 566 (FR 566). Pass over a cattle guard and continue through private property on the forest road right-of-way for 1.4 miles to dead-end at the wilderness boundary. The parking area has picnic tables and fire rings, and can make for a late-arrival campsite.

THE HIKE

Leave the parking area and take the trail leaving east away from the trailhead.

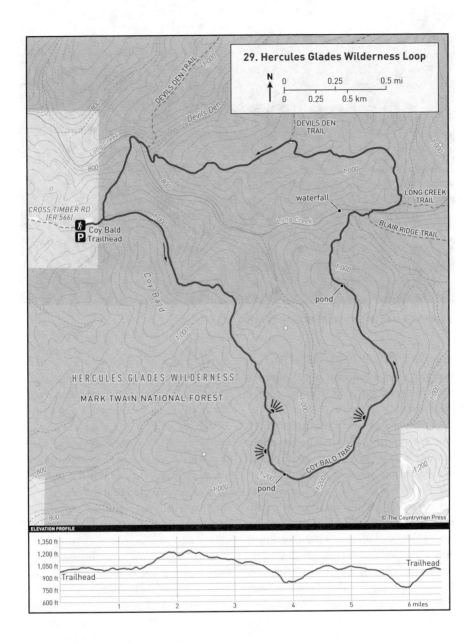

29. Hercules Glades Wilderness Loop

DEVILS DEN TRAIL

Long Creek

Devils Den

DEVILS DEN TRAIL

800

1,000

CROSS TIMBER RD
[FR 566]

Coy Bald
Trailhead

800

1,000

waterfall

Long Creek

LONG CREEK TRAIL

BLAIR RIDGE TRAIL

Coy Bald

1,000

pond

1,000

HERCULES GLADES WILDERNESS

MARK TWAIN NATIONAL FOREST

1,000

1,000

800

1,000

COY BALD TRAIL

1,200

1,200

1,200

pond

800

© The Countryman Press

ELEVATION PROFILE

1,350 ft
1,200 ft
1,050 ft
900 ft
750 ft
600 ft

Trailhead

Trailhead

1   2   3   4   5   6 miles

You are immediately entering cedars mixed with grassy glades. Shortly, you'll pass the official wilderness boundary at a fence line to reach a trail junction. Here you can go right to Coy Bald or forward to Long Creek. Stay right here toward Coy Bald, following the old Cross Timbers Road, which has reverted to trail inside the wilderness. Long Creek will be your return route. The path continues mostly level over a rock-and-dirt path, winding through little glades that seem to occur without rhyme or reason; in fact they are related to the soil and rock composition and exposure. Cedars thrive in these thin soils and thus are

LOOKING OVER THE EXPANSE OF HERCULES GLADES AND BEYOND

abundant. A wooded hillside rises to the right as you continue over long rock slabs. Where the glades are long or wide, the surrounding landscape becomes visible, including the ridgeline on which you are circling. The path meanders through a long open glade, with views of the surrounding wilderness.

The trail continues drifting in and out of small glades mixed with full-blown woods. Climb a hill to reach an open glade and vista at 1.7 miles. Enjoy views to the northeast, across Long Creek, into the wilderness, and beyond. The trail stays right, away from the open glade. Now gain more views to the west. The forest evolves from rock and cedar to include more hardwoods. The usual Ozark hardwood suspects are present—oak, hickory, dogwood. Cedars still have a fair representation. Even within this hardwood realm, though, small cedar glades can be found.

At 2.1 miles, pass an old farm pond on trail left. Look around for rolled-up barbed-wire fence as well, revealing a farming past in what's now wilderness. Make your way up the hill beyond the pond. The pathway is now making its big curve around a tributary of Long Creek. Watch for wolf trees in the forest. These are larger trees with widespread arms that were here before the ridgeline was completely wooded, as it is today. Open onto extensive glades at 2.6 miles. Look for the wildflower Indian paintbrush growing in the meadow. The westward views as well as some to the north extend beyond what you might expect, even beyond what you might hope for, and would surprise many a visitor to the Missouri Ozarks. The vistas keep on coming in the open glades, into the heart of the wilderness and also at other glades from a distance. Continue cruising along the rim of this ridge in mostly woods, passing another farm pond on your left at 3.4 miles.

Begin a descent just beyond the farm pond, drifting through scattered glades. Continue down, making the wide bed of Long Creek at 3.9 miles. A spur trail leads left to a campsite and falls that will only be running at higher flows. At this point the creek cuts through a rock outcrop, creating a beautiful scene. Just downstream is a large pool suitable for swimming. When the water level is low, you can rock-hop and explore the area. The trail continues upstream a short distance to make a junction and another campsite; a spur trail leads right to Blair Ridge Road. This hike turns left and crosses Long Creek, and then continues upstream to shortly reach another junction. A lesser-used trail continues up the creek, whereas this loop veers left, climbs, and turns back north, then west. The climbing is easy as you join a rock-lined woods track. Watch for rock piles in the woods here, an indicator that this thin soil may have been tilled at one time. The climb ceases and the trail just undulates through mostly canopied woods, passing an occasional streambed, to make a junction at 5.0 miles. There is a dried-up farm pond to your left. A trail leads right toward Upper Pilot Knob, but this loop continues forward toward the Devils Den. The path is flanked by cedars as if they were a crowd of spectators watching you hike.

The stony track sharpens as it aims for the Devils Den, finally making a loping switchback to reach it at 5.9 miles, just above the confluence with Long Creek, passing a nice flat and campsite, too. The Devils Den is a steep, rocky hollow. Curve back to cross Long Creek just upstream of a gorgeous bluff line above the stream. Reach another campsite and leave left away from Long Creek. Break one last sweat on the climb before reaching a trail junction to complete your loop. It's just a short distance back to the parking area.

LONG CREEK FLOWS CLEAR BESIDE A BLUFF IN THE HERCULES GLADES WILDERNESS

30

Ha Ha Tonka State Park Loop

TOTAL DISTANCE: 3.9-mile loop	

HIKING TIME: 2 hours

VERTICAL RISE: 225 feet

RATING: Moderate

MAPS: USGS 7.5' Ha Ha Tonka; Ha Ha Tonka State Park Trails

TRAILHEAD GPS COORDINATES: N37° 58.534', W92° 46.028'

CONTACT INFORMATION: Ha Ha Tonka State Park, 1491 State Road D, Camdenton, MO 65020, (573) 346-2986, www.mostate parks.com

The following suggested loop allows you to see many of the wonderful and varied features of Ha Ha Tonka State Park, including the Castle Ruins, Natural Bridge, Devils Kitchen and Promenade, Lake of the Ozarks, Trout Glen Pool, Ha Ha Tonka Spring, Whispering Dell, Colosseum, and more. You may get turned around at the many trail junctions, but all the trails are interconnected, so your hike may turn into an unexpected adventure. In any case, you simply can't pass this destination by, as it offers so many features in one short hike.

HOW TO GET THERE

From Exit 129 off I-44, head north on MO 5 for 27 miles to Camdenton and US 54. Take US 54 west for 2.5 miles, then turn left onto Highway D. After 1.5 miles on Highway D, the park visitor's center is on your right. Continue past the visitor's center for 0.4 mile and turn right toward the Castle Ruins. Keep forward and uphill to reach the Dell Rim trailhead.

THE HIKE

Your first order of business is to check out the Castle Ruins. Take the concrete path uphill, passing a couple of overlooks. Ahead stand the concrete foundation and walls of the structure, which was burned in a fire. Circle the house, admiring its grace. You can also see the steep drop-off from here and the grassy glades just below; Lake of the Ozarks lies beyond.

Backtrack to the trailhead and join the Dell Rim Trail, passing the castle water tower to your left. A wooden walkway leads past the spur trail to the tower. The Whispering Dell Sinkhole is below. Continue along the boardwalk. To your right is the sinkhole. Leave the board-

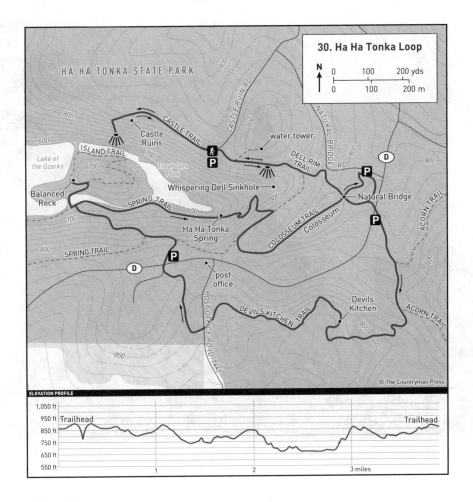

ELEVATION PROFILE

walk and turn left toward the Natural Bridge, passing by picnic tables, still on a gravel path. Before you know it, you are crossing over the Natural Bridge. Keep forward for now—you'll be circling under this feature later. Cross Highway D, reaching the Ha Ha Tonka Oak Woodland Natural Area trailhead. This area is fire-maintained to keep its open look, which once occurred naturally in the Show Me State. Leave the pavement and enter the savanna area. Keep climbing along the Savanna Trail as the Acorn Trail leaves left. Join the Devils Kitchen Trail, passing a slope of open grassy savanna to dip into a valley. Just as you

dip, a spur trail leaves left to a rock overhang and wet-weather waterfall.

You won't miss the crevice on your right, a narrow cut in the rock. You might say this is the chimney hole to the Devils Kitchen, which is below. Curve around the rock line, descending into the Devils Kitchen. Notice, while you curve, how the ferns and mosses grow on this side of the rock wall. Enter the overhang of the Devils Kitchen, which is a partially collapsed rockhouse, with ample dry room for several people. Walk to the back of the rockhouse and peer up the crevice that you were just looking down. Curve along a very rugged bluff

THE CASTLE RUINS AGAINST AN OZARK SKY

line, with many caves and overhangs. At one point the rock line becomes very narrow, forcing you to jump out onto a fallen rock, then return to the main cliff line. The curved overhang ahead is the Devils Promenade, a rock overhang with an elevated floor.

Reach and cross gravel road D-144. Climb away from the gravel road and wind for County Road 2 (CR 2). A trail comes in just before the paved road. There's a picnic shelter to your left. Cross paved Highway D. To your right is the post office of the old community of Gunter's Spring. The spring for which it was named is now known as Ha Ha

Tonka Spring. Join the Spring Trail. Stay left here, passing bare rock pillars to reach an intersection. Continue forward downhill as a blue-blazed trail turns left. The rock-and-gravel track has large wooden water bars to check erosion. When you reach stillwater, turn left and see the remains of an old mill bridge, milldam with its millstone, and Lake of the Ozarks. There is a shelter here also. A paved trail continues beyond the shelter.

You may want to see Balanced Rock, which is just a short distance away. Cross the old bridge over the former mill run. Head up along a cliff line until the trail splits. Stay left; you'll make Balanced Rock in short order. It is about 8 feet high. If you want to extend your hike, go ahead and make the circle on the Island Trail, which will add about 0.6 mile.

Backtrack to the shelter and now enjoy a paved path leading away from Lake of the Ozarks. Come alongside Trout Glen Pool, then Ha Ha Tonka Spring, framed in white cliffs. Join a boardwalk circling the spring. Pass by the spring outflow, then climb on wooden stairs along the sheer bluff line above Ha Ha Tonka Spring. A few hundred steps later, you'll pass the Whispering Dell Sinkhole. Climb more steps to reach a junction. It's left to the Castle—but this hike isn't over. Stay right, then veer left onto the Colosseum Trail. If you hit the road, you have gone the wrong way.

The correct trail climbs just a bit and then descends to enter the Colosseum, which is a natural rock cathedral. At the far end you'll reach the Natural Bridge again. Pass under the bridge, enjoying a different perspective of this geological wonder, and keep forward, climbing steps. Leave the Colosseum Trail and reach a parking area. Stay right here, circling back to the top of the Natural Bridge. You are now backtracking for the

ANOTHER VIEW OF THE CASTLE RUINS

stone water tower. Enjoy some last great Ozark views before regaining the Dell Rim trailhead.

31

Paddy Creek Wilderness Loop

TOTAL DISTANCE: 10.3-mile loop

HIKING TIME: 5 hours, 30 minutes

VERTICAL RISE: 330 feet

RATING: Moderate to difficult

MAPS: USGS 7.5' Slabtown Spring; Mark Twain National Forest—Houston, Rolla, and Cedar Creek Districts, Paddy Creek Wilderness

TRAILHEAD GPS COORDINATES: N37° 33.499', W92° 2.845'

CONTACT INFORMATION: Mark Twain National Forest, 108 S. Sam Houston Boulevard, Houston, MO 65483, (417) 967-4194, www.fs.usda.gov/mtnf

Paddy Creek Wilderness covers more than 7,000 acres of wildland and formerly homesteaded land returned to a wild state. This loop, using the Big Piney Trail, traverses the northeastern segment of the wilderness, which is part of the Mark Twain National Forest. It's shared by hikers and equestrians. Leave Paddy Creek Recreation Area, a fine destination unto itself, to cross Big Paddy Creek. The trail switchbacks up a ridgeline southwest before meeting the Old Military Road Trail near a homesite that is disappearing into the wilderness. Trace the Military Road Trail down to crystal-clear Little Paddy Creek prior to rising into the high country again, traveling piney hills and hardwood hollows to emerge onto a bluff line and a grand vista from a rock outcrop of Big Paddy Creek. From the vista, the trail drops to this stream's bottomlands to complete the loop.

This is a good backpacking hike, as Paddy Creek and Little Paddy Creek flow year-round. The entire Big Piney Trail is 17 miles long; combined with 2.1 miles of the Old Military Road Trail, this makes for over 19 miles of wilderness paths. Alternatively, Paddy Creek Recreation Area offers a nice campground located in the bottoms of Paddy Creek—a good base camp as you explore the wilderness, fish, and float the Big Piney River.

HOW TO GET THERE

From the junction of MO 32 and MO 137 in Licking, take MO 32 west for 4.0 miles to County Road N (CR N). Turn right and follow CR N for 2.2 miles to County Road AF (CR AF). Turn left; take CR AF over the Big Piney River as the road turns to gravel, continuing for a total of 9 miles from CR N. Turn left onto

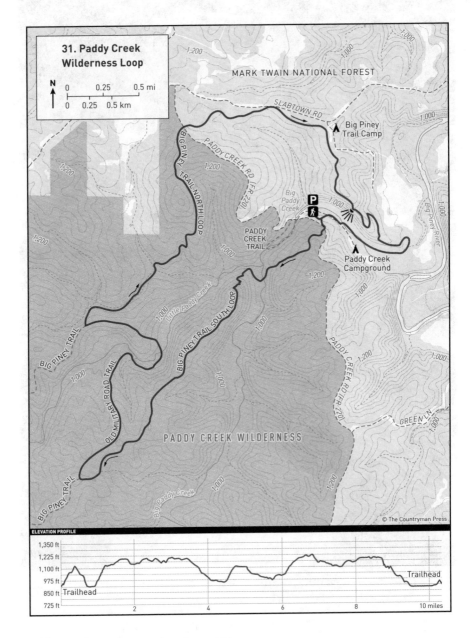

31. Paddy Creek Wilderness Loop

MARK TWAIN NATIONAL FOREST

SLABTOWN RD

Big Piney Trail Camp

BIG PINEY TRAIL NORTH LOOP

PADDY CREEK RD (FR 220)

Big Paddy Creek

PADDY CREEK TRAIL

Paddy Creek Campground

Little Paddy Creek

BIG PINEY TRAIL SOUTH LOOP

BIG PINEY TRAIL

OLD MILITARY ROAD TRAIL

BIG PINEY TRAIL

PADDY CREEK WILDERNESS

Big Paddy Creek

PADDY CREEK RD (FR 220)

GREEN LN

Big Piney River

© The Countryman Press

ELEVATION PROFILE

1,350 ft
1,225 ft
1,100 ft
975 ft
850 ft — Trailhead
725 ft

Trailhead

2   4   6   8   10 miles

Paddy Creek Road, Forest Road 220 (FR 220), and follow it for 1.8 miles, crossing the low-water bridge over Paddy Creek, and then turn left into the Paddy Creek Recreation Area. The Piney Creek Trail starts on your right just beyond a set of picnic tables.

THE HIKE

The trail system in the Paddy Creek Wilderness comprises a large loop, the Big Piney Trail, with a shortcut in the middle. The naming is confusing, however, because the Forest Service has named

SYCAMORE LEAVES LIE STILL IN THE WATERS OF LITTLE PADDY CREEK

the south half of the loop the South Loop and the north half of the loop the North Loop, when it is essentially one loop. This hike traverses the eastern part of the greater loop, using the Old Military Road Trail to bisect it.

Leave the trailhead, immediately ascending into woods to reach a trail junction. Turn right here to take the South Loop. The other way will be your return route. The narrow gravel track leads uphill to cross gravel FR 220. Continue uphill, entering the wilderness boundary on a trail that switchbacks uphill to top out in pines.

Assume a downgrade in hickory-oak forest, growing amid scattered rock outcrops. Level out in the wide and brushy bottomland of Big Paddy Creek, with walnut trees aplenty. Paddy Creek was named for an early settler and timber man, Sylvester Paddy, who logged the area, sending the timber to St. Louis by water; it was used in construction. Cross Paddy Creek at 0.8 mile. It will have pools even in the driest of times, though the crossing is on gravel bars between pools. This translucent, scenic stream winds beside tan rocks overhung with trees growing from the gravel bars. Continue rambling in the flats beneath sycamore, yucca, and cedar. Come very near Little Paddy Creek just above the confluence of Big and Little Paddy Creek. A short trail leads right to the confluence, but you stay left, joining a ridgeline dividing the two drainages, ascending by switchbacks. Don't short-cut the switchbacks the way others before you have. It causes erosion and damages the trail.

Top out on the dividing ridge, making your way southwesterly beneath the sturdy oaks and short-leaved pines that occupy the highest points on the ridge. The mostly level dirt-and-pebble track makes for easy going. Slip over to the left side of the ridge before dipping to reach a sandy gap at 2.0 miles. The Big Piney Trail continues undulating southwest, crossing a couple of wet-weather drainages flowing from right to left across the trail. Continue traveling on the ridge to reach a trail junction at 3.0 miles.

The South Loop continues left toward Roby Lake and the Big Piney Trailhead. You, however, turn acutely right, toward the North Loop, on the Old Military Road Trail. Before leaving, note the copse of persimmon trees at this junction.

The Old Military Road Trail shortly passes a standing chimney to the left of the trail. Wonder what the family who lived here would make of their homestead, which they carved from the wilderness, now returning to wilderness. Just ahead the doubletrack passes an old farm pond, now ringed in trees. You have turned 180 degrees, traveling nearly parallel to your path of just a few minutes ago. The trail drifts north down to a hollow leading into the bottomland of Little Paddy Creek. Turn downstream and work through reforesting fields, twisting and turning amid cedars reclaiming the old roadbed. Osage orange grows here, too, and cacti. The area is an amalgamation of nearly all the flora of the wilderness.

Cross Little Paddy Creek, between clear pools, at 4.5 miles. A campsite is located on the far bank. The Old Military Road Trail quickly leaves the valley for higher and drier woods, making a trail junction at 5.1 miles.

You have now reached the North Loop, part of which leads left to Roby Lake and the Big Piney Trailhead. Our loop turns acutely right, toward Big Piney Trail Camp. The singletrack trail drifts into a shallow valley beneath lush woods. The streambed lies off to your left; you cross it at 5.5 miles. A campsite is on the right bank in some pines, but water is not guaranteed here. Continue down, crossing the wash where boulders constrict the drainage. Intersect a tributary stream at 5.8 miles, and turn away from the hollow, entering pines, where golden needles carpet the trailbed. Bisect some intermittent drainages, and then begin climbing to join an old roadbed at 6.3 miles.

Continue climbing before saddling alongside a high knob that rises to your left. Enter a gap between two knobs at 6.7 miles. The trailbed becomes extremely rocky, as do the surrounding woods. A knob now rises to your right as you mostly travel downhill on a stony track.

OUTCROP OFFERS VIEWS INTO PADDY CREEK VALLEY

32

Devils Backbone Wilderness Loop

TOTAL DISTANCE: 10.1-mile loop	

HIKING TIME: 5 hours

VERTICAL RISE: 320 feet

RATING: Difficult

MAPS: USGS 7.5' Dora, Siloam Springs, Pottersville, Cureall NW; USDA Forest Service Devils Backbone Wilderness; Mark Twain National Forest—Asa, Cassville, and Willow Springs Ranger Districts

TRAILHEAD GPS COORDINATES: N36° 45.160', W92° 9.011'

CONTACT INFORMATION: Mark Twain National Forest, P.O. Box 188, 1103 South Jefferson, Ava, MO 65608, (417) 683-4428, www.fs.usda.gov/mtnf

The Devils Backbone Wilderness comprises nearly 7,000 acres of preserved backcountry, centered on the hills and hollows bordering the beautiful North Fork River. This loop leaves North Fork Recreation Area and soon reaches Blue Spring, which fills the North Fork with more crystalline water. Leave the spring and climb along the North Fork, stopping to gain vistas from riverside bluffs. You'll then enter the wilderness proper, following McGarr Ridge before returning to the river at another scenic bluff. Head up aptly named Crooked Branch, twisting and turning up a forgotten hollow. A side trip to the wilderness's namesake, Devils Backbone, offers limited vistas. Continue the hike, now traveling Mary Hollow to rejoin McGarr Ridge, completing the loop with one last trip by the bluffs of the North Fork and Blue Spring. Long pants are recommended on this hike during the growing season, as much of the trailside in Crooked Hollow is brushy.

HOW TO GET THERE

From the intersection of US Business 63 and US 63 on the south side of West Plains, take US 63 north for 4.1 miles to Highway CC. Turn left and follow Highway CC for 16.3 miles to North Fork Recreation Area, on your left. (If you bridge the North Fork River, you just passed the turn.) Turn left into the recreation area. Next, turn left toward the campground and continue forward to reach the trailhead at the end of the road. There is a parking fee.

THE HIKE

Two trails leave from the trailhead. None of the trails here are marked or signed, but they're all easily followed.

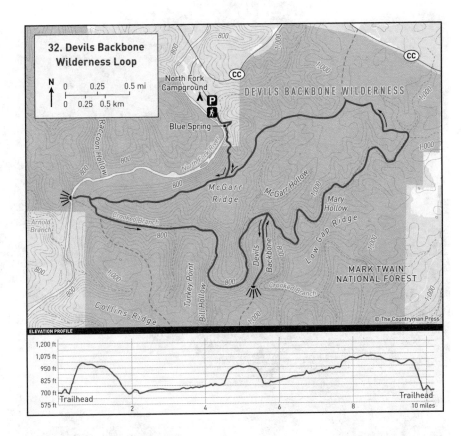

32. Devils Backbone Wilderness Loop

N

| 0 | 0.25 | 0.5 mi |
| 0 | 0.25 | 0.5 km |

North Fork Campground

CC

DEVILS BACKBONE WILDERNESS

CC

Blue Spring

Raccoon Hollow

North Fork River

800

800

800

McGarr Ridge

McGarr Hollow

Mary Hollow

Low Gap Ridge

MARK TWAIN NATIONAL FOREST

Arnold Branch

Crooked Branch

800

Devils Backbone

800

Crooked Branch

800

1,000

Turkey Point

Bill Hollow

Collins Ridge

© The Countryman Press

ELEVATION PROFILE

| 1,200 ft |
| 1,075 ft |
| 950 ft |
| 825 ft |
| 700 ft |
| 575 ft |

Trailhead

Trailhead

2   4   6   8   10 miles

Take the trail leading left to immediately span a streambed on a bridge. Continue on a hillside, paralleling the trail that departed from the right side of the trailhead. The North Fork River is off to your right. A short spur trail soon leads right to a promontory overlooking the North Fork and Blue Spring below. The beautiful aqua-blue water emerges from the bluff upon which you were standing.

To reach the spring, veer left and turn up the hollow, passing a small cave on your left before you cross the streambed. Curve back to again overlook Blue Spring, which emerges on bluffs directly adjacent to the North Fork River, immensely increasing its flow and adding a bluish cast to its already crystalline appearance. Leave the riverside

spring scene, clambering up a rocky track in woods. Join a bluff line above the river and enjoy more views. Here, you can look over a colorful vista from the gray bluffs: sapphire water flowing alongside russet gravel bars, bordered by verdant forests against a bluish white sky. Missouri is a land of big springs, and many are called Blue Spring, thanks to the water color.

Continue winding your way steeply through hickory-oak woods, officially entering the Devils Backbone Wilderness and reaching the top of McGarr Ridge and a trail junction at 0.6 mile. Turn right here, heading west on McGarr Ridge, beginning the loop portion of the hike westerly toward the river. Enjoy the easy walking on an old roadbed beneath a fairly young forest. The North Fork

LOOKING DOWN ON THE GRAVEL BARS OF NORTH FORK WHITE RIVER

River is to your right; Crooked Branch is to your left. The ridge narrows and drops steeply off on both sides, especially the river side. Continue running parallel to the river, eventually making a downgrade. The trail receives moderate use from equestrians, so be prepared to step aside for horses.

Leave the roadbed on its descent and enter grassy areas pocked with walnut trees aplenty. Be mindful here in a walnut-grass area: The loop part of the trail leaves left at 1.8 miles. You'll take this path in a moment, but for now, follow the more heavily used track keeps forward and downhill. The woods thicken and the trailbed becomes sandy before you reach the North Fork River in sycamore-dominated bottomlands. Look over a scenic bluff on the river; the water is difficult to access at this spot. Backtrack to reach the intersection again, this time veering right onto the loop. Shortly pass through pines and curve into Crooked Branch watershed.

Soon you'll cross the wash of Crooked Branch in bottomland to reach an intersection at 2.2 miles. A trail leaves right and uphill for Collins Ridge, but you stay left up Crooked Branch, entering Crooked Hollow on an old roadbed. The intermittent stream is to your left as you head up the hollow—remote in aura if not reality. The hollow initially doesn't live up to its name as it maintains an easterly course amid dogwood, sassafras, hickory, and oak, with the bottomland species thriving on the gravel streambed below.

Pass the outwash of a tributary at 2.9 miles. Keep east, passing below Turkey Point. The hollow begins to curve and the trail crisscrosses the gravel streambed, sometimes heading straight up. This makes for slow going, though you'll occasionally travel less stony terrain. Watch for gray bluffs along parts of this valley, especially as the trail curves back to the north and passes beneath the Devils Backbone, which isn't visible from the bottom of the valley.

Reach an intersection at 4.5 miles. A trail leads right up the Devils Backbone to meet Collins Ridge. Detour up this rocky track as it makes a southerly ascent into piney woods. The climb

eases, and the ridge is wider than you expect. Be patient: The ridgeline narrows and becomes rocky, dipping to a narrow saddle—the Devils Backbone. Here, Crooked Branch has nearly circled back on itself, leaving only a slender spine of terra firma between its meanderings. The tree canopy is absent overhead. You can peer east and west at nothing but wilderness through the trees from the Devils Backbone, though there's no single outstanding view.

Backtrack from the saddle after 0.5 mile, returning to Crooked Branch, continuing up the hollow. Ahead, leave Crooked Hollow left, entering Mary Hollow and its streambed. This hollow has some crooks of its own but is much narrower than Crooked Hollow. Mary Hollow is rocky and hemmed in—you continually crisscross the wash and its side tributaries. The tight hollow favors moisture-loving plants, such as ferns and vines. Also note the increase in red maples.

You leave Mary Hollow left at 7.6 miles, though a faint path does continue up it. The main track is quite evident as it heads northwesterly up a rocky ridge. The ascent is gentle—you've been slowly but surely gaining elevation since the North Fork River, miles back. Soon you'll level off in pine woods to reach a junction at 8.3 miles. A trail leaves right to make CR CC. To complete this loop, stay left, again on McGarr Ridge. Travel just a short distance to another intersection. Here, an unmaintained trail leads left and uphill. The main path veers right, immediately passing a small wildlife pond to the right of the trail. Enjoy a nearly level forest walk, heading westerly with the slope of the ridge dropping off to your right.

The walking is easy under the oaks and hickories, and you soon reach

LOOKING DOWN AT THE CONFLUENCE OF BLUE SPRING AND THE NORTH FORK WHITE RIVER

another junction at 9.5 miles, completing the loop portion of the hike. Turn right, leaving the wilderness to return to the North Fork River. This time, when you get to Blue Spring, take some time to enjoy it, as paths circle it three-quarters of the way around. Return by the riverside trail, passing under a low-hanging bluff before reaching to the trailhead at 10.1 miles.

33

Devils Well
and Cave
Spring Circuit

TOTAL DISTANCE: 5.4-mile loop with spurs	

HIKING TIME: 2.5 hours

VERTICAL RISE: 290 feet

RATING: Moderate

MAPS: USGS 7.5' Round Spring, Lewis Hollow; Devils Well Trail

TRAILHEAD GPS COORDINATES: N37° 22' 35.5", W91° 29' 28.8"

CONTACT INFORMATION: Ozark National Scenic Riverways, P.O. Box 490, Van Buren, MO 63965, (573) 323-4236, www.nps.gov/ozar

This rewarding trek takes you to two fascinating aquatic geological features. First, check out the Devils Well, where you can peer down at an underground lake through a hole linking the underworld to the land above. Next, trek through glades and bluffs above the Current River, gaining a vista, before descending to the river's edge. There, in a richly wooded flat, discover the mouth of cool and colorful Cave Spring, as it flows from a cave into the Current. Climb the bluffs again for a second view, then visit the river once more. The final part of the hike heads up Devils Well Hollow, crisscrossing a crystalline stream in an untamed wooded valley.

HOW TO GET THERE

From the junction of MO 19 and MO 106 in Eminence, head north on MO 19 for 24 miles before turning left on MO KK. Follow MO KK for 2.1 miles, then turn left onto Devils Well Road. Trace the gravel track for 1.5 miles to dead end at the trailhead parking area.

THE HIKE

Back in 1954, curiosity had finally got to Bill Wallace, landowner of a rugged Ozark tract in Missouri's Current River Valley. Ol' Bill just had to see what was down that hole in the ground—locals had always called it the Devils Well—and see once and for all what was at the bottom. Bill was a little worried just what he might encounter down there—maybe the horned one itself. Luckily, Bill's brother Bob Wallace volunteered to go first. Brother Bob was crazy enough and always the daring type. The adventurous siblings set up a hand-cranked winch to drop crazy Bob through the hole in the

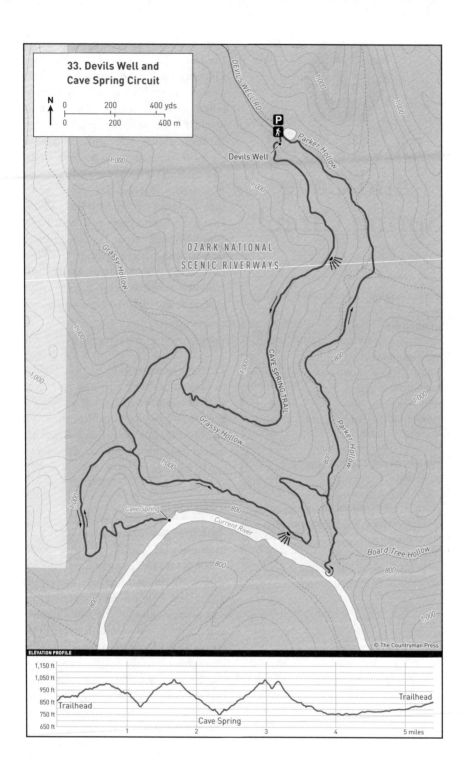

33. Devils Well and Cave Spring Circuit

N

| 0 | 200 | 400 yds |
| 0 | 200 | 400 m |

DEVILS WELL RD.

P

Parker Hollow

Devils Well

1,000

1,000

OZARK NATIONAL
SCENIC RIVERWAYS

Grassy Hollow

1,000

1,000

1,000

CAVE SPRING TRAIL

800

Parker Hollow

1,000

Grassy Hollow

1,000

800

800

Cave Spring

Current River

Board Tree Hollow

800

800

1,000

© The Countryman Press

ELEVATION PROFILE

| 1,150 ft |
| 1,050 ft |
| 950 ft |
| 850 ft |
| 750 ft |
| 650 ft |

Trailhead

Trailhead

Cave Spring

1   2   3   4   5 miles

HIKER GLANCES AT WATERFALL BEFORE PEERING DOWN INTO THE DEVILS WELL

surface into the dark unknown depths, through the same hole that water often fell, creating a waterfall.

Bill lowered Bob about 100 feet to reach a pool of water. Bill shined his flashlight around, and to his surprise, there stretched an underground lake bigger than a football field! Neither of the brothers knew it at the time, but that underground lake was 80 feet deep! To this day, this concealed tarn remains Missouri's largest subterranean lake, yet another piece of the complex plumbing system of the Ozarks. Bill and Bob probably also didn't know that if a man accidentally fell down the hole into the hidden lake, he would eventually die of hypothermia in chilly water where blind, translucent cavefish dwelled.

On this hike, you can not only peer into the Devils Well but also see Cave Spring, a riverside rock opening emitting cool air and water into the Current River. But to get there requires a little hiking. The trek first leaves the Devils Well parking area, passing around a pole gate to enter a grassy picnic area. From there, follow the trail and circular staircase leading down to the viewing spot into the Devils Well. Here, part of the cave roof above the Devils Well collapsed, creating a window to the netherworld below. When you reach the window, park-placed lighting illuminates the falling water as it spills into the lake below.

This initial highlight comes quick. You then join the Cave Spring Trail as it heads south, joining a bluff above Devils Well Hollow. Cedars, hickories, and oaks line the rock-strewn path. Occasional flowery glades open in the woods. At 0.4 mile, the trail opens to a rock outcrop and view into the Current River valley. Stay along the rim of the hollow before dropping to a streambed, which you cross at 1.2 miles. Climb to the crest of the ridge above the Current River, making a trail intersection at 1.7 miles. Head right here, taking a spur path toward Cave Spring. Drop off the ridge at 1.8 miles. Step over a streambed at 2.2 miles.

Ahead, the path courses through a riverside flat populated with tall sycamores and stinging nettle in the summertime. A campsite lies in the flat. At 2.4 miles, the trail leads to the edge of the Current and the mouth of Cave Spring. A narrow rocky passage leads you to the entrance of the rock maw, where the spring upwells then courses a short distance, adding its flow to the Current River. It's dark and cool in Cave Spring during the steamy Ozark summer. Backtrack to the main loop and continue the circuit, traversing a bluff above the river. Rock outcrops and cliffs mix with cedars, pines, and small grassy glades where wildflowers grow. Open onto an overlook of the Current River at 3.5 miles. The shoals of the Current sing below.

Just ahead, the Cave Spring Trail turns away from the river, and winds down along a wildflower-rich vale to reach and cross the stream of Parker Hollow at 3.9 miles. Here, a double-track spur heads right for a quarter mile down to a flat, allowing you another close-up look at the Current River, the aquatic heart and soul of the Ozark National Scenic Riverways. After viewing the Current, backtrack then resume up the Devils Well Hollow, repeatedly rock hopping the rock- and gravel-bar-laden watercourse that seasonally gushes or trickles through a riot of vegetation.

At 4.9 miles, the doubletrack path you have been following curves right, but you cross an incoming streamlet and head left. The spot is signed. The upper portion of the Parker Hollow has been managed with prescribed fire by the National Park Service. Note the blackened tree trunks and brushy undergrowth. The Ozarks, to maintain their biological integrity, need prescribed fire. The final part of the hike works up Devils Well Hollow on a singletrack path. Emerge at the Devils Well picnic area near a quiet pond at 5.4 miles, completing the hike.

34

Alley Spring Mill Loop

TOTAL DISTANCE: 1.9-mile loop

HIKING TIME: 1 hour

VERTICAL RISE: 225 feet

RATING: Easy

MAPS: USGS 7.5' Alley Spring; Alley Spring Campground, Ozark National Scenic Riverways

TRAILHEAD GPS COORDINATES: N37° 9.080', W91° 26.523'

CONTACT INFORMATION: Ozark National Scenic Riverways, P.O. Box 490, Van Buren, MO 63965, (573) 323-4236, www.nps.gov/ozar

Alley Spring Mill is an Ozarks icon. The red structure, located adjacent to the azure waters of Alley Spring, is often photographed and is a busy place in summer, when the National Park Service offers interpretive displays and events at the mill—the centerpiece of a former Ozark community now preserved as part of Ozark National Scenic Riverways. Luckily for hikers, a trail winds through the old community, passing the spring and mill, and then rises along a slope to an overlook, where you can peer down on the valley below. After meandering through upland woods, the trail then works its way back down to Alley Spring, passing along the spring run and its impressive bluffs. As mentioned, visiting the area in summer can be hectic, though you may enjoy the active park interpretations. Solitude is found much more easily in spring and fall. A large picnic area lies adjacent to the mill, and a campground is located just across the Jacks Fork River.

HOW TO GET THERE

From the junction of MO 19 and MO 106 in Eminence, head west on MO 106 for 5.7 miles, crossing the Jacks Fork River. Shortly beyond, turn right into the Alley Spring area, and immediately left into a large parking area. The hike starts on a sidewalk at the rear.

THE HIKE

From the parking area, take the sidewalk/trail leading toward Alley Mill, Alley Spring, and Story Creek School. Pass a picnic shelter above you on a hill before entering the valley of Alley Spring and site of a small community centered on the mill. The quaint white structure of Story Creek School comes

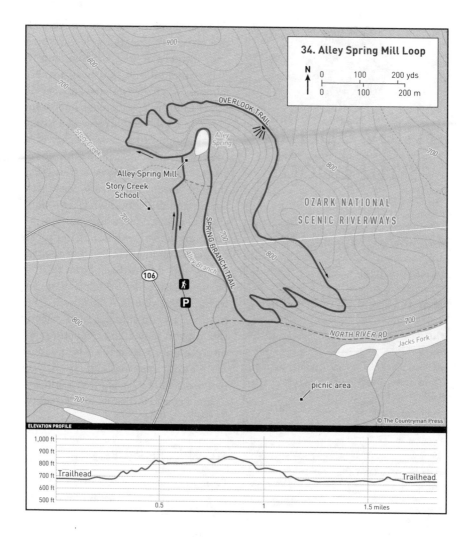

into view. The structure was donated to the park and moved here in 1971; Alley already had its own school, which doubled as a church on Sunday. Ahead, a bridge leads right, over Story Creek. Cross the span and the famed red Alley Spring Mill comes into view. A trail leads right to a bridge over the outflow of Alley Spring. Stay left, reaching the red rectangular building of Alley Spring Mill.

The multistory mill structure is open daily in summer, and weekends only during May, September, and October; it's closed the rest of the year. If the mill

is open for touring, you can explore the back porch, and then the first floor where grain entered the mill and was ground. Unfortunately for the owners and area residents, Alley's roller mill was designed to grind wheat to flour in an area where corn was the main crop. Above, on the second floor, grain was sifted in machines called swing sifters, so it could achieve uniform consistency. The attic held the belts that operated the sifters, while the basement headquartered the machinery that transmitted power to the mill.

The reliable flow of Alley Spring made locating a mill here a natural choice, as many Ozark streams run dry or nearly dry in summer and fall. Alley Spring's 81-million-gallon daily output meant a mill would always have a power source. The trouble came when too much water was flowing and nearby Alley Branch above the valley flooded the mill. Though this mill was designed to control how much water entered its turbine by means of a system of belts and wheels, as opposed to the typical waterwheel design, it couldn't handle floods. The mill was completed in 1894, replacing one built shortly after the Civil War.

The springwater loudly surges through the mill spillway and lures you to look over this scene. Alley Spring comes into view. Its colorful waters rise forth from the depths below—32 feet below, to be exact—and are backed by an impressive sheer bluff. A short loop trail circles the springhead. No wonder this slice of Americana is so often photographed and visited. Interpretive displays are scattered throughout the area. Wander around and enjoy the setting.

This hike leads away from the mill area on the Overlook Trail. The wide gravel track passes alongside upper Alley Branch and limestone bluffs to your right. Begin switchbacking up the mountainside that forms one edge of the Alley Mill Valley. Dark boulder outcrops form lichen-covered sentinels in the trailside forest of dogwoods, sassafras, and pines along with the ever-present oaks and hickories. Despite the elevation gain, the rushing roar of Alley Branch is clearly audible below.

The trail levels out before reaching a cleared overlook at 0.6 mile. Enjoy the

ALLEY SPRING MILL IN THE MORNING LIGHT

ALLEY SPRING MILL REFLECTED IN THE ALLEY SPRING POOL

view of the bucolic valley below, where mown grassy areas contrast with the wooded hillsides and stream bottoms. Story Creek School appears quainter than ever. The Overlook Trail continues beyond the overlook, in deciduous woods, to reach the top of a ridge. The park service has been using prescribed burning to restore this forest to its natural state. The understory is kept thin via burns. Look for blackened trunks at the base of trees along this ridgetop.

Begin circling the valley in oaks, running parallel to Alley Branch, which gurgles below. The well-constructed trail then curves downhill, descending by wide switchbacks toward Alley Branch. Wind through more lichen-covered outcrops before reaching the valley floor again, meeting gravel North River Road, a horse trail. Turn right here and pass through a picnic area with horse hitching posts. Ahead, a bridge spans Alley Branch, but don't go that way—it leads back to the parking area, shortcutting your walk.

Instead, keep right, now joining the Spring Branch Trail. Saddle alongside clear Alley Branch, where water weeds wave in the rapid gush, soon to meet Jacks Fork. A steep hillside rises to your right, and you are pinched in between the hillside and the stream. Rugged bluffs soon rise. Notice the mini caves and intricate, eroded formations in the bluffs. Take your time in this extremely scenic area, where overhanging bluffs form grottoes large enough to shelter someone from the rain.

All too soon you reach a bridge leading left over Alley Branch. Alley Spring Mill is in sight. Continue forward, but don't cross the bridge; keep following the spring run up to its source and the large pool that is Alley Mill Spring. Enjoy more bluffs, eventually curving along the amphitheater-like bluff that encloses the spring to return to Alley Mill. You may want to ramble around this area more, examining Story Creek School, before backtracking the final distance to the trailhead.

35

Current River Vista–Blue Spring Double Hike

TOTAL DISTANCE: 6.0 miles total for both there-and-back hikes	
HIKING TIME: 3 hours	
VERTICAL RISE: 180 feet	
RATING: Moderate	
MAPS: USGS 7.5' Powder Mill Ferry; Ozark Scenic Riverways; Ozark Trail—Current River 1	
TRAILHEAD GPS COORDINATES: N37° 10.898', W91° 10.533'	
CONTACT INFORMATION: Ozark National Scenic Riverways, P.O. Box 490, Van Buren, MO 63965, (573) 323-4236, www.nps.gov/ozar	

These two relatively short there-and-back treks emanate from the same destination. First, you'll take the Ozark Trail northbound to reach a great view of Owls Bend on high, dry bluffs. Next, return to the trailhead and head south along the Current River bottom on the Blue Spring Trail, which takes you beside the wild and scenic Current River to reach Blue Spring State Natural Area. Blue Spring is widely regarded as the most colorful of all Missouri's springs and is the state's eighth largest. It puts out 87 million gallons per day and sounds like a whitewater river after it emerges from its famous indigo hole. At an amazing 310 feet, it is Missouri's deepest spring. As a bonus, the trails start at the Powder Mill area of Ozark National Scenic Riverways, administered by the National Park Service, and include a campground, restrooms, and a gravel river access area.

HOW TO GET THERE

From the junction of MO 21 and MO 106 at Ellington, take MO 106 west for 13.6 miles to the left turn into the Powder Mill Area on Shannon County Road 106531 (CR 106531). Follow the signs to Powder Mill. At 0.4 mile, watch for the sign for the OZARK RESEARCH CENTER. Turn right here to access the Ozark Trail. For the Blue Spring Hike, continue forward on CR 106531 to the left turn into Powder Mill Campground, and the sign for FLOATER PARKING AND THE BLUE SPRING TRAIL.

THE HIKE

The first hike of this pair starts at the Ozark Research Center, within easy walking distance of the Blue Spring trailhead. Leave the center on the Ozark Spur Trail, which starts on your left as

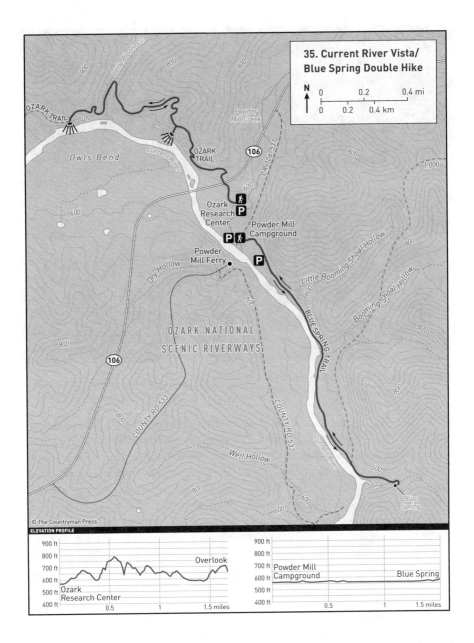

35. Current River Vista/ Blue Spring Double Hike

ELEVATION PROFILE

you face the research center building. Cross a small grassy area, and then enter rich, viney woods. Shortly you'll reach and cross MO 106, now entering rocky, dry woods; cedars and oaks dominate. Join the Ozark Trail, which has come across MO 106 and ascends a slope. Reach a gladey area that offers a good view of the Current River. The path now switchbacks and opens into the upper gladey area; there's a great vista to the left of the trail. Walk down into the grass to get the best look. The Current River is making its curve around Owls Bend—another name for the Powder Mill area.

BLUE SPRING REALLY IS BLUE—AND 310 FEET DEEP

Continue beyond this first view. The trail curves into the woods, then back out to a point. A faint track leads downhill through grassy glades to reach an outcrop and view. The expanse of Owls Bend opens before you. The fields on the south side of the river are easily visible; you can also see the bend of Owls Bend curving out of sight. These bluffs are lower than the first set.

The Ozark Trail turns away from the river and descends to cross a hollow, before once again curving back out toward the river. It seems like you are going to gain another view, but the trail instead dips to reach the thickly wooded hollow of Little Bloom Creek at 1.3 miles. The perennial stream is flowing left-to-right, following gravity's rules to feed the Current River.

The Ozark Trail ascends from the hollow, first heading toward the river, which is just out of sight. The path turns away, trying to moderate the rise. Inevitably, the trail is drawn back toward the Current, now well below you. Enter an area of cedars shading a campsite, then open onto the third and best bluff of Owls Bend at 1.5 miles. Southward views await from this perch at the apex of the bend, where the river curves in both directions. Cedars cling to the bluff's edge, while in other spots only rock and grass lie atop the cliffs that drop to the Wild and Scenic River below. Wooded ridges rise forth in the distance. It is quite a view. Backtrack to the research center.

The Blue Spring Trail begins at the rear of the floater parking area. Enter woods as a trail leads left to the area's restrooms. Turn right here, heading through a shady bottomland forest dominated by ash and ironwood. Look for a

VIEW OF OWLS BEND

tall bluff to your left through the woods. Soon you'll pass a side trail leading right, to the lower end of the campground. The singletrack proceeds downstream sandwiched by the bluff to the left and the Current River to the right. At 0.3 mile, bridge a steep-sided wet-weather tributary flowing through Little Booming Shoal Hollow. The trailbed is primarily dirt—soft on the feet, unlike most rocky Ozark trails. Grass also borders the way. The park service keeps it mown, however. The path saddles alongside the Current River and offers first-rate views of this clear, swift, and wide watercourse. The trail runs so close to the Current that the trees give way, exposing you to the sky overhead and great sweeps up- and downriver. Look left just after the trail reenters woods to see an overhanging rock outcrop that forms a small rock shelter.

Cross a seasonal wet drainage flowing out of Booming Shoal Hollow without benefit of a footbridge at 0.6 mile. This drainage is normally rock, dry and easy on the feet. Keep traveling downriver in bottomland dominated by sycamores. Reach the Blue Spring Picnic Area at 1.2 miles. A spur trail for boaters leads right to the river, while a separate trail leads left to a small picnic area and restroom. Keep forward in woods and reach a junction with another trail reaching the Blue Spring parking area. A large gravel bar lies across the river as

you enter the Blue Spring Natural Area, a 17-acre tract protected by the state of Missouri.

The Blue Spring Trail now turns left, away from the Current and into the Blue Spring drainage. The spring run is loudly flowing over rocks, making whitewater noises. The depth of the roar hints that this is a big spring, and it is. If you could paddle a canoe or kayak up to the springhead, the spring run could easily carry it down to the river.

The forest is exceedingly lush here. Reach the springhead at 1.5 miles. The upwelling is backed against a sheer bluff. Nearing the water, you will see that the spring really is deep blue, almost an inky shade, colored by minerals. The hue depends on the season and on the interplay between light and sky. Come here when the sun is directly overhead, and you will gain an understanding of just how deep the spring is. Notice the plants in the water, and the fish—maybe even a muskrat. A platform leads to the edge. From this platform a second trail leads to an elevated overlook where you can get the spring view from on high. Make sure to stay on the trail and platforms, to protect fragile plants growing around the upwelling. No swimming, fishing, or diving is allowed.

Backtrack to Powder Mill Campground—itself a worthwhile destination, with its riverside campsites, restrooms, and potable water in-season.

36

Stegall Mountain Vista via Rocky Falls

TOTAL DISTANCE: 6.2-mile there-and-back

HIKING TIME: 3 hours, 30 minutes

VERTICAL RISE: 530 feet

RATING: Moderate to difficult

MAPS: USGS 7.5' Stegall Mountain; Ozark National Scenic Riverways, Ozark Trail—Current River 2 Miles 9 to 18

TRAILHEAD GPS COORDINATES: N37° 5.671', W91° 12.596'

CONTACT INFORMATION: Ozark National Scenic Riverways, P.O. Box 490, Van Buren, MO 63965, (573) 323-4236, www.nps.gov/ozar

Missouri's Ozark Trail (OT) has many highlights, and the view from atop Stegall Mountain may be one of the best. From this peak, protected as part of Missouri Department of Conservation's Peck Ranch, hikers can peer upon an unbroken forest extending as far as the eye can see. The hike starts out well, too, on Ozark National Scenic Riverways land near Rocky Falls, a cascade that tumbles 40-plus feet over volcanic rock to reach a clear pool.

Once you leave Rocky Falls and its developed recreation area, you'll head east along perennial Rocky Creek to meet the Ozark Trail. Travel southbound on the OT up Kelley Hollow, a wooded flat formerly inhabited by Ozark highlanders, where you can observe pioneer relics. Leave Ozark National Scenic Riverways land and enter Peck Ranch. A series of switchbacks leads up the north slope of Stegall Mountain to peak at an open rock pinnacle where the views display Missouri in all its finery. The trailhead offers an attractive picnic area with restrooms; the falls are just a short distance away.

HOW TO GET THERE

From Eminence, drive east on MO 106 for 7 miles to Highway H. Turn right and follow Highway H for 3.9 miles to Highway NN. Turn left; proceed on Highway NN for 2 miles to the signed right turn for ROCKY FALLS, Shannon Highway 526. Turn right and follow this gravel road for 0.3 mile to the signed left turn to ROCKY FALLS PARKING AREA, where it soon dead-ends.

THE HIKE

Leave the parking area and take the gravel path leading toward Rocky Falls.

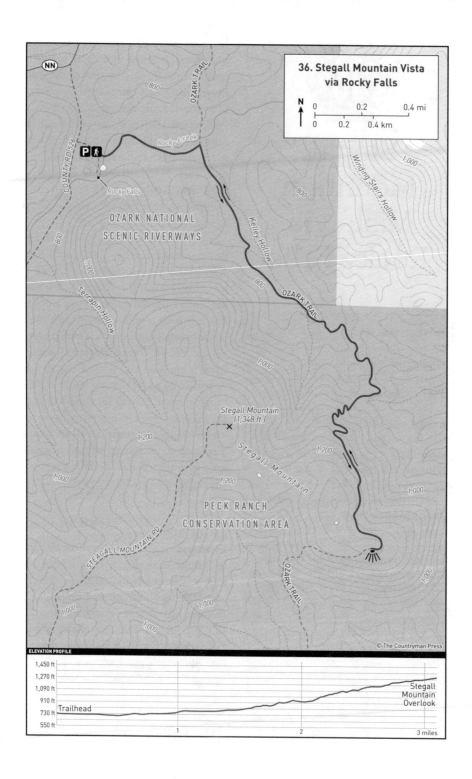

36. Stegall Mountain Vista via Rocky Falls

N
0   0.2   0.4 mi
0   0.2   0.4 km

NN

OZARK TRAIL

800

Rocky Creek

COUNTY RD 526

P

Rocky Falls

OZARK NATIONAL
SCENIC RIVERWAYS

800

1,000

Terrapin Hollow

Kelley Hollow

800

OZARK TRAIL

Winding Stairs Hollow

1,000

800

1,000

Stegall Mountain
(1,348 ft.)
×

Stegall Mountain

1,200

1,000

1,200

1,200

1,000

PECK RANCH
CONSERVATION AREA

STEGALL MOUNTAIN RD

1,000

1,000

OZARK TRAIL

1,000

© The Countryman Press

ELEVATION PROFILE

1,450 ft			
1,270 ft			
1,090 ft			Stegall
910 ft			Mountain
730 ft	Trailhead		Overlook
550 ft			

1   2   3 miles

LOOKING OUT FROM ATOP STEGALL MOUNTAIN

Check out this cascade before you continue the hike. Erosion-resistant volcanic rock forms a craggy spillway over which Rocky Creek descends 40 feet into a large, crystalline catch pool bordered by a large gravel bar. This pool makes for a fine swimming hole as well. In times of low flow, you can clamber along the waterfall with its stony borders, which form a classic Ozark shut-in.

After visiting the falls, backtrack just a short distance to the trailhead, starting the hike again. Now look to your left for a gravel trail leading into the woods. The connector path immediately crosses stone-filled Rocky Creek,

then passes a pine-shaded campsite on your right. Continue downstream along Rocky Creek, which gurgles to meet the Current River. The wooded trail enters a field dotted with pines and sumac before meeting the OT at 0.5 mile. Turn right here, southbound on the OT, heading up heavily wooded Kelley Hollow. Dogwoods are the prevalent understory tree here and light up the forest with their blooms in spring and red leaves and redder berries in fall.

Work up the hardscrabble hollow, where braided stony streambeds normally run dry. The thin underbrush allows extensive forest views below the spindly trees. This hollow was once cleared as farmland. Old relics such as rusted cans, pots, and broken crockery can be spotted; please leave them for others to discover. The trail hangs close to the upsloping right side of the hollow. At 1.4 miles, the OT leaves national park land and enters the Peck Ranch. Continue up the hollow just a short distance and look carefully for the OT, which leaves to your right from an old roadbed you've been tracing. The path is marked with OT signs; when they are placed angling left or right, this indicates the direction of the path.

Shortly leave Kelley Hollow as you circle a fast-disappearing clearing and begin angling up the north slope of Stegall Mountain. Note the use of prescribed fire here. The trunks of the pines and oaks are fire scarred, and the rocky soil is exposed in places or lightly covered in leaf litter. Work up the head of the hollow to reach a gap at 1.9 miles. Cross an old woods road winding up the mountain. Continue aiming for Stegall, crossing the road a second time. The broad crest of the mountain is dead ahead.

The OT meets a dry wash flowing off the ridgeline. Ascend by switchbacks to cross the dry wash. Continue angling up the slope in oak-dominant woods. White stones are scattered throughout the landscape. A couple more switchbacks lead higher still as the OT continues its southbound march up the east flank.

Watch for a significant rock clearing to the right of the trail at 2.6 miles. Bisect another old road just before an opening atop Stegall Mountain at 3.1 miles. Flat lichen-covered rock slabs are broken by grasses and wildflowers at the broad crest, which is effectively an open glade. The trail can be hard to follow here. Look for cairns—piles of rock indicating the way. Soon you'll top out on the rock slabs and enjoy the views, which open to the east and south, framed by oaks where the trees begin on the lower mountaintop. At this point you will begin scrambling among the rocks, looking this way and that, trying to absorb the beauty of both the mountaintop and the land beyond. Immediately in front of you, pinkish slabs top the peak with additional big boulders. The unbroken forests of southeast Missouri extend to the limit of the horizon. A few reasons for the extensive forestlands: the Mark Twain National Forest, the 23,000-acre Peck Ranch, and the lands of the Ozark National Scenic Riverways. Try to come here on a clear spring or fall day to make the most of this excellent outlook.

When you're ready, retrace your steps to the trailhead.

37

Boomhole Vista and Beyond from McCormack Lake

TOTAL DISTANCE: 7.9-mile loop

HIKING TIME: 4 hours, 15 minutes

VERTICAL RISE: 380 feet

RATING: Moderate to difficult

MAPS: USGS 7.5' Greer; Ozark Trail Eleven Point River Miles 0 to 15; Mark Twain National Forest—Doniphan, Eleven Point, and Poplar Bluff Ranger Districts

TRAILHEAD GPS COORDINATES: N36° 49.357', W91° 21.028'

CONTACT INFORMATION: Mark Twain National Forest, #4 Confederate Ridge Road, Doniphan, MO 63935, (573) 996-2153, www.fs.usda.gov/mtnf

This hike travels the bluffs and hollows of the Eleven Point National Wild and Scenic River and the Mark Twain National Forest. You'll start at McCormack Lake Recreation Area, dipping into McCormack Hollow to near the Eleven Point River before ascending to riverside bluffs that offer scenic vistas from rock bluffs and open glades, including the Boomhole. Stop by a sink, traveling through pine-oak woods to reach Duncan Hollow. Course in wide bottomland flats where sycamores and other trees tower to reach Greer Crossing Recreation Area before looping around a ridgeline. After finishing the loop portion of the hike, backtrack, grabbing a second look from the Boomhole Vista and other overlooks, returning to quiet and pretty McCormack Lake.

HOW TO GET THERE

From the intersection of MO 19 and US 160 in Alton, drive north on MO 19 for 13.1 miles to Forest Road 3155 (FR 3155) and the signed turn to MCCORMACK LAKE. Turn left onto FR 3155 and follow it for 1.9 miles to the recreation picnic area, on your left. As you face out to McCormack Lake, the trail starts at the edge of the grassy picnic area to your left.

THE HIKE

Leave the picnic area, heading left, keeping McCormack Lake to your right. Enter woods only to open to a second picnic area with restrooms on your left. By the way, the recreation area has not only a picnic area but also a free, but nice, primitive campground on the far side of the lake. McCormack Lake offers stillwater fishing. This is officially the McCormack Greer Trail, though you

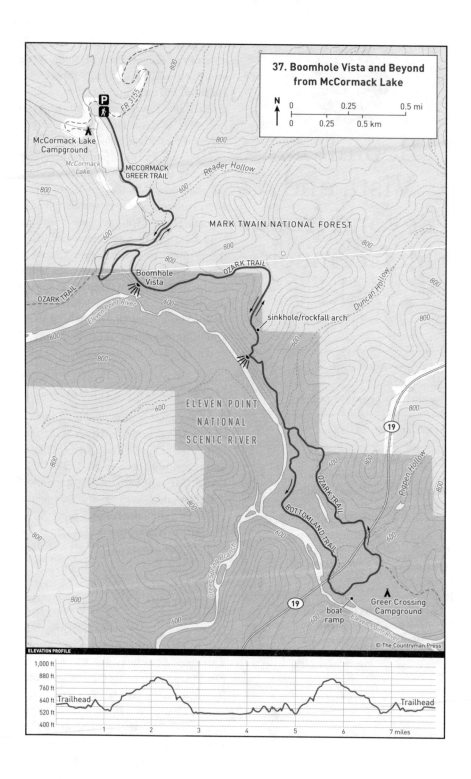

37. Boomhole Vista and Beyond from McCormack Lake

N

0   0.25   0.5 mi

0   0.25   0.5 km

FR 3155

P

McCormack Lake
Campground

McCormack
Lake

MCCORMACK
GREER TRAIL

Reader Hollow

MARK TWAIN NATIONAL FOREST

800

OZARK TRAIL

Duncan Hollow

Boomhole
Vista

OZARK TRAIL

Eleven Point River

sinkhole/rockfall arch

ELEVEN POINT

NATIONAL

SCENIC RIVER

19

Pigpen Hollow

OZARK TRAIL

BOTTOMLAND TRAIL

Green Spring Branch

19

boat
ramp

Greer Crossing
Campground

Eleven Point River

© The Countryman Press

ELEVATION PROFILE

1,000 ft
880 ft
760 ft
640 ft Trailhead   Trailhead
520 ft
400 ft
        1   2   3   4   5   6   7 miles

will see an OZARK TRAIL sign, as it is a spur of the greater Ozark Trail. Trace the grassy path along the impoundment. You may see beaver activity on this impoundment, maybe even a lodge.

The lake is backed by a wooded ridge. Reach the lake dam. Here, the McCormack Greer Trail heads left up into woods, whereas anglers can continue across to the lake dam. Ascend past the noisy outflow of the dam, passing an overlook of the spillway. Cruise a wooded bluff line aiming for McCormack Hollow. Cedar, pine, maple, redbud, and dogwood shade the trail. Cross the wash of McCormack Hollow at 0.6 mile. Turn downstream along the gravel wash, looking for an old stone fence in the woods to your right. The gravelly track crosses the wash of Reader Hollow to intersect the official Ozark Trail at 1.1 miles, near the Eleven Point River. Head left, eastbound, on the Ozark Trail.

The Ozark Trail immediately climbs a hillside of mossy rock before turning away from the river, making a wide lope, and returning to the river, now on a high bluff. Open onto a rocky glade and reach the Boomhole Vista at 1.5 miles. Around 1900, when this area was being timbered, a giant wooden chute was located at the bluff to the southwest, across the

VIEW OF ELEVEN POINT RIVER VALLEY

Eleven Point River. Massive pine logs were rolled into the chute; from there they shot down into the river, making a tremendous boom, giving the area its name. Once on the river, the logs were floated to Mary Decker Shoal, where they were extricated from the water, loaded onto a train, and taken to the mill at Winona. Enjoy the views. Cedars hang on atop the craggy cliffs, while the open glade behind the view has grasses and black-eyed Susans in fall. A large flat extends downstream.

The trail continues downstream along the bluff, passing more views amid the pines and cedars before turning away from the river. Now the path makes a pleasant forest cruise in upland oak-hickory woods. Briefly join a woods track at 2.4 miles before reaching a stony sinkhole just to the left of the trail. In the middle of the sink, fallen blocks of stone have connected to form a very small rockfall arch. A natural arch is created through erosion of soil, whereas a rockfall arch, as the name implies, is created by rocks falling together to create a passageway beneath.

The trail opens into a rocky glade and a second major view—some argue that this one's superior to the Boomhole View—at 2.6 miles. Scramble around and enjoy the scenes in the Eleven Point Valley before dropping to Duncan Hollow. The trail now turns up heavily wooded Duncan Hollow, crossing its streambed before saddling alongside the Eleven Point River. Note the size of the river here; it'll soon increase with the inflow of Greer Spring, downstream, coming in on the far side.

Reach the loop portion of the hike at 2.9 miles. The Bottomland Trail keeps right along the Eleven Point. The official Ozark Trail, your return route, leaves left. Stay right with the River Trail.

Enter a wide bottomland, where sycamores are king, along with ash, pawpaw, river birch, and vines. Notice the contrast in the trailbed. Sand and soft dirt are easy on the feet as opposed to the stony hillsides. The heavily-forested flat extends far to the left, and to the light gap that is the Eleven Point River on your right. Before reaching MO 19, the trail splits. Stay right, toward the river, soon passing under the MO 19 bridge at 3.8 miles. (The left fork heads to MO 19.) Beyond the bridge, the main trail heads through a brushy area before emerging at the Greer Crossing Recreation Area, near the boater access, at a picnic area. A water spigot stands near the put-in if you are thirsty. Greer Crossing also has an auto-accessible fee campground.

To continue the hike, turn left onto the paved road leading into the picnic area, away from the river. You'll soon come to the gravel entrance road to the campground. Here, you will see the Ozark Trail entering the woods. Rejoin the foot trail, walking just a few feet before reaching a trail junction. The southbound portion of the Ozark Trail continues right, downstream on the Eleven Point River. You, however, leave left, continuing the loop on the northbound portion of the Ozark Trail leading uphill. Leave the foot-friendly bottomland to make a short but steep uptick, level out in cedars, and then return to reach MO 19. Turn right and walk along the road for a short distance before veering left, crossing the road to reenter woods, and ascending to step over an incised drainage. Continue along the slope to complete your loop at the junction you were at before, reaching it at 5.0 miles. Backtrack to McCormack Lake, enjoying more of those blufftop vistas along the Eleven Point River, completing your hike at 7.9 miles.

ANOTHER VIEW OF THE ELEVEN POINT RIVER VALLEY

38

Irish Wilderness Loop

TOTAL DISTANCE: 18.4-mile loop

HIKING TIME: 10 hours

VERTICAL RISE: 350 feet

RATING: Difficult

MAPS: USGS 7.5' Wilderness, Riverton; USDA Forest Service Irish Wilderness; Mark Twain National Forest—Doniphan, Eleven Point, Poplar Bluff Ranger Districts

TRAILHEAD GPS COORDINATES: N36° 45.940', W91° 8.127'

CONTACT INFORMATION: Mark Twain National Forest, #4 Confederate Ridge Road, Doniphan, MO 63935, (573) 996-2153, www.fs.usda.gov/mtnf

The Irish Wilderness, at 16,500 acres, is the largest federally designated wilderness in the Missouri Ozarks. Bordering the Eleven Point National Wild and Scenic River in the Mark Twain National Forest, the Irish is home to steeply cut creeks, springs, and bluffs, in addition to rich and remote hardwood forests. The Whites Creek Trail makes a large loop through the northern half, and is an excellent backpacking venue. The trail leaves from the Camp Five Pond trailhead, making its way west to cross Whites Creek and its tributaries before reaching Bliss Spring, near the Eleven Point River. From here, it traverses the bluffs of the Eleven Point, offering river vistas.

After reaching the mouth of Whites Creek, you'll turn away from the Eleven Point and pass Whites Cave, which is open to the public during the warm season. Beyond the cave, travel up the often dry bed of Whites Creek before climbing to upland hardwood forests typical of the Ozarks. Meander old logging roads on the final leg of this trek. Water is limited, but reliable springs make finding aqua a sure thing. This wilderness trail is lightly maintained, so expect to walk around or over fallen trees along your hike.

HOW TO GET THERE

From Alton, take US 160 east for 19.7 miles—passing the Riverton Access on the Eleven Point River along the way—to reach Highway J. Turn left and follow Highway J for 6.9 miles to the Irish Wilderness trailhead, on your left. A gravel road leads 0.1 mile to the parking area, which has picnic tables.

OLD CHIMNEY NEAR BLISS SPRING

THE HIKE

As you face Camp Five Pond from the parking area, the Whites Creek Trail starts to your left. Head through the trees toward the left side of the dam pond, crossing it. A second picnic area lies on the far side of the dam. Begin the trail here, entering Ozark upland hardwoods of oak and hickory on a narrow, rocky singletrack. The understory is generally light. The trail is marked with

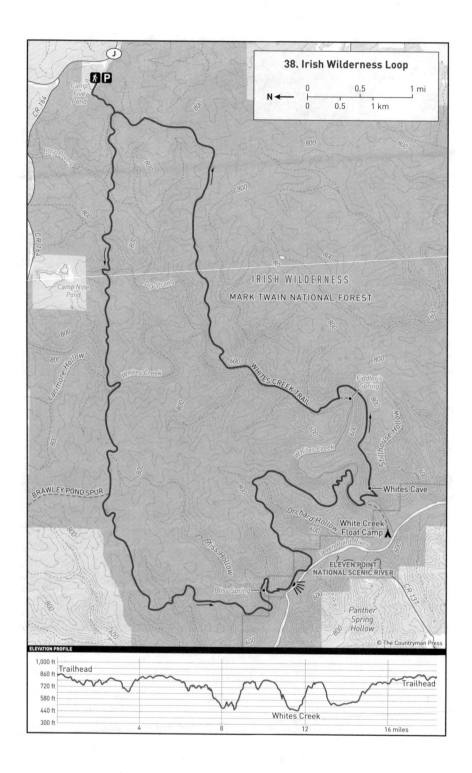

38. Irish Wilderness Loop

N ←

| 0 | | 0.5 | | 1 mi |
| 0 | 0.5 | | 1 km | |

CR 164

CR 164

Camp Five Pond

Dry Prong

800

800

800

800

Camp Nine Pond

Dry Prong

IRISH WILDERNESS

MARK TWAIN NATIONAL FOREST

800

800

800

800

600

Larimore Hollow

Whites Creek

800

800

800

WHITES CREEK TRAIL

600

Fiddler's Spring

800

Stillhouse Hollow

600

800

BRAWLEY POND SPUR

800

Whites Creek

600

Whites Cave

Orchard Hollow

White Creek Float Camp

800

Bliss Hollow

600

Eleven Point River

600

CR 137

Bliss Spring

ELEVEN POINT NATIONAL SCENIC RIVER

Panther Spring Hollow

600

800

600

© The Countryman Press

ELEVATION PROFILE

1,000 ft
860 ft
720 ft
580 ft
440 ft
300 ft

Trailhead

Trailhead

Whites Creek

4   8   12   16 miles

white diamond blazes. Slip into a drainage to reach the loop portion of the hike at 0.4 mile. Turn right, taking the north loop.

The trail shortly dips into Dry Prong, an aptly named feeder branch of Whites Creek. Typical of many Ozark streams, Dry Prong flows in winter and spring, or after heavy rains. Climb out of the drainage, only to dip past two unnamed feeder branches. At 2.9 miles, the trail makes a sharp left near an old farm pond, now filled with trees and vegetation. Cruise the uplands before meandering down to Larimore Hollow and not-likely-to-be-flowing Whites Creek at 3.6 miles.

The path makes its steepest climb yet on a rocky slope before resuming a westerly tack atop a piney plateau. At 4.2 miles, you'll draw near a water-filled pond about 50 yards off the trail. You may see a nearby fire ring—backpackers use this site. The trail shortly picks up old roadbed, traveling west to reach a junction at 4.8 miles. Here, a spur trail leads right 1.1 miles to the Brawley Pond trailhead. Keep forward on the old roadbed. The walking is easy as the trail angles to the southwest, meeting another old roadbed. Watch for rock piles and metal fencing, relics from pre-wilderness days. The Irish Wilderness got its name from a group of Irish settlers who migrated here from St. Louis in the 1860s. The Civil War broke out, and the area became lawless. Legend has it that a traveling salesman entered the Irish Wilderness selling pots, pans, needles, and dry goods. When he reached the settlement he found wagons, buildings, and other structures . . . but no living creatures, not even a horse or dog. The settlers may have been victims of violence or simply fled. The relics you see in this area likely came from settlers after the Irish group.

Continue on the ridgeline, aiming for the Eleven Point River. The path then turns south and dives into a hollow. Stay in sloped country before resuming level land, where shallow depressions mark sinkholes in the making. Drop yet again amid outcrops, cedars, and small glades. Listen for moving water. Meet lush woods full of pawpaw and cane and reach a trail junction at 8.1 miles. A spur trail leads right to the head of Bliss Spring, offering reliable water and a campsite. Straight ahead, a trail leads along the Bliss Spring outflow to shortly reach an old cabin chimney, another campsite, and the Eleven Point River. This is a very scenic area. To continue your hike, head left (south) on the Whites Creek Trail. The Eleven Point is audible below. The path climbs to reach a vista at 8.4 miles, where you can look down upon the river and the sloping countryside beyond. The vista on the Eleven Point might make you want to canoe the river. If so, call Eleven Point Canoe Rental at (417) 778-6497. They service trips of any length on this wild and scenic river.

The narrow track twists amid the scenic cedars, rock outcrops, and small flowery glades, which offer obscured river looks. Turn away from the river as the path works around Orchard Hollow, dipping into its head, where several rocky drainages come together. Reach tableland again after an uptick, now heading southwest along the far side of Orchard Hollow on an old roadbed plying a peninsula between the hollow and Whites Creek. This is the easiest hiking of the entire trek, sandwiched between two rugged stretches.

Drop off the peninsula to cross an interesting area where a gray boulder field stretches across the landscape, shaded by cedars. Gently curve into moist Whites Creek Valley. Look for the

HIKER PEERS INTO WHITES CAVE

sheer bluff across the streambed from the trail. Small fissures and mini caves pock the bluff. Sycamores grow amid the tan rocks of the streambed.

At 11.7 miles, you'll reach a trail junction. A spur trail leads right for 0.3 mile to White Creek Float Camp, which is most often used by boaters but also available to hikers. It has a fire grate, lantern post, and tent pad. The main trail continues forward, ascending by switchbacks to reach Whites Cave at 12.0 miles. This is the most used part of the trail, because boaters walk from the float camp to reach the cave. The cave is fronted by metal bars, but has a door. Don't worry about being tempted to get in—the door will be locked, as the cave is closed year-round to protect the endan-

gered Indiana cave bat. The trail continues climbing to reach ridgetop flats, joining an old logging track. The valley of Whites Creek is visible to your left.

The trail then curves into a rocky drainage, making its way into the deep woods of Whites Creek to reach a trail junction at 13.3 miles. A spur leads left 150 yards to Fiddler's Spring and a campsite. To continue this hike, work your way up Whites Creek Valley through thick woods with overgrown brush in the warm season. The trail becomes harder to follow due to the heavy growth, especially where it crosses rocky drainages of feeder branches and Whites Creek itself. These crossings could be wet in winter and spring. Even in the driest of times you'll find pools of stillwater. Sycamores and ironwood thrive in these bottoms.

At 14.6 miles, the trail leaves the valley, working into piney woods atop a ridge. It then joins another old roadbed and meanders along an easterly-running ridge, making only minor undulations in elevation. You will see scattered campsites and rock fire rings on ridgelines, where backpackers toted their water to the camp. Consider carrying your water from the springs to ridgeline camps for maximum solitude.

At 17.6 miles, the trail reaches another roadbed, where it turns abruptly and begins aiming for the trailhead. The old road is arrow straight. Gorgeous hardwood-and-pine forest borders the track. Begin descending the ridge to reach a trail junction, ending the loop portion of your hike. Turn right here and backtrack to the trailhead.

39

Big Spring Loop

TOTAL DISTANCE: 7.1-mile loop

HIKING TIME: 4 hours

VERTICAL RISE: 400 feet

RATING: Moderate to difficult

MAPS: USGS 7.5' Big Spring, Van Buren South; Big Spring Trails

TRAILHEAD GPS COORDINATES: N36° 57' 10.64", W90° 59' 35.21"

CONTACT INFORMATION: Ozark National Scenic Riverways, P.O. Box 490, 404 Watercress Drive, Van Buren, MO 63965, (573) 323-4236, www.nps.gov/ozar

This loop hike at Ozark National Scenic Riverways starts off with a splash as you visit truly big Big Spring, following its outflow along the gorgeous Current River. Suddenly, the loop turns away from the water and climbs to the historic Big Spring Lookout Tower. Next, loop through hardwood-draped ridges before turning back toward the Current River, deep in the backwoods. Consider adding other activities such as camping, paddling or picnicking while at this large recreation area, complemented by the historic overlay of Civilian Conservation Corps (CCC) buildings.

HOW TO GET THERE

From Van Buren, MO, take US 60 west 0.5 mile across the Current River, then turn left on MO 103 south. Follow MO 103 south for 3.8 miles, then cross the outlet of Big Spring before turning left at the sign for Big Spring picnic pavilion. The hike starts at the trail kiosk just beyond the picnic pavilion.

THE HIKE

This hike shows many facets of the Big Spring area along the Current River, just a few miles outside of Van Buren, Missouri. Big Spring is not only the largest spring in the Ozarks, but one of the largest in the United States, emitting an average of 470 cubic feet of water per second—that's 286 million gallons of water per day! The overall beauty of the area was first recognized as a Missouri state park in 1924, and the spot was later developed by the Civilian Conservation Corps (CCC) in the 1930s. Rustic wood and stone structures from that era enhance the natural beauty of

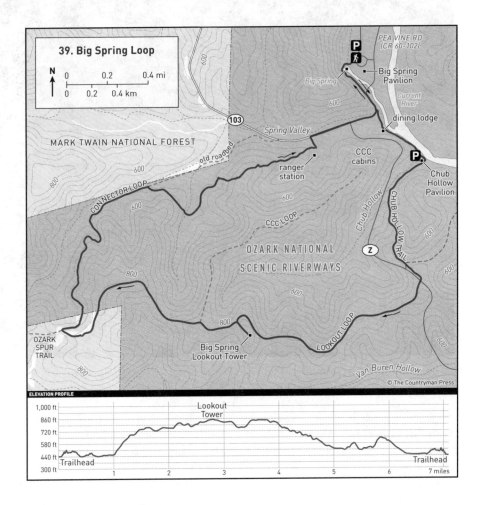

39. Big Spring Loop

N

0	0.2		0.4 mi
0	0.2	0.4 km	

PEA VINE RD
(CR 60-102)

Big Spring
Pavilion

Big Spring

Current
River

600

dining lodge

103

Spring Valley

MARK TWAIN NATIONAL FOREST

600

old roadbed

ranger
station

CCC
cabins

Chub
Hollow
Pavilion

800

CONNECTOR LOOP

600

600

CCC LOOP

Chub Hollow

CHUB HOLLOW TRAIL

600

OZARK NATIONAL
SCENIC RIVERWAYS

Z

400

800

600

LOOKOUT LOOP

600

OZARK
SPUR
TRAIL

800

Big Spring
Lookout Tower

Van Buren Hollow

© The Countryman Press

ELEVATION PROFILE

	Lookout Tower	
1,000 ft		
860 ft		
720 ft		
580 ft		
440 ft	Trailhead	Trailhead
300 ft		
	1　2　3　4　5　6　7 miles	

the locale. In 1969, the state park was donated to the Feds, becoming part of the national riverway.

Start near the Big Spring Pavilion, then follow the flagstone path to circle behind the large, crystalline-blue pool of Big Spring. The hike then leads to the spring emergence. Here, Big Spring gushes forth from a rock bluff, an immediate watercourse, then flows a quarter-mile to where it melds with the Current River. The hike follows the outflow, crossing MO 103 at 0.4 mile, on a curve. Continue along the Big Spring outflow, passing a paddler's access to

your left and the historic CCC-built dining hall on your right.

Ahead, saddle alongside the swiftly flowing Current River. Enjoy views of the protected waterway, just below the inflow of Big Spring. By the way, Big Spring is the second-largest tributary of the entire Current River. Reach an alternate parking area at 0.7 mile. Just ahead, bridge a stream, then find the Chub Hollow Pavilion off to your right. Turn right here, passing the pavilion, and join the Chub Hollow Trail (a user-created trail continues along the Current River, but soon dead ends at private property). The

BIG SPRING SWIRLS FROM ITS SOURCE

singletrack, packed-gravel Chub Hollow Trail climbs away from the river in hickories, pines, and oaks after bridging a stream valley.

At 1.4 miles, cross a gravel road, then climb to cross paved Highway Z at 1.5 miles. Keep straight, passing around a pole gate, now tracing a doubletrack trail through oak-heavy woods, prototypical Ozark forest. Undulate along the ridgeline, reaching a trail intersection at 2.6 miles. Here, turn left and climb the final part to the historic Big Spring Lookout Tower, erected in 1939. It once housed men who scanned the skies for conflagrations, but was eventually abandoned. Efforts are underway to restore the structure. Hopefully, upon your arrival it will be refurbished and you can gain the views the fire watchers once had. For now, the summit alone is a worthy goal.

From the tower, backtrack, then continue the circuit hike, making another intersection at 3.0 miles. Here, stay left with the Connector Loop. A right turn leads you down the CCC Loop to the Big Spring cabins. The Connector Loop makes an easy track atop a forested ridgeline, heading westerly to enter the Mark Twain National Forest, identified with a sign, at 3.7 miles.

Descend off the ridge, then come to another intersection at 4.0 miles. Here, the Ozark Trail heads left, but our loop heads right, northeasterly, soon reentering Ozark National Scenic Riverways domain. Work down into a hollow, and the path becomes doubletrack. At 5.1 miles, the path suddenly turns right, off the doubletrack and away from the hollow, surprisingly working along a slope. This signed turn is easy to miss. The unmaintained doubletrack keeps

HIKER WATCHES BIG SPRING BOIL FORTH FROM ITS SOURCE

straight for MO 103, while the official but sometimes faint trail works along a rocky side slope, cutting across a gravelly hollow. Watch closely for trail signs nailed to trees and rock cairns. Keep easterly to emerge onto a park road at 6.2 miles. Here, a ranger station and park maintenance area stands to your right. Our hike heads left on the gravel road, then reaches MO 103 at 6.3 miles. Here, turn right and follow paved MO 103 toward Big Spring, passing the road intersection with Highway Z at 6.4 miles. Keep straight on MO 103 and

come to the outflow of Big Spring and head left, back onto the foot trail, circling around Big Spring one last time. Return to the parking area and complete the circuit at 7.1 miles.

While here, consider camping at Big Spring. The attractive campground, with electric and nonelectric sites, is but a short distance from the trailhead. Or stay at one of the restored CCC cabins. Picnic areas abound. Paddling the Current River is a sure winner. Outfitters operate in nearby Van Buren, providing canoes, kayaks, and shuttles.

Deer Run Loop at Onondaga Cave State Park

TOTAL DISTANCE: 2.5-mile loop

HIKING TIME: 1 hour, 40 minutes

VERTICAL RISE: 230 feet

RATING: Moderate

MAPS: USGS 7.5' Onondaga Cave; Deer Run Trail

TRAILHEAD GPS COORDINATES: N38° 3.413', W91° 14.094'

CONTACT INFORMATION: Onondaga State Park, 7556 Highway H, Leasburg, MO 65535, (573) 245-6576, www.mostateparks .com

This hike explores some of the aboveground features of Onondaga Cave State Park. You'll leave the campground on the Deer Run Loop to enter lush woods, passing a closed entrance of Cathedral Cave, one of two caves here open for tours. The trail surmounts a ridge, passing through grassy glades while heading for the Meramec River, where more blufftop glades offer inspiring vistas that are a fine hiker's reward. Overall, the hike is a great leg stretcher that will complement a ranger-led tour of Onondaga Cave or Cathedral Cave.

If you're still looking for exercise afterward, try 3-mile-long Oak Ridge Trail, which starts down the hill within sight of this trailhead and makes a loop. Speaking of the campground, it adds another activity that can be enjoyed at this state park, in addition to paddling and fishing the Meramec River. One more thing: The tours of Onondaga and Cathedral caves should not be bypassed. After all, these caves are the focal point of this fine recreation destination easily accessible from the Greater St. Louis area. Onondaga Cave is famed for its water-created formations, such as columns, stalactites, and stalagmites, with named features like King's Canopy and the Twins. Onondaga Cave is special enough to be a registered National Natural Landmark.

HOW TO GET THERE

From Exit 214 off I-44, Leesburg, take County Road H (CR H) south for 7 miles to the Onondaga State Park Visitor Center. Continue beyond the center, bearing right at the sign for the campground. Reach the campground and keep forward to park near the shower house. The Deer Run Trail starts nearby on a wide gravel track.

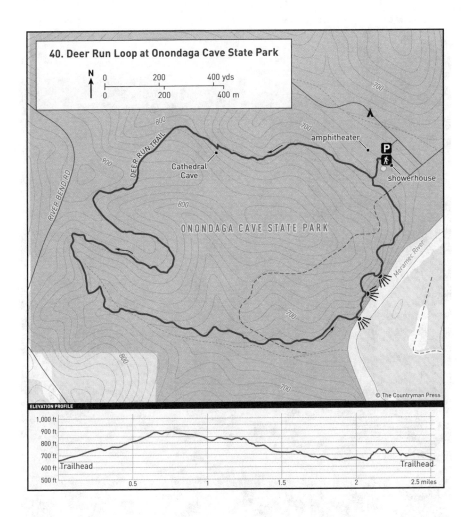

40. Deer Run Loop at Onondaga Cave State Park

N
0   200   400 yds
0   200   400 m

amphitheater

showerhouse

Cathedral
Cave

DEER RUN TRAIL

RIVER BEND RD

ONONDAGA CAVE STATE PARK

Meramec River

© The Countryman Press

ELEVATION PROFILE

1,000 ft
900 ft
800 ft
700 ft
600 ft   Trailhead   Trailhead
500 ft
            0.5   1   1.5   2   2.5 miles

THE HIKE

Walk just a short distance toward the park amphitheater then bear left, following the hiker symbol. You'll soon enter lush forest and reach a junction. Stay right; the other way is your return route. Oaks dominate the landscape, with an understory of maple, sassafras, and dogwood as well as emergent boulders on a steep hillside. The gravel track takes you through the woods, curving in and out of gentle hollows. At 0.4 mile, you'll reach Cathedral Cave. The entrance has a concrete cover over it, and the door is

quadruple bolted to prevent break-ins. Lantern tours of Cathedral Cave are offered on weekends, however, and last about two hours. Check with the visitor center.

Cathedral Cave is 15,639 feet long. It was threatened in the 1970s by a proposed Meramec Park Lake project that would have flooded portions of both Onondaga and Cathedral caves, but the proposal was defeated in a regional referendum, and Onondaga became part of the state park system in 1981. Part of the official management policy for the cave now forbids unsupervised trips. Cav-

VIEW OF MERAMEC RIVER FROM HIGH BLUFF

ers and citizens have been working for many years to restore Cathedral Cave by removing construction debris, concrete, and wire from its days as a private tourist attraction. The aim is to return it to the most natural appearance possible.

The trail levels off, passing an old roadbed. Reach the top of a ridgeline and the now closed old Riverbend Road, which runs along the ridgeline. The trail begins to curve around a steeply cut valley. The walking stays nearly level

VIEW OF MERAMEC RIVER FROM BLUFF NEAR TRAIL

here. Enter some grassy glades. These were once overgrown, but the park has restored them by cutting and then letting fire do the rest of the work. Glades such as these need fire to be kept open, otherwise cedars will creep in. Pick up a bluff line as you travel in and out of glades. Notice how thin and gravelly the soil is here.

Leave the bluffs area and continue rambling through woods, enjoying a gorgeous forest cruise. Enter a dry streambed and begin working your way down this lush hollow, which will have wildflowers galore in spring. Cross back over to the left-hand side of the tributary. Now climb or stay level as the hollow you just crossed continues descending toward the Meramec River. At 1.6 miles, a wooden span takes you over a normally dry streambed. Continue aiming for the Meramec, curving into its valley, which drops off to your right. The trail opens onto grassy glades overlooking the waterway. Ascend along a bluff line, gaining great views up and down the river.

Keep descending to enjoy more good looks on the Meramec. The trail turns away from the sheer bluff line and curves around moderate slopes. Return to the cliff line to enjoy more views, then circle away from it again to reach a third vista point. Turn away from the cliffs, this time for good. Enter another hollow with a wooden bridge. A spur trail leads right for small cave. The campground comes into sight and a trail splits off right—some people are cutting from the campground to the bluffs. However, the full loops stay left, crossing a gravel maintenance road before returning to the loop portion of the hike. Backtrack just a few feet to the trailhead.

Council Bluff Loop

TOTAL DISTANCE: 11.7-mile loop

HIKING TIME: 7 hours

VERTICAL RISE: 200 feet

RATING: Moderate to difficult

MAPS: USGS 7.5' Johnson Mountain; Council Bluff Trail; Mark Twain National Forest—Salem, Potosi, and Fredericktown Ranger Districts

TRAILHEAD GPS COORDINATES: N37° 43.861', W90° 55.843'

CONTACT INFORMATION: Mark Twain National Forest, P.O. Box 188, 10019 West State Highway 8, Potosi, MO 63664, (573) 438-5427, www.fs.usda.gov/mtnf

The waters of Council Bluff Lake, within the confines of Mark Twain National Forest, are alluringly clear. Its shoreline rises in hills away from the impoundment. This loop makes for a long but doable day hike or an overnight trip, great for novice backpackers. Offering varied terrain, it's not too steep, and there are escape routes if you need them. The lake also makes for an ideal destination in fall, when you can see the season's colors blazing and reflecting off the shoreline; in spring bright greens color the forest. The parking area has restrooms and a fine picnic area, as well as several secluded woodland tables with grills. The greater recreation area also has a large and underutilized campground, swim beach, and boat ramp.

HOW TO GET THERE

From the junction of MO 8 and Highway P in Potosi, take Highway P south for 14.4 miles to reach Highway C. Turn right and follow Highway C for 0.2 mile, then turn left onto Highway DD. After 7 miles, turn left into Council Bluff Recreation Area. Bear left toward the Wild Boar Hollow boat ramp. Drive 0.4 mile farther, then bear right to the boat ramp, for a total of 1.3 miles beyond the recreation area entrance. There is a parking fee.

THE HIKE

As you face the lake from the Wild Boar Hollow boat launch, head left, immediately crossing a wooden bridge. The Council Bluff Trail is marked with metal blazes. Enter the picnic area to cross another wooden bridge; you begin to enjoy the first of many, many, many lake views. Continue along the Wild Boar Hollow arm of the lake. The undulations are moderate but consistent as the sin-

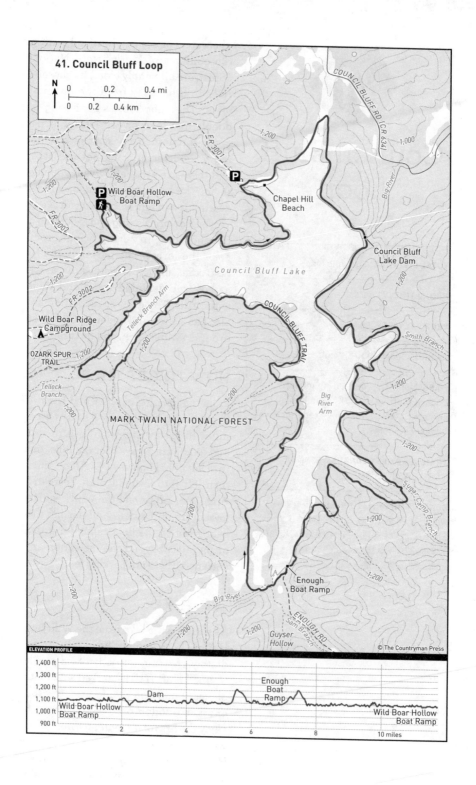

41. Council Bluff Loop

N
0   0.2   0.4 mi
0   0.2   0.4 km

FR 3001

1,200

1,200

1,000

COUNCIL BLUFF RD. (CR 634)

Big River

P

P Wild Boar Hollow
Boat Ramp

FR 3002

1,200

1,200

1,200

Chapel Hill
Beach

Council Bluff
Lake Dam

1,200

Council Bluff Lake

COUNCIL BLUFF TRAIL

Telleck Branch Arm

Wild Boar Ridge
Campground

OZARK SPUR
TRAIL

Telleck
Branch

1,200

1,200

Smith Branch

1,200

MARK TWAIN NATIONAL FOREST

1,200

Big
River
Arm

Sugar Camp Branch

1,200

1,200

1,200

Enough
Boat Ramp

ENOUGH RD

Sam Branch

Big River

1,200

1,200

Guyser
Hollow

© The Countryman Press

ELEVATION PROFILE

1,400 ft
1,300 ft
1,200 ft   Enough
1,100 ft   Dam   Boat
1,000 ft   Wild Boar Hollow   Ramp
900 ft   Boat Ramp

Wild Boar Hollow
Boat Ramp

2   4   6   8   10 miles

JOHNSON MOUNTAIN RISES FORTH FROM COUNCIL BLUFF LAKE

gletrack path rolls over piney rib ridges emanating from the mountainside in a mixed pine-oak-hickory forest. It stays near the lakeshore at all times, curving away only when steeply cut hollows force it from the lake into the hollow and back around to the shoreline.

Most of the streambeds that you curve in and out of will be dry, except after a rain or in winter. Johnson Mountain rises to the east and adds to the lake scenery. At 0.9 mile, the trail passes through an interesting boulder field mixed with cedars. Hundreds of rocks jut from the soil. The lake dam comes into view just beyond the boulder field, but it will be awhile before you actually walk on it.

Curve over low hills and around a deep embayment toward Chapel Hill swim beach, reaching the beach access road at 1.4 miles. Turn right here, following the access road. The swim beach also has a picnic area and camp store in-season. You can either walk along a paved track by the beach or cut over the picnic area hill; either way, you'll end up on a wide gravel track with the lake directly to your right. Follow the track through grassy fields, then turn off it to your right to cross the dam overflow area.

Reenter woods, resuming your circuit of Council Bluff Lake, traveling through planted pines. Continue undulating along the lakeshore, looking at where you just walked—the swim beach and the fields beyond. That's the beauty

SPIDERWORT AFTER A RAIN

of this hike: You can see where you're going and where you've been. When the shoreline slopes steeply, the trail rises well above the lake. At 2.7 miles, cross the dam. A stellar view of Johnson Mountain opens to your left.

The elevational undulations continue in young rocky woods, but are never steep or troublesome. At 3.2 miles you'll cross an old roadbed, traveling directly into the water. Obviously this was a road before the lake was a lake! Just beyond, the loop trail enters an interesting field of lichen-covered boulders. You're entering Big River Arm—the largest arm of the lake. It has many arms of its own, where standing dead tree snags add a scenic component to Council Bluff. The path stays level through these relatively flat woods.

Cross the drainage of this first embayment of the Big River area at 3.8 miles. Return to the Big River Arm on more sharply sloped land amid thick cedars. At 4.7 miles, the trail has joined an oak-lined roadbed that curves into yet another embayment of this arm. Watch for musclewood and sugar maple trees growing deep in the hollows here. Cross the tributary, then make your biggest climb of the loop. The trail now extends out onto a ridgeline. Slowly descend the nose of the ridge to rejoin the lakeshore. Surprise—curve into another embayment of the Big River Arm. Finally you rejoin the lakeshore, getting your best views in a long time, especially fields across the water.

At 6.6 miles, you'll reach Enough Boat Ramp, which has a gravel launch and shaded picnic tables. Continue across the parking area and rejoin the hiking trail just beyond some posts. The walking is quite easy on a level track here in lower Guyser Hollow. Span the Big River on a wooden footbridge, then turn left, upstream. The singletrack path is overlaid on a partly canopied old farm road bordered with oaks and cedars. Large fields extend beyond. Enter Enough Savanna and the Enough Wildlife Habitat Improvement Project. The wider, straighter path stays well away from the lakeshore, which is temporarily out of sight.

Leave the roadbed at 7.6 miles, once again on a singletrack. Undulate through steep hills, only to rejoin the old forest road. The trail stays on the lakeshore, now in a gravelly, shallow-soiled oak forest. The trail again joins the old forest road, which has emerged from the lake. The dam comes into view through the trees to your right as you leave the Big River Arm at 8.7 miles. Also look for the Wild Boar Hollow boat ramp to your left, west. But you still have a good way to go before reaching it.

Begin working toward the Telleck Branch Arm of the lake. Enter the campable bottomland of this last embayment, circling the watersheds that feed it in a mix of field and wood. Cross the Telleck Branch on a wooden footbridge at 10.3 miles. A spur trail leads left 0.5 mile to the Ozark Trail. To complete this loop, however, turn right to stay on the Council Bluff Trail, making your way downstream on a steeply sloped hill to rejoin the lakeshore. Enjoy some last views of Johnson Mountain from the point before curving into Wild Boar Hollow. Pass two spur trails leading left, uphill, to the recreation area campground. Soon you'll open onto the parking area, ending your hike.

42

Bell Mountain Wilderness Loop

TOTAL DISTANCE: 12.2-mile loop	
HIKING TIME: 7 hours, 30 minutes	
VERTICAL RISE: 700 feet	
RATING: Difficult	
MAPS: USGS 7.5′ Edgehill, Johnson Mountain, Banner, Johnson Shut-Ins; Bell Mountain Wilderness and Trail, Ozark Trail—Trace Creek 3 Miles 19 to 26, Mark Twain National Forest—Salem, Potosi, and Fredericktown Ranger Districts	
TRAILHEAD GPS COORDINATES: N37° 37.546′, W90° 54.661′	
CONTACT INFORMATION: Mark Twain National Forest, 10019 West State Highway 8, Potosi, MO 63664, (573) 438-5427, www.fs.usda.gov/mtnf	

This is a challenging loop within the confines of the Bell Mountain Wilderness. Leave the trailhead on the Ozark Trail (OT), climbing the west slope of Bell Mountain to shortly gain views from rock outcrops and grassy glades. Leave the OT, joining the Bell Mountain Trail, only to descend into Joes Creek. Ply the hollows here before climbing to the high point of Bell Mountain; easterly and westerly views open among the rocks and stunted trees. The loop then works westerly along Bell Mountain, and backtracks to the lowlands along Ottery Creek. The trail is well marked and maintained, unlike many designated wilderness routes in Missouri.

HOW TO GET THERE

From Potosi, take MO 21 south to MO 32. Turn right and follow MO 32 westerly for 7.5 miles to Highway A. Turn left onto Highway A and head south, ignoring the left turn for the north Bell Mountain Wilderness trailhead at 0.5 mile (this hike starts at the west trailhead). Continue down Highway A for a total of 5.5 miles; the west trailhead is on your right.

THE HIKE

Leave the trailhead, heading north, the way you drove in. Ottery Creek flows to your left. Open onto the grass and cross Highway A, joining the Ozark Trail. The singletrack path travels uphill on a narrow, rocky tread through a mixed forest of dogwood, oak, maple, redbud, and a few cedar trees. The rocks have a red hue due to their iron content. After all, this is Iron County, Missouri. Up, up, up the trail travels, to shortly enter the wilderness boundary, still angling up the mountainside. The OT begins cruising among very

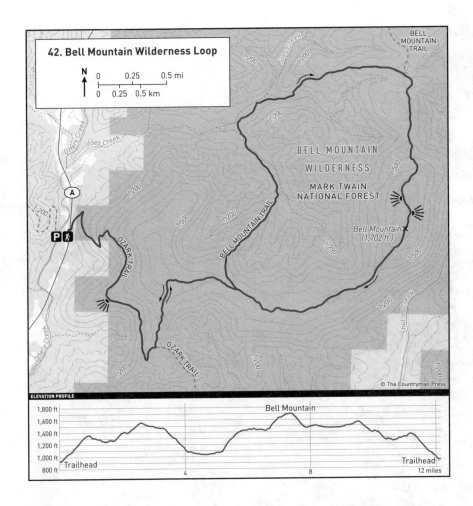

42. Bell Mountain Wilderness Loop

N

| 0 | 0.25 | 0.5 mi |
| 0 | 0.25 | 0.5 km |

BELL MOUNTAIN WILDERNESS

MARK TWAIN NATIONAL FOREST

Bell Mountain ✕ (1,702 ft.)

BELL MOUNTAIN TRAIL

OZARK TRAIL

OZARK TRAIL

BELL MOUNTAIN TRAIL

Joes Creek

Ottery Creek

Shut-in Creek

© The Countryman Press

ELEVATION PROFILE

Bell Mountain

Trailhead

Trailhead

| 1,800 ft | 1,600 ft | 1,400 ft | 1,200 ft | 1,000 ft | 800 ft |

4   8   12 miles

large boulders embedded in the soil and shortly makes a switchback—the first of several—ascending the west side of Bell Mountain. Outcrops here are quite gorgeous and colorful with the pinkish red rock, emerald moss, and lime-colored lichens. Begin getting looks across the valley as you gain elevation. The sounds of Ottery Creek fade below.

Continue up among all these boulders, some of which become so thick that they've prevented trees from taking root—these rocky glades are more rock than glade. At 0.6 mile, vistas open of the mountains on the far side of

Ottery Creek. Leave the view and continue angling up the mountain, again in woods, to join a bluff line heading west where more views open to your right. The rocky track levels out here, amid an increase in pines. Portions of this level track may be muddy. Continue passing more outcrops and more views.

At 1.3 miles, you'll reach an extensive rocky glade bordered by a big rock outcrop to your right. Views open to the southeast. Resume angling up the mountainside, passing through more boulder glades to top out on the ridgeline of Bell Mountain at 2.1 miles. Leave

VIEW FROM ATOP BELL MOUNTAIN

ANOTHER VIEW FROM ATOP BELL MOUNTAIN

the OT left and join Bell Mountain Trail. Dip to a saddle, then rise to a knob of Bell Mountain. Once you get atop this first knob, curve right, easterly. You are now descending through forest. Keep east in a semi-stunted woods with little grassy clearings.

At 3.2 miles, you'll reach another trail junction and the loop portion of this hike. Turn acutely left here, tracing what is obviously an old roadbed. Join the nose of a ridge, gaining views to the north of the Joes Creek Valley where you're heading. Steadily descend a hollow, crossing a tributary coming in on your left. Walk alongside a feeder branch of Joes Creek, crossing over to its right-hand bank at 4.5 miles. Keep downhill, entering a flat field transforming to forest. Just ahead, turn right up the Joes Creek Valley. A faint trail continues downstream—but don't take it. Continue up the valley, looking for rock piles, and

then come alongside Joes Creek at an old rock fence from pre-national-forest days. Cross over the left-hand bank at 5.2 miles. Continue in the flat for just a short distance, leaving to ascend a piney ridge. Climb moderately as maple-oak woods replace the pines. The ridgeline you have joined is level in spots. Trees crowd the trail.

At 6.2 miles, meet the Bell Mountain Trail once again. Turn right here, as the other way heads toward the northern Bell Mountain Wilderness trailhead. Make a mostly level track in oak woods, traveling south. Work up the ridgecrest of Bell Mountain, seeking its highest point. Pass an old stock pond just before coming to the rocky crest of the mountain. The trail slips to right of the crest; you can easily scramble among the boulders here to the top.

Reach a grand westerly trailside view at 7.3 miles, from a rocky area inter-

Elephant Rocks State Park Loop

TOTAL DISTANCE: 1.1-mile loop	

HIKING TIME: 1 hour

VERTICAL RISE: 80 feet

RATING: Easy

MAPS: USGS 7.5' Graniteville; Braille Trail

TRAILHEAD GPS COORDINATES: N37° 39.182', W90° 41.336'

CONTACT INFORMATION: Elephant Rocks State Park, 7406 Highway 21, Belleview, MO, (573) 546-3454, www.mostateparks .com

The Elephant Rocks are among the most unusual rock formations in the Ozarks—and that's saying a lot. This geological wonder is situated in the scenic Arcadia Valley, and the state park here offers an excellent interpretive trail. You'll learn the history of this granite, prized for building construction and known worldwide as "Missouri Red" for its excellent quality and reddish tint. Here in the St. Francois Mountains, not only can you walk among these giants and learn a few things, you can also have fun, as thousands before you have, scrambling over the formations beyond the trail system. And while you're up there, you will enjoy views of the surrounding countryside.

HOW TO GET THERE

From the junction of MO 21 and MO 72 in Ironton, take MO 21 north for 6.3 miles to the entrance of Elephant Rocks State Park, on your right.

THE HIKE

The hiking loop at Elephant Rocks State Park is known as the Braille Trail. Interestingly, this trail has Braille interpretive signage for the blind, as well as strategically placed carpeting and ropes alongside parts of the trail to aid blind hikers. The parking area offers picnic tables and restrooms. Water fountains and circular stone resting benches are salted along the trail. A shaded information kiosk offers your first glimpse into the Elephant Rocks, detailing the quarry beginning just after the Civil War, the mining techniques of the past, and how the area eventually became a state park thanks to a previous owner by the name of . . . well, you can learn all about how this park came to be when you get here.

Leave the trailhead on a paved

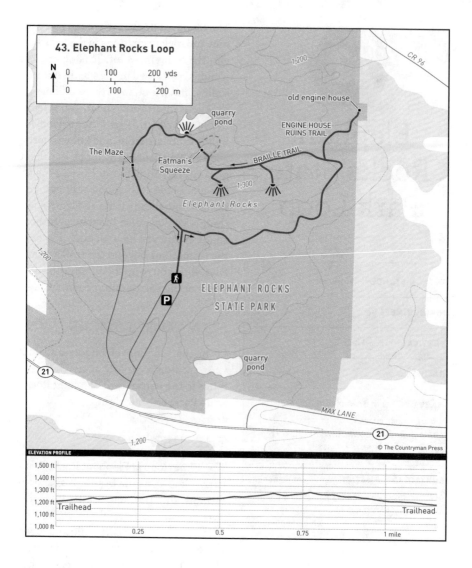

43. Elephant Rocks Loop

N

| 0 | 100 | 200 yds |
| 0 | 100 | 200 m |

CR 96

1:200

old engine house

ENGINE HOUSE
RUINS TRAIL

quarry
pond

BRAILLE TRAIL

The Maze

Fatman's
Squeeze

1:300

Elephant Rocks

1:200

ELEPHANT ROCKS

STATE PARK

quarry
pond

21

MAX LANE

21

1:200

© The Countryman Press

ELEVATION PROFILE

| 1,500 ft |
| 1,400 ft |
| 1,300 ft |
| 1,200 ft | Trailhead | | | | Trailhead |
| 1,100 ft |
| 1,000 ft |

0.25   0.5   0.75   1 mile

path and soon reach the loop portion of the trail. Turn right amid volcanic rocks in every shape and size. This stone was volcanic molten magma that cooled and was later covered by a shallow sea, only to lift up and rise forth, become exposed to the elements, and then weather into the formations visible today. It really is amazing to see the effects of earth's long existence on display. Boulders border the track, and

trees grow where they can gain purchase in the shallow soil.

The Braille Trail twists and turns among lichen-covered boulders. These small plants—the lichens—slowly break down these rocks over time. Already, you can see spur paths leading to the rock formations, made by rock scramblers who couldn't wait to start climbing. By the way, climbing equipment, such as ropes, is not allowed in the state park.

Stop and enjoy the interpretive information offered at periodic stops. As a hiker of too many treks to count, I consider this trail among the best anywhere at interpretation. The methods of presenting the information to the blind are also intriguing. Curve around the main rock upthrust to reach the side trail leading right to the old engine house. Follow the crushed-granite track to a beautiful roofless relic of marble; this spot once housed engine repair areas for the railroad that shipped the quarry's stone all over the United States. Many structures in St. Louis feature this granite, most notably the piers on the famed Eads Bridge, a span completed in 1874 that connects St. Louis, Missouri to East St. Louis, Illinois, across the Mississippi River. Granite not up to snuff for construction purposes was made into paving stones for the streets of St. Louis. And it all started here, at the quarry's shipping yard. Look for the old railroad tracks in the buildings heading off into what is now woodland.

Return to the Braille Trail and pass broken rock jumbles that were once underground and only brought to the surface as the granite was quarried. Reach a spur trail leading left to a scenic overlook. Take this path to stone promontory that offers a view across the valley. To your right, a mass of exposed rock lures other rock scramblers and leads to the actual Elephant Rocks themselves, but you must use all fours to get there. If you aren't adept at scrambling, you can backtrack to the main trail, which reaches the same destination but requires only two limbs.

The Braille Trail continues a short

VIEW OF THE ELEPHANT ROCKS

LOOKING ON THE QUARRY POND

distance farther, reaching the afore-mentioned spur trail leading left to the Elephant Rocks. Climb just a bit and open onto a wide rock slab topped by what resembles—if you use your imagination—a circus train of elephants. This geological wonder is great for exploring and also offers good views. By this point you will notice the names, mostly neatly carved, of the men who worked at the quarry, which was in operation from the 1860s to the 1940s. The largest of the Elephant Rocks is known as Dumbo; at 27 feet high, 35 feet long, and 17 feet wide, it makes for one big elephant. And it weighs in at 680 tons! Notice the small depressions up here. Pools of water form after rains, and vegetation grows in them. This vegetation, like the lichens noted above, is breaking the granite down, but at such a slow pace we can hardly see any effect in the span of our lifetimes.

Return to the Braille Trail and reach another highlight—Fatman's Squeeze. An alternative wheelchair-accessible trail bypasses this narrow, crevice-like passage between parallel boulders. The squeeze extends upward of 100 feet. Next, come to a water-filled quarry. The marble-bordered pond now harbors aquatic life and is a nice addition to the stony landscape. "The Maze" may be the trail's only disappointment. The path winds among rocks but really isn't mazelike at all—maybe the trail builders got carried away in their enthusiasm for this 131-acre state park that needs no artificial enhancement. A wheelchair-accessible path circles the Maze.

Circle back a little more and complete the loop at 1.1 miles. You may want to make another round, or abandon the trail altogether and explore previously unseen parts of the unique Elephant Rocks.

Missouri High Point Loop at Taum Sauk Mountain

TOTAL DISTANCE: 3.0-mile loop

HIKING TIME: 2 hours

VERTICAL RISE: 375 feet

RATING: Moderate to difficult

MAPS: USGS 7.5' Ironton; Mina Sauk Falls Trail

TRAILHEAD GPS COORDINATES: N37° 34.383', W90° 43.651'

CONTACT INFORMATION: Taum Sauk Mountain State Park, Highway CC, Ironton, MO 63656, (573) 546-2450, www .mostateparks.com

This is a hike of superlative caliber. Leave the trailhead at Taum Sauk Mountain State Park, and take a walk to Missouri's high point, Taum Sauk Mountain, visiting the granite marker on the wooded high point. Then take a hike. Cruise the tableland of the mountain crest before dropping off the mountainside to travel over rocky treeless glades that allow far-reaching views beyond the Taum Sauk Creek Valley. Drop to a low point to meet the Ozark Trail and check out Mina Sauk Falls—the highest waterfall in Missouri—tumbling over an open ledge that not only offers watery vistas but also features a backdrop of breathtaking mountain scenes. What goes down, of course, must sometimes come up; thus, the Ozark Trail ascends along the stream forming the falls, continues up more bouldery glades with still more views, and then enters woodland and returns to the tableland of Taum Sauk Mountain.

HOW TO GET THERE

From the junction of MO 21 and MO 72 in Ironton, take MO 21 south for 4.6 miles to reach Highway CC. Turn right and follow Highway CC for 2.9 miles. The road turns to gravel here. Continue forward, passing the park campground on your left and a developed overlook on your right to reach the trailhead at a dead end 1 mile beyond the road's switch to gravel.

THE HIKE

The Mina Sauk Falls Trail leaves the parking area as a concrete path entering the woods. To your right are restrooms and an information board. You will be surprised at the nearly level nature of the path, since it's going to a high point.

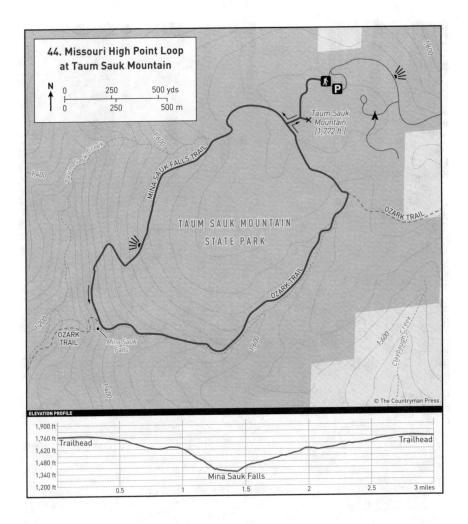

44. Missouri High Point Loop at Taum Sauk Mountain

Taum Sauk Mountain State Park

Taum Sauk Mountain (1,772 ft.)

OZARK TRAIL

MINA SAUK FALLS TRAIL

Taum Sauk Creek

OZARK TRAIL

Mina Sauk Falls

Claybaugh Creek

© The Countryman Press

ELEVATION PROFILE

Trailhead

Mina Sauk Falls

Trailhead

Classic Ozark hickory-oak woods cover the plateau-like crest of Taum Sauk Mountain. Maples have a fair representation as well. Wind through the highland woods to reach a trail junction. The actual hike leaves right, but first you must follow the concrete path a few feet to your left to reach Missouri's highest point. The height differential on this crest of the mountain is nearly imperceptible, but a certain boulder rises just a bit higher and is thus the spot. A "Missouri Red" marble monument marks the point, officially 1,772 feet in elevation.

After pictures have been taken, backtrack to the last trail junction and take off on the hike.

The trail changes from gravel to natural surface, and you soon reach the actual loop of the hike. Turn right, taking the Mina Sauk Falls Trail, cruising a dirt-and-rock track with roots. Begin drifting off the crest of the mountain just above the headwaters of Taum Sauk Creek, passing through the first of many boulder glades at 0.5 mile. Soon pass another. Views open to west and southwest, but hang on as you reach the

INSCRIBED GRANITE SLAB MARKS MISSOURI'S HIGH POINT

third glade at 0.9 mile. This glade goes on and on; you walk its margin. A few scattered hickories and sumacs grow in the shallow soil and provide a scenic contrast with the open glades, habitats that host the striped scorpion, among other unique species. Striped scorpions hang out in damp, cool areas, like under rocks. These 2.5-inch critters use their pincers to grasp and crush spiders, crickets, and flies. Then they swing their tail around, sting their victims, and eat

VIEWS OPEN FROM ROCKY GLADES ON TAUM SAUK MOUNTAIN

them. Don't worry about getting bitten yourself, however, as the scorpion comes out only at night to feed. Interestingly, their outer shell shines under fluorescent light, which is how biologists observe them at night.

The view from this rocky glade opens into the Taum Sauk Creek Valley below. In the background Wildcat Mountain lies to your right, Proffitt Mountain is in the distance, and Church Mountain is to the left. This is one spectacular view. Begin dropping off the boulder field, entering mixed woods and boulder glades. The going is quite slow—the trail is excessively rocky here. But with scenery like this, what's the hurry? The trail becomes even more rocky and bouldery, if that's possible, just before reaching a trail junction at 1.5 miles. Here, the Mina Sauk Falls Trail meets the Ozark Trail. Mina Sauk Falls is dead ahead, and perhaps you have heard it by now (except in autumn, when the falls nearly dry up). To get the best of both aspects of this hike—views, and the falls—consider coming here in spring, after a rain-bearing cold front has blown though. That way the falls will be flowing and the skies will be clear, allowing you to enjoy the expansive views. Much of this trail is uncanopied and will be quite hot in summer.

A tributary of Taum Sauk Creek is the source of the falls. It has come off the southwest side of Taum Sauk Mountain and dives over a granite face into a vertical rock garden. Craggy pines cling to the edges of the granite face, which offers views of the oak-covered mountains in the distance. This whole falls area is worth a closer look—it's the best exploration spot on the entire hike.

The trail then turns uphill, along this perennial stream, which is flowing downhill to your right. Ascend some more of those special boulder glades, and don't forget to look back for more great views. Watch as the trail comes alongside a second, upper waterfall. It doesn't have quite the punch of the first, but is scenic nonetheless.

Continue ascending along the creek valley, often bordered by sumac trees. The gradient moderates; the path becomes more wooded, and the glades decrease. At 2.5 miles, you'll reach a trail junction. The Ozark Trail leaves right, and a connector trail leads left toward the top of Taum Sauk Mountain. At 3.0 miles, you'll come to another junction. You have been here before. Turn right and return to the parking area, maybe stopping at Missouri's high point one last time.

45

Crane Lake Loop

TOTAL DISTANCE: 4.8-mile loop

HIKING TIME: 2 hours, 15 minutes

VERTICAL RISE: 230 feet

RATING: Moderate

MAPS: USGS 7.5' Glover, Des Arc NE; Ozark Trail Marble Creek Miles 0 to 9, Mark Twain National Forest—Salem, Potosi, and Fredericktown Districts

TRAILHEAD GPS COORDINATES: N37° 25.504', W90° 37.575'

CONTACT INFORMATION: Mark Twain National Forest, 10019 West State Highway 8, Potosi, MO 63664, (573) 438-5427, www.fs.usda.gov/mtnf

This loop offers some stillwater scenery and some rugged hiking beside a creek, along with views from some rocky hillside glades in the Mark Twain National Forest. The lesser-trod trek features some navigational challenges as well. Leave the Crane Lake boat ramp on a seemingly forgotten segment of the Ozark Trail to enjoy some waterside forest cruising, with detours into side hollows thrown in. Reach the lake dam and geological features of a shut-in, where volcanic rock borders Crane Pond Creek through the narrow upper reaches of Reader Hollow. You'll then depart from the Ozark Trail to cross Crane Pond Creek, bisecting scenic meadows. Travel through thick woods before emerging onto more rocky glades with shut-in vistas before returning to the shore of Crane Lake. From here, the going is easy as the trail takes a mostly level path, allowing you to appreciate the scenic body of water instead of watching your next step or trying to figure out where to go. In places, parallel trails make things confusing, but there is little danger of actually getting lost.

HOW TO GET THERE

From just south of Ironton, take Highway E for 9 miles to Iron County Road (CR 124). Turn right and follow CR 124 for 2.6 miles to the signed left turn to CRANE LAKE. Follow this gravel road for 2 miles to the boat launch area. Alternative directions from Fredericktown: From US 67 just south of town, take Highway E west for 18.5 miles to Iron Highway 124. Turn left onto CR 124 and follow the directions as above.

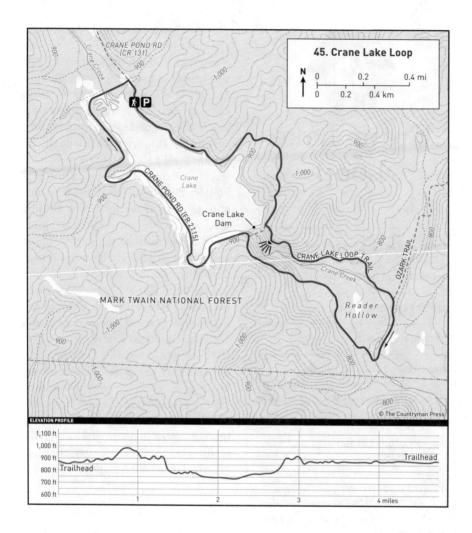

45. Crane Lake Loop

ELEVATION PROFILE

© The Countryman Press

THE HIKE

This hike leaves left from the parking area as you face out to the lake. Take the gravel track beyond vehicle barrier boulders, passing through the former national forest picnic area. In places on your right the bank has been stabilized for shore anglers. The wide gravel track narrows underneath the oaks, hickories, and pines. Soon you'll descend to cross a trickling stream.

The trail is marked with white diamonds here, though you may also see Ozark Trail markers. Shortly, you'll drop to a dry drainage. The path drifts back from the lake and onto a hill, offering a good lake vista, before working around a relatively large embayment. Step over the gravel wash of the drainage. The path then meanders through rocky hillside woods and loses Crane Lake entirely. After a while the path turns south and the water returns to view. Stay with the blazes as the trailbed becomes ultra-rocky. The outflow of Crane Lake Dam becomes audible.

You may see a path leading right,

down toward Crane Creek below the dam, at 1.2 miles. This hard-to-find and hard-to-follow spur path leads to the creek and the attendant boulder jumbles below to cross the stream and shortcut the loop. You can also access the creek this way just for fun, the rocky, bouldery landscape is great for rock-hopping and scrambling, especially in fall, when the water is down. The engineers who designed this dam put it at the head of a shut-in, to take advantage of the tight course through which the creek had to pass; that's why the balance of the shut-in begins just below the dam.

The official trail continues up a bouldery hill and glade. These outcrops offer fantastic views toward the head of the lake. Also, gaze across the creek at rock stacks and terrain similar to what you're standing on. You will be over there in a few miles on your return trip, looking at where you stand now. Watch for painted blazes on the rocks as you continue through this gorgeous area. The trail reenters woods, still in boulder heaven. The creek is noisily flowing to your right. The shut-in gives way, as you continue downstream, dancing in and out of hollows. Open onto a large, partially wooded meadow at 1.8 miles. Keep the meadow to your left, traversing the margin where the meadow meets the woods. The creek is still to your right. Reach the end of the meadow at 2.0 miles. The Ozark Trail leaves left for Marble Creek Campground and the Crane Lake Loop veers right, soon crossing a gravel bar in riparian woodland. Keep downstream, with another meadow to your left and Crane Creek flowing to your right. In some places, however, Crane Creek may not be flowing, as beavers are active in the area. You might see a dam.

Enter a huge gravel wash, and keep an eye peeled for the trail leaving right to cross Crane Pond Creek by rock-hopping. Once you're across, turn right, heading upstream through brushy woods to soon open onto a large and attractive meadow, colorful with wildflowers in-season. Stay left here on an old roadbed, keeping the meadow to your right, though it seems as if you should stay directly along the creek heading upstream. Travel in the margin of woods and field; keep watch for remnant barbed-wire fence growing into the edge trees.

Pay close attention here when the roadbed begins to rise left, away from the meadow. The actual foot trail veers right, staying alongside the meadow. (If you follow the roadbed instead, it reconnects to the main foot trail above the dam—the actual foot trail parallels the meadow and does not climb.) However, the correct trail will be very brushy in the growing season, and is bordered by trees. Look for markers indicating that this is the proper trail. The path enters a cedar copse where the trailbed is very faint—many hikers miss this turn and trace the aforementioned roadbed. Remain in this bottomland woods before working up a wooded hillside to level out onto pink volcanic boulders enmeshed in grasses and wildflowers. Cedars ply the edges of these glades. The trail now continues along an open boulder plateau that offers vistas of the lake ahead and the hillside across the creek. The real trail begins angling down to reach the lake dam at 3.1 miles.

At the dam, a spur trail leading right cuts across to Crane Pond Creek, where you were earlier. The trail leading left continues the loop. Enjoy easy walking around the lake to soon reach the roadbed that most hikers and trail users follow. This old roadbed continues around the lake and is the actual trail

VIEW OF CRANE LAKE FROM DAM

most of the way beyond here. However, one more rugged, little-used foot-only segment works around an embayment. If you follow this, stay with a very faint path that runs closest to the lake.

After circling the embayment, the trail is wide and almost level. Enjoy the nearly continuous lake views, the melding of water and woods. Watch for an old roadbed coming in on your left at 3.9 miles; at 4.0 miles, you'll reach a tributary and cross it on an old concrete bridge. The trail enters a brushy riparian zone. Curve right to span Crane Creek on a concrete former auto bridge and follow potholed Forest Road 2115 (FR 2115) to meet the road on which you arrived. Turn right and follow the gravel track a short distance to complete your loop.

Tiemann Shut-Ins via Silver Mines

TOTAL DISTANCE: 5.4-mile there-and-back

HIKING TIME: 3 hours

VERTICAL RISE: 150 feet

RATING: Moderate to difficult

MAPS: USGS 7.5' Rhodes Mountain; Silver Mines Recreation Area, Mark Twain National Forest—Salem, Potosi, and Fredericktown Districts

TRAILHEAD GPS COORDINATES: N37° 33.283', W90° 26.271'

CONTACT INFORMATION: Mark Twain National Forest, 10019 West State Highway 8, Potosi, MO 63664, (573) 438-5427, www.fs.usda.gov/mtnf

This hike is packed with scenery, especially at the beginning and end. Leave Silver Mines Recreation Area, part of the Mark Twain National Forest, and travel up the St. Francis River Valley, replete with granite formations that are a feast for the eyes and beg further exploration. The waters of the river, popular with kayakers in spring, are alluring, bordered by bluffs and cliffs and interspersed with boulders that make paddling a challenge, possibly the most formidable white water in the state of Missouri. Travel the geological fantasyland before turning away from the river for a woodland walk that makes you wonder if you are on the right trail. The path leads into Tiemann Shut-Ins on Missouri Department of Conservation Land, and a second spot where rock, water, and the things that grow on and in them will make every step worthwhile. Check out the view from Pine Rock Overlook, and see water still carving its way through monstrous boulders. Check out more views from other developed overlooks that feature white water rapids. While you are enjoying the big picture, don't forget to appreciate some of the unique flora of these rock bluffs. A picnic shelter and alternative trail access wait at the end of the hike, but this is one trip where you certainly won't mind backtracking, for you are bound to enjoy the trip from a different perspective. By the way, Silver Mines Recreation Area offers two nice campgrounds as well as picnic areas.

HOW TO GET THERE

From the intersection of US 67 and MO 72 just west of Fredericktown, take MO 72 for 4.3 miles to Highway D. Turn left and follow Highway D for 2.9 miles to the Silver Mines Recreation Area. Turn right

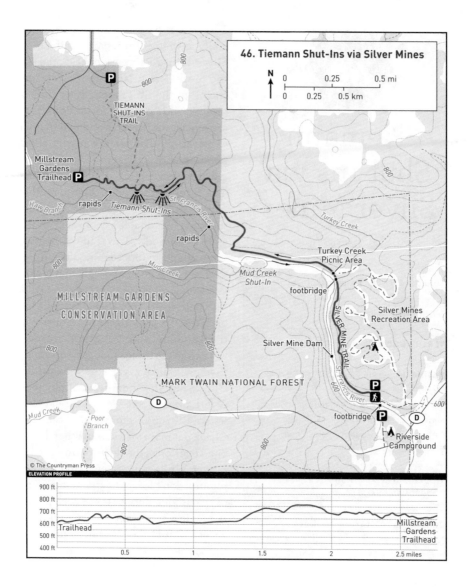

46. Tiemann Shut-Ins via Silver Mines

here and continue forward, passing a right turn into the campground. The trail starts at the dead end. Picnic tables and a restroom are located at the trailhead. If the parking area is full, backtrack to Highway D, cross the St. Francis River, reach the Riverside Camping Area, and turn right into another picnic area. The trail can be accessed by crossing the low-water bridge over the St. Francis. There is a parking fee at this recreation area.

THE HIKE

This trail can be appreciated in multiple seasons, whether it be in the third weekend in March, when the Missouri Whitewater Association's kayaking championships are held on the river; later in spring, when the flowers are blooming; or in fall, when the St. Francis River is low, more rock is exposed, and autumn colors complement the granite boulders. Winter offers icy

LOOKING INTO TIEMANN SHUT-INS

formations, bridging water and rock in a powerful river beside which leafless trees reveal even more rock formations. Take a swim or fish in summer.

Leave the parking area and enter boulder-strewn woodland dominated by cedar trees, the Silver Mines Shut-Ins. The south-facing slope is dry but still has oaks and hickories aplenty. Pines tower above all. The St. Francis River flows below you, dancing through rocks. Work your way up

a bluff offering views below. At 0.3 mile, a side trail leads left and down to the river, where two-thirds of the old Silver Mine Dam arcs across the valley. The side closest to you is gone.

The trail then makes its way along an incredible bluff line where exposed rock shoots skyward. More boulders and rocks are scattered all about. In places, the trail is rough enough for children to ask for a helping hand, but rest assured, they will

GNARLED PINE TREE MARKS THE MILLSTREAM GARDENS TRAILHEAD

be having a ball clambering around. Spur trails lead uphill and to the right, toward the campground and other facilities up top. Continue straight at all junctions for the time being.

Car-sized boulders and more bluffs wait. The hike is a continual geological overload as you keep upriver. The rapids and pools of the St. Francis below will change character with the seasons. In summer and fall, the river will seem more pool than rapid; in winter and spring you'll find the opposite.

Drift down to span Turkey Creek on an arched bridge and reach Turkey Creek Picnic Area at 0.8 mile. Continue upriver though the grassy riverside retreat to pick up the hiking trail once again on the far side, next to the St. Francis. The trail now plies rich wooded bottomland, rife with brush. Look for moisture-loving trees such as river birch and sycamore. You may notice suspended fodder in the tree branches beside the path. This debris is left over from the times when the river has flooded. Imagine being here when the river is such a torrent!

The trail remains level and reaches the concrete foundation of a house at 1.3 miles. A faint path continues forward, only to peter out near the river's edge—although a bouldery bluff here offers some good rock scrambling. The real trail curves right and uphill just before the home foundation, leading away from the river. This is where you wonder if you are on the correct path. Stay with it, as it ascends into classic Ozark hickory-oak forest.

Keep winding through woods, and resume a westward direction with significantly fewer rock formations. Enter Missouri Department of Conservation lands at 2.0 miles. This is known as the Millstream Gardens Conservation Area. The trail widens here, and you are once again near the St. Francis River. Look for signs indicating riverside features, such as Double Drop Rapids. Open glades, where yuccas grow in abundance, offer a look down on the river. At 2.2 miles, a spur trail leads left to Pine Rock Overlook. Walk a short distance and open to a great view of Tiemann Shut-Ins. The river, the boulders through which it flows, the bordering forests, and the hills all form a majestic mosaic of Ozark beauty.

More lies ahead. Continue on a now wide old roadbed, complete with crumbled asphalt. Further views await, including one of the Sharks Fin, a river feature. Cross a wet-weather drainage and reach an observation deck hailing the Cat's Paw. Here, the wheelchair-accessible Tiemann Shut-Ins Trail leads right and to a parking area. The next overlook is at Double Drop Rapids. Did I mention that this stretch of the St. Francis is the Show Me State's most challenging whitewater? You ought to see this river when it hits the Arkansas Delta. It's muddy, brown, slow, and full of trees—all it seems to share with this stretch of river is its name.

Keep winding to reach a final observation area. The trail then crosses a wooden bridge and returns to bottomland before opening onto a field with a picnic pavilion at 2.7 miles. This is the end of the line and the alternative trailhead, but I wouldn't want to leave a shuttle car here—the return trip is too tempting. This area is a paddler put-in when the water is up. Before you turn around, check out one more feature—a pine tree that rises upward only to have its trunk do a complete loop before turning for the sky again. To reach the Millstream Gardens trailhead from Fredericktown, take MO 72 west for 8 miles, and look for the left turn into the conservation area. Follow the main road, staying left at the split to reach the trailhead and picnic pavilion.

47

Mudlick Mountain Loop at Sam A. Baker State Park

This is a challenging hike at one of Missouri's oldest state parks, located in the St. Francois Mountains. Start on the Shut-Ins Trail and head up the flats of Big Creek. Check out the bluffs of the stream before ascending along the rugged east slope of Mudlick Mountain, where CCC-built trail shelters from the 1930s overlook the watercourse below. Continue upward; a sense of remoteness falls over the peak. The trail rolls along high ridges, offering occasional vistas before cutting into a super-rocky mountainside where travel slows to a crawl. The loop winds in and out of rocky gorges and over mountainside rock jumbles that will tax your feet before you're done with your loop. The Mudlick trail system also has two backpacking sites, for those inclined.

HOW TO GET THERE

From downtown Piedmont, take MO 34 east for 10.6 miles to MO 143. Turn left (north) and follow MO 143 for 4 miles to the stone entrance of the park. From this entrance, continue through the park for 2 miles to the hiking trailhead's parking area across from the park store. A sign here states, RESTROOMS AND LAUNDRY. If you cross the bridge over Big Creek, you have gone too far. Additional parking is available at the park store's lot across MO 143 from the trailhead.

THE HIKE

Sam A. Baker State Park has an extensive trail system; this is but one of many potential hikes here. Leave the parking area and descend to a streambed, crossing it on a wooden bridge. You'll reach the first of many trail junctions here, so pay attention. Keep forward

TOTAL DISTANCE: 7.4-mile loop

HIKING TIME: 5 hours

VERTICAL RISE: 750 feet

RATING: Difficult

MAPS: USGS 7.5' Brunot, Patterson; Sam A. Baker State Park Shut-ins Trail, Mudlick Trail

TRAILHEAD GPS COORDINATES: N37° 15.581', W90° 30.426'

CONTACT INFORMATION: Sam A. Baker State Park, Rt. 1 Box 18150, Patterson, MO 63956, (573) 856-4411, www.mostateparks .com

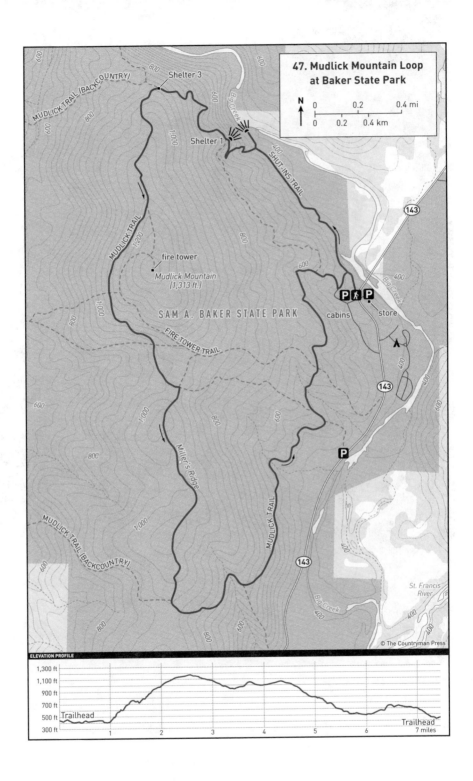

47. Mudlick Mountain Loop at Baker State Park

N

0	0.2	0.4 mi
0	0.2	0.4 km

MUDLICK TRAIL (BACKCOUNTRY)

Shelter 3

Big Creek

Shelter 1

MUDLICK TRAIL

SHUT-INS TRAIL

fire tower

Mudlick Mountain
(1,313 ft.)

143

SAM A. BAKER STATE PARK

Big Creek

FIRE TOWER TRAIL

cabins   store

MUDLICK TRAIL (BACKCOUNTRY)

Miller's Ridge

MUDLICK TRAIL

143

143

P

St. Francis
River

Big Creek

© The Countryman Press

ELEVATION PROFILE

1,300 ft	
1,100 ft	
900 ft	
700 ft	
500 ft	Trailhead
300 ft	

Trailhead

1   2   3   4   5   6   7 miles

BLUFFS RISE FROM BIG CREEK AT SHUT-INS

beyond the bridge on the blue-blazed Shut-Ins Trail. Shortly cross a decaying paved road. The Shut-Ins Trail travels the margin between the steep slope of lower Mudlick Mountain and the flats of Big Creek to your right. Soon you'll drop on wooden steps to the creek bottoms, lush with cane, maple, ash, and sycamore. While enjoying the soft dirt track at your feet, look left for desiccated side canyons, topped in ferns and mosses dropping into the flats. These gorges flow only during rains, and it's hard to imagine the amount of water and time it took to erode these marvels into what we see today.

You'll reach a split in the trail at 1.1 miles. Take the right fork and open onto a gravel bar that leads to the Big Creek Shut-Ins. This is where Big Creek is hemmed by the bluffs closing in on it. As the shut-in opens, the large gravel bar upon which you walk is formed. Backtrack to the junction, this time taking the other path. Here, you can gain a close-up look at one of the aforementioned side canyons. Boulders and loose rock have been carved into shapes and formations from which explorers shy away. Also look for cacti growing to the right of the trail. They like south-facing, well-drained slopes such as the one on which you're switchbacking upward.

Continue climbing to Shelter 1. This two-fireplace rock building, open at the front, was built by the Civilian Conservation Corps in the 1930s. Many park facilities feature CCC handiwork. A rock outcrop in front of the shelter affords a view out to Big Creek and the mountains on the far side. You'll reach a trail junction just beyond the shelter. Here, the yellow-blazed Mudlick Mountain Trail leaves left and right. Stay right, joining an old roadbed that ultimately leads to the top of the mountain. Enjoy this wide track—it makes for easy walking, albeit uphill. Continue on to meet Shelter 2. This shelter is identical to the first, minus the view. Reach Shelter 3 at 1.9 miles. Stay left at the nearby trail junction, heading up the crest of Mudlick Mountain, now on the Mudlick Trail. This national recreation trail encompasses several different trails that make a large loop and also include spurs, so the term Mudlick Trail can be misleading. Stay with the hike narrative and you will be fine.

Keep upward to meet the side trail leading to the fire tower at 2.6 miles. You may want to see the historic tower, built in 1936, but climbing it is prohibited. The grade eases but the trail now leaves the roadbed and evolves into a narrow singletrack that winds among hickories and oaks. The stony path is rough, and your travel slows considerably. Get used to it, however: A lot of irregular walking lies ahead. The slow pace will allow you to look to the west across the Logan Creek Valley and the heights of Green Mountain. Views are sporadic through the trees and will be improved in winter. This area exudes a real sense of isolation, a feeling of being in the back-of-beyond.

Work around the crest of Mudlick Mountain to reach an old roadbed at 3.4 miles. This roadbed leads right into Logan Creek Valley and the park backcountry. Keep straight on the official trail in more level country, despite the fact that it bisects several dry washes. Look left in the woods at an old pond that now serves the park's wildlife.

At 3.7 miles, you'll reach another junction. This loop turns right to head south over Miller Ridge. If you've had enough, keep forward to cut 2 miles off your hike via the Fire Tower Trail.

Continue south, ascending Miller Ridge back on a roadbed. Top out over a knob and descend into a meadow with another pond at 4.0 miles. Keep south in this brushy area before returning to woods, topping over a second knob, and reaching a trail junction at 4.8 miles. Turn left here, beginning the northbound return leg of the loop. The

HIKE TRAVERSES ULTRA ROCKY EAST SLOPE OF MUDLICK MOUNTAIN

Mudlick Trail leaves the roadbed again and begins a long stretch of slow going over stony soil.

Watch for rock outcrops aplenty beside the trail and in the nearby forest. Continue angling downhill to meet another junction at 5.3 miles. A trail leads right to Camping Area 1 and the Equestrian Campground. Stay left on the hiker-only trail.

This is where the path becomes ultrascenic and ultrachallenging. Look for views to the east across the deep gorge of Big Creek, but you may find yourself watching your feet as you make your way along the nothing-but-rock east slope of Mudlick Mountain. The soil is so stony, you begin to wonder how trees can grow here, but the path remains in forest.

Cross rock jumbles and keep descending to cross a bridge spanning an incised gully at 5.7 miles. Begin winding in and out of scenic yet picturesque stony drainages. Reach a trail junction at 6.3 miles. Here, your hike meets the Fire Tower Trail, which leads to the equestrian trailhead. Turn left and walk 100 yards to another junction. Leave right, continuing north on the foot-only trail. The path remains rocky and crosses a road leading right to the park office.

Cross a power line at 6.8 miles and keep trucking to reach another trail junction at 7.2 miles. Turn right onto a wider path heading downhill to cross a crumbling asphalt road. Dip to bisect one last drainage and meet the Shut-Ins Trail. You have been here before. Leave right and backtrack just a short distance to complete the loop.

48

Pickle Springs Natural Area Loop

TOTAL DISTANCE: 2.0-mile loop

HIKING TIME: 2 hours

VERTICAL RISE: 175 feet

RATING: Moderate

MAPS: USGS 7.5' Sprott, Pickle Springs Natural Area trail map

TRAILHEAD GPS COORDINATES: N37° 48.101', W90° 18.113'

CONTACT INFORMATION: Missouri Department of Conservation, St. Louis Regional Office, 2360 Highway D, St. Charles, MO 63304, (636) 441-4554, www.mdc.mo.gov/

This path, built in 1985, is known as the Trail Through Time. Situated in the uppermost Pickle Creek drainage, numerous streams, combined with wind, temperature, and the ages, have carved all kinds of geological features from the plateau. This trail travels to most of them. After an innocuous start, the path cuts into the Slot, where you think it won't go, before opening onto Double Arch, a pair of rock arches. Giant rocks form other features, such as the Cauliflower Rocks and the Keyhole, before dropping to cross upper Pickle Creek. From here, the path cuts over to Bone Creek, where Mossy Falls and Owls Den Bluff await. A view can be had after climbing to Dome Rock, where you can see more stony features above the trees. A trip into Rockpile Canyon and to Head Wall Falls, then a ramble over Piney Glade, completes the trek. Take your time and savor every step of this 2-mile path. The significant features are marked with signs. The Pickle Springs trailhead has a shaded picnic area, should you choose to bring a lunch.

HOW TO GET THERE

From Exit 150 off I-55, take MO 32 west for 16.7 miles to Highway AA. Turn left and follow Highway AA for 1.6 miles to Dorlac Road. Take Dorlac Road for 0.3 mile to the trailhead on your right.

THE HIKE

Head beyond the wooden fences on mulched track and walk just a short distance to reach a split. Go left. You will immediately come upon a rock wall, which will be long forgotten after all the forthcoming features. The path

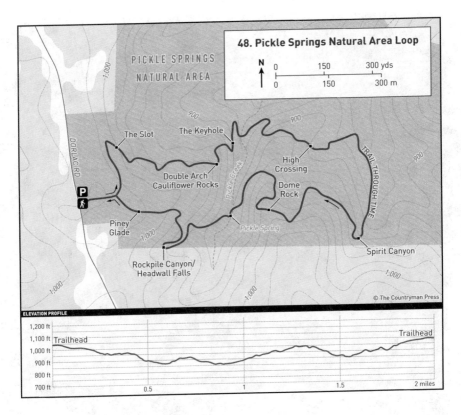

48. Pickle Springs Natural Area Loop

N

| 0 | 150 | 300 yds |
| 0 | 150 | 300 m |

PICKLE SPRINGS
NATURAL AREA

The Slot   The Keyhole

High
Crossing

Double Arch
Cauliflower Rocks

Dome
Rock

DORLAC RD

TRAIL THROUGH TIME

Piney
Glade

Pickle Spring

Spirit Canyon

Rockpile Canyon/
Headwall Falls

© The Countryman Press

ELEVATION PROFILE

1,200 ft				
1,100 ft	Trailhead			Trailhead
1,000 ft				
900 ft				
800 ft				
700 ft	0.5	1	1.5	2 miles

turns abruptly right into the Slot. Many hikers have kept forward, not thinking that the path enters the narrow slit, but it does. This unbelievable crevice is still being eroded by water. Fern and moss add a colorful touch. Cruise along an incredible multi-tiered bluff line that after rain features numerous small, dripping falls. Before you catch your breath, you'll reach an area of hoodoos—rock outcrops that stand above the land in rounded shapes carved over time. Descend wooden steps, passing under Double Arch. From the opposite direction the arch resembles a pair of windows, and in a sense it is a window into geological time.

Watch for another hoodoo on an elevated rock. More boulders on your right beckon exploration. Next comes the Key-hole, where you slip under an arch that looks like the slot for a key. Continue coursing among mighty boulders. Look around you—each set of rocks makes you want to explore, and you should. Descend past Terrapin Rock. If you look at this from the correct angle, you will see the head of a turtle. Shortly, you'll cross upper Pickle Creek on a wooden footbridge. This clear stream flows perennially down through Hawn State Park and into the River aux Vases, which in turn flows into the Mississippi.

Regain elevation to make the High Crossing, which is a bridge over a tiny stream that will run dry in fall. Cruise well above the stream, which has cut its own little gorge. Curve into Bone Creek; rich fern beds and flowers border small bluffs along its banks. Cross

EMERGENT ROCKS ARE GEOLOGICAL WINDOWS AT PICKLE SPRINGS

Bone Creek twice in quick succession on a bridge to reach Mossy Falls, which is but a small drop entering a much larger pool than you would expect. Above here the creek flows over rock slabs in chutes and pools that form a quaint and picturesque setting. Come along a significant bluff line and rock cathedral. This locale is quite scenic and deserves its name: Spirit Canyon. Watch for the low-flow waterfall here, along with an overhanging rockhouse, ferns carpeting its base.

Climb away from Spirit Canyon, regaining the main ridgeline, where you come upon more emergent boulders, including one rock with a smaller natural arch. Ascend onto Dome Rock, an open boulder flat mixed with pines, where views open. Look for a little rock shelter near where you stand. Farther, a hoodoo stands in the distance, to the northwest.

The trail cruises below Dome Rock in piney woods with azaleas. Look left for a rock wall with many embedded caves. You'll have to look at them from afar, though, because rock climbing is prohibited. Descend to reach Pickle Springs, crossing the outflow on a bridge. Climb into another bluff canyon area, taking the time to appreciate the geology of the area known as Rockpile Canyon. The fallen stones have separated from the main cliff line, creating a boulder jumble. Head Wall Falls is deeper in the canyon. Not only are the falls worth admiring, but you'll also find some unusual hoodoos up here. Leave Rockpile Canyon to travel beside Piney Glade, slab rock interspersed with evergreens that dot the shallow soil. Just ahead, complete the loop, backtracking a short distance to the trailhead.

49

Whispering Pines Loop

TOTAL DISTANCE: 6.2-mile loop

HIKING TIME: 3 hours, 15 minutes

VERTICAL RISE: 300 feet

RATING: Moderate

MAPS: USGS 7.5' Coffman; Hawn State Park —Pickle Creek Trail, Whispering Pines Trail

TRAILHEAD GPS COORDINATES: N37° 49.809', W90° 13.825'

CONTACT INFORMATION: Hawn State Park, 12096 Park Drive, Sainte Geneviève, MO 63670, (573) 883-3603, www.mostate parks.com

This hike travels through what many consider to be the finest state park in Missouri. Make your own determination about that, but I can assure you that this loop will meet your qualifications for a good hike. First explore Pickle Creek, a classic Ozark shut-in, with boulders forming rocky ramparts along a gorgeous perennial stream. Leave the shut-in, continuing up the creek amid other rock formations to make a wooded ridge. A pair of knobs offer rocky vistas. Pass a spur trail to a backpack campsite before making a tributary of Pickle Creek, which drops in cascades. Travel over high bluffs atop lower Pickle Creek before returning to the trailhead, which has a picnic area and restroom facilities.

HOW TO GET THERE

From Exit 150 off I-55 south, take MO 32 west for 12.7 miles to MO 144. Turn left onto MO 144 and travel 3.1 miles to reach the Hawn State Park. Alternative directions: From Farmington, take MO 32 east for 13 miles to MO 144. Turn right onto MO 144 and continue for 3.1 miles to enter Hawn State Park. Once you're in the park, proceed 1.2 miles farther to reach the picnic area, on your right. Park at the Pickle Creek trailhead. The Whispering Pines trailhead will be your return route.

THE HIKE

Leave the parking area on the Pickle Creek Trail. Cruise through a pretty pine-shaded picnic area. Pickle Creek flows to your left, but to your right a grassy pine savanna rises away from the stream. The trail lies between them. Deeply shaded Pickle Creek flows over rapids in a lush hollow. It isn't long before you enter a shut-in and the des-

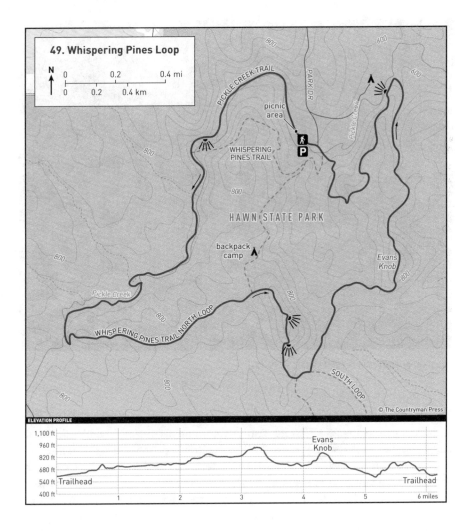

49. Whispering Pines Loop

N

| 0 | 0.2 | 0.4 mi |
| 0 | 0.2 | 0.4 km |

PICKLE CREEK TRAIL

PARK DR

Pickle Creek

picnic
area

WHISPERING
PINES TRAIL

P

HAWN STATE PARK

backpack
camp

Evans
Knob

Pickle Creek

WHISPERING PINES TRAIL NORTH LOOP

SOUTH LOOP

800

800

800

800

600

600

600

800

© The Countryman Press

ELEVATION PROFILE

1,100 ft						
960 ft				Evans	
820 ft				Knob	
680 ft					
540 ft	Trailhead				Trailhead
400 ft	1	2	3	4	5	6 miles

ignated state natural area. Pickle Creek has cut into the rocks, forming a tight little gorge. The trail is quite rocky where the valley closes in. Sometimes you'll have to dance over and between boulders, getting quite a rock-and-water show. Be apprised that during wet times, parts of the trail will be flooded. Where the stream's edge is particularly ornery, the path will climb above the water, traveling through scree, boulders, and rocks by the thousands, all jumbled up and covered with lichens. In places, the trail acts as the boundary between the pine savanna and the lush streamside forest. Since the park has used fire as a management tool, the savanna is restored and provides a good contrast with the Pickle Creek drainage—the trail is the actual burn line. Reach an area open to the sky, which allows a wonderful vantage of Pickle Creek.

The Pickle Creek Trail then enters an area of bigger boulders mixed with smaller ones, together forming a scenic rock garden that must be seen to be enjoyed. You don't know whether to admire the stream or the boulder field,

TRIBUTARY OF PICKLE CREEK FORMS SMALL WATERFALL

so take the time to stop and appreciate both. At 0.9 mile, the Pickle Creek Trail ends and the Whispering Pine Trail begins. A sign notes the Whispering Pines Trail as being 10 miles long, but that includes both loops of the trail. This loop goes for 5.3 miles beyond this point.

Join the Whispering Pine Trail as it continues up Pickle Creek. Red metal reflectors mark this path. Leave the gorge portion of Pickle Creek and continue upstream, where the trail is much quieter. Enter a pine-dominated flat along Pickle Creek. Pickle Creek shows off more muted rock formations, less spectacular but beautiful nonetheless, including overhanging bluffs where azaleas bloom in spring. Pass a small, shallow cave on your right at 1.5 miles, then cross a tributary of Pickle Creek just beyond.

Shortly, you'll cross Pickle Creek itself. This can usually be rock-hopped. Continue up the left-hand bank, climbing. Briefly drift out of sight of the creek, entering a pine savanna. Once again, the trail itself forms the boundary between a burned savanna to your left and the lush river gorge to your right. The lesser-vegetated forest floor reveals more rock formations, including a castle-like fortress on your left at 2.2 miles. The trail leaves Pickle Creek to switchback onto the fortress rock. This scene is quite colorful, what with the green moss, the red needles of the pines, the dark green cedars with brown trunks, and the auburn trunks of short-leaved pines. Your ears will tune into the lack of water sounds atop this ridge where the pines and oaks reach high in the sky.

While working your way up the ridge, look for traces of old roadbeds like that upon which you're traveling. Once again

FOGGED-IN BLUFFS OVERLOOK CAMPGROUND AT HAWN STATE PARK

the state in Missouri has stepped in to preserve a special swath of land after it was settled and utilized. Dogwoods, maples, oaks, and a few hickories complement the towering pines here. At 3.0 miles, a spur trail leads left to the park's backpack campsites. Beyond, the Whispering Pines Trail climbs to slip around the left side of an unnamed knob, coming along the edge of a precipitous cliff at 3.3 miles. Look to the southwest. Descend from the unnamed knob, opening to more southerly views. The very rocky track makes for slow going as it leads off the knob. Notice on the descent how people are shortcutting the switchbacks. Please do not do so yourself: It causes erosion and makes Hawn State Park a little less beautiful. Off the knob, the trail again enters big woods, where pines and oaks grow tall versus the more stunted trees atop the knob with the poor soils.

At 3.6 miles, the blue-blazed South Loop leaves to your right; you'll continue forward on the red-blazed track. Just a short distance later, the trail meets the other end of the South Loop, which again leaves right. Here, the red-blazed Whispering Pines Trail leaves left into a sometimes mucky area. The unnamed knob you just climbed rises to your left. Descend to a saddle, then up Evans Knob. Rock becomes more prevalent as you work amid large boulders and outcrops, with views opening up to the west. Evans Knob levels out and reveals many alluring picnic and relaxation spots. Drop sharply off the knob, resuming a more foot-friendly walk in cedars and pines. Start making your way downhill for a tributary of Pickle Creek, toward the main watercourse. This feeder stream cuts its own bluffs, spreading wide while flowing over rock slabs. In other places it drops over rock edges noisily, forming small waterfalls. These cascades increase in size as you near Pickle Creek.

Return to Pickle Creek at 5.2 miles. The state park campground is visible across the stream. Turn left, heading upstream at this point, now traveling a particularly steep bluff. The trail diverges into numerous user-created paths, although the correct pathway is marked and stays high atop the bluff above Pickle Creek. The sounds of the campground below are audible, especially on weekends. Stay with the red-blazed track, which rises high along this ridge only to leave the bluffs. Descend to step over a tributary of Pickle Creek, then reach a bridge. You can see the Whispering Pines Trail to your left. This loop ends after you cross a pair of bridges over Pickle Creek. Across the bridge, the Pickle Creek trailhead and this hike's beginning lie to your left.

50

White Oaks Loop at Hawn State Park

TOTAL DISTANCE: 4.0-mile loop	
HIKING TIME: 2 hours	
VERTICAL RISE: 125 feet	
RATING: Moderate	
MAPS: USGS 7.5' Coffman, Sprott; Hawn State Park—White Oaks Trail	
TRAILHEAD GPS COORDINATES: N37° 49.984', W90° 14.408'	
CONTACT INFORMATION: Hawn State Park, 12096 Park Drive, Sainte Geneviève, MO 63670, (573) 883-3603, www.mostateparks.com	

This is a get-back-to-nature hike. If you want to leave the crowds behind and enjoy some of the beauty for which Hawn State Park is known, give this lesser-traveled trail a try. Why the lack of use? It has no single spectacular feature, such as a waterfall, overlook, bluff, or cave. It does, however, offer a sense of remoteness where nature reigns supreme. The trek rolls over hills, passing a superlative cedar tree to reach the loop portion of the hike. From there it crosses in and out of tributaries feeding Pickle Creek, traveling on and off old roads that once passed through these now tall woods. Surmount a rocky and piney knob before completing the loop and backtracking to the trailhead.

HOW TO GET THERE

From Exit 150 off I-55 south, take MO 32 west for 12.7 miles to MO 144. Turn left onto MO 144 and travel 3.1 miles to reach Hawn State Park. Alternative directions: From Farmington, take MO 32 east for 13 miles to MO 144. Turn right onto MO 144 and follow it for 3.1 miles to enter Hawn State Park. The White Oaks trailhead is on your right just as you enter the park.

THE HIKE

Leave the trailhead and its kiosk and restroom area to begin heading westerly along an oak ridge. You can see rock outcrops here. The forest floor is generally more open and grassy than other parts of the park because of the aggressive use of prescribed fire here. This resembles what Missouri looked like before white settlement, when low-level fires caused by lightning kept forest understories open and weren't suppressed as soon as they flared up. Nowadays, land

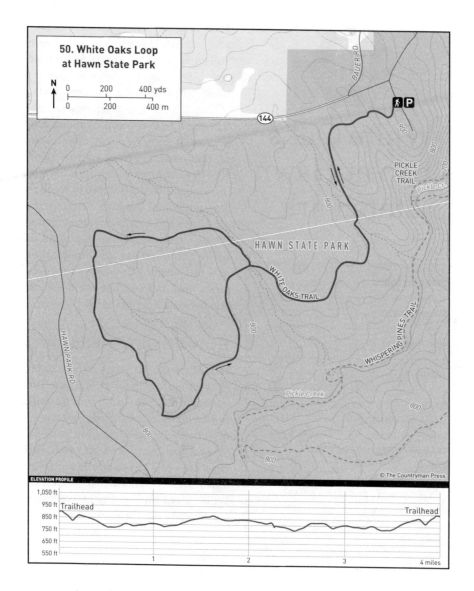

50. White Oaks Loop at Hawn State Park

N

| 0 | 200 | 400 yds |
| 0 | 200 | 400 m |

BAUER RD.

144

PICKLE
CREEK
TRAIL

Pickle Cr.

HAWN STATE PARK

WHITE OAKS TRAIL

WHISPERING PINES TRAIL

HAWN PARK RD.

Pickle Creek

800

800

800

800

900

800

700

© The Countryman Press

ELEVATION PROFILE

1,050 ft
950 ft Trailhead
850 ft
750 ft
650 ft
550 ft   Trailhead

1   2   3   4 miles

managers know that certain ecosystems simply cannot be in their natural state without fire. To restore and preserve ecosystems is one of the missions of Missouri's state parks.

The blazed White Oaks Trail curves and descends to a streambed, where it crosses a little branch flowing south toward Pickle Creek. Many of the streams here run dry during late summer and fall. Leave the branch flat and

climb. Keep an eye out for the shagbark hickory tree, whose loose bark plates make identification simple. It's found throughout Missouri and the Ozarks, but its range ends not far west of the Show Me State's border. Tennessee and Kentucky are the center of its range, which extends from east Texas to New York. Squirrels, foxes, rabbits, and turkeys, among other species, are fond of shagbark hickory nuts. The trail slips

HIKER CLIMBS HILL ON WHITE OAK LOOP

over the right-hand side of a knob on a rocky but narrow tread, revealing its infrequent use compared with other Hawn State Park trails. Cross a second branch in another hollow. Abruptly turn away from the hollow, skirting the edge of a field underneath a cloak of pines. The White Oaks Trail levels off on the ridge and passes one of the larger cedar trees in the Ozarks, to the left of the trail. Eastern red cedars are known to live 500 years!

Dip to cross a branch in an isolated hollow, then reach the trail junction with the loop portion of the hike at 1.1 miles. Turn right here, heading upstream along this branch. Hickory, sassafras, and maple shade this hollow. Note how the stream keeps meandering back and forth, cutting deeper into its valley.

Yet you can see old channels that were once cut off, making oxbows. Eventually floods cut across the oxbows, creating new channels; the old channels are filled only during floods. Ferns aplenty grace the streamside woods. The streambed is quite sandy if you get a close look. The oaks that give this trail its name grow quite tall in this valley, which exhibits a wild character and remoteness. All too soon, you'll curve left away from this subtle and picturesque vale.

Head up a tributary where the oaks grow in abundance. Level off and continue in remote woodlands, where pines have joined the mix. At 1.6 miles, the White Oak Trail abruptly turns left, south, joining an old wagon track through what once was pastureland. The forest is younger here, and the canopy is

FROG-EYE VIEW OF STREAM ON WHITE OAK LOOP

somewhat open in places. Dip across a wide rock slab and more small tributaries of Pickle Creek. At 2.4 miles, curve around to reach a picturesque rocky knob wooded with pines. Unfortunately views are limited, but the emergent gray boulders and the fallen red pine needles offer a contrast with the woods through which you've been walking.

Dip across a rocky branch flowing left-to-right, toward Pickle Creek. Make your way over one last hill before completing the loop portion of the hike at 2.9 miles. From here, retrace your steps 1.1 miles to complete your day's outing.

Hawn State Park's other trails, the Pickle Creek Trail and the Whispering Pines Loop, are themselves worthy treks (see Hike 49). The nearly 5,000-acre park, acquired in 1955, also has a clean, quality 50-site campground located in a flat along Pickle Creek. It offers sites for tents and RVs in a variety of settings, including creekside sites across from bluffs on the stream. Consider camping overnight and tackling all the hikes here. Also take note of naturalist programs that are held on weekends from May through August, including ranger-led hikes that will enhance your appreciation of the preserve that is Hawn State Park.

Index